T0408284

TITANIC

COLLECTIONS

— VOLUME 2 —

FRAGMENTS OF HISTORY: THE PEOPLE

MIKE BEATTY, GEORGE BEHE, JOHN LAMOREAU, DON LYNCH, TREVOR POWELL AND KALMAN TANITO

TITANIC

COLLECTIONS

— VOLUME 2 —

FRAGMENTS OF HISTORY: THE PEOPLE

The History Press

First published 2024

The History Press
97 St George's Place, Cheltenham,
Gloucestershire, GL50 3QB
www.thehistorypress.co.uk

British Library Cataloguing in Publication Data.
A catalogue record for this book is available from the British Library.

ISBN 978 1 80399 334 8

Typesetting and origination by The History Press
Printed and bound in India by Thomson Press India Ltd

CONTENTS

INTRODUCTION

A 'tragedy' cannot happen to a ship, because a ship is an unfeeling inanimate object whose individual fate is immaterial both to itself and to the other inanimate objects that surround it. A sinking ship is just a 'thing' that has no memory and feels no emotion or pain. It is the loss of life among a sinking vessel's passengers and crew that adds meaning to that incident and turns a mere ship 'disaster' into a true tragedy. Tragedy happens only to living creatures.

The book you hold in your hands deals with the human side of the *Titanic* saga and will present individual items representing the lives of some of the men and women who sailed on the great vessel's ill-fated maiden voyage. The book has been divided into two sections, with the first offering photographs of a wide variety of items that commemorate *Titanic*'s passengers and crew in general. These photos depict period items like 1912 newspapers, letters, religious pamphlets, memorial cards, poetry, sheet music, programmes from fundraising concerts, announcements of relief funds, memorial paintings, books and postcards showing public monuments dedicated to the *Titanic*'s dead. We've limited ourselves to presenting only early items, because many hundreds of newer commemorative items have been created in recent years as a direct result of the discovery of the *Titanic* wreck site in 1985.

Part 2 of this book presents items that were once connected in various capacities with individual *Titanic* passengers and crew. We won't focus exclusively on *Titanic*-related artefacts, because each of the *Titanic*'s passengers and crew had a personal life that existed long before (and, for the lucky ones, long after) the *Titanic* tragedy itself. With that being the case, we intend to give our readers a rare glimpse into these people's personal lives by showing items that spotlight their humanity instead of focusing exclusively on a five-day ocean voyage that came to a tragic end on 15 April 1912.

We hope these rare memorial items and physical reminders of the *Titanic's* passengers and crew will highlight the fact that the *Titanic* disaster was a *human* tragedy that affected not only the passengers and crew themselves, but devastated the families of all those people who lost their lives when the great ship went down.

George Behe
Mike Beatty
John Lamoreau
Don Lynch
Trevor Powell
Kalman Tanito

NEWSPAPERS

▲ Newspaper

Early reporting on the sinking of the *Titanic* published in the *Arizona Gazette* newspaper, 15 April 1912. The article contains numerous mistaken statements, such as: 'All passengers safe and *Titanic* taken in tow by the *Virginian*.' (John Lamoreau collection)

▲ **Newspaper Clippings**
Articles from Halifax, Nova Scotia, where recovered bodies from the *Titanic* were taken. What makes this collection more unusual than most is the care taken by the person assembling the articles. If an article started on one page and ended on another, the compiler would attach them together with sewing thread. An example of this can be seen towards the lower middle of the picture. (John Lamoreau collection)

LETTERS

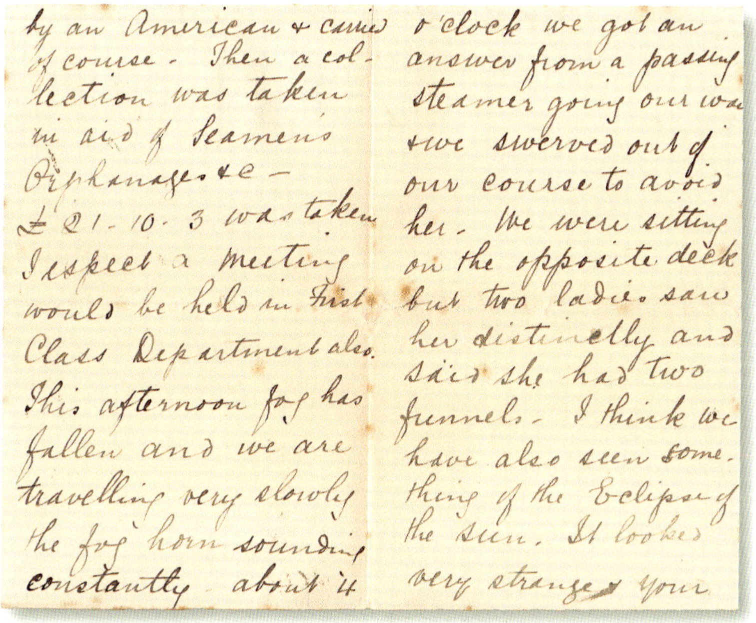

by an American & came of course. Then a collection was taken in aid of Seamen's Orphanages &c – £21-10-3 was taken. I expect a meeting would be held in First Class Department also. This afternoon fog has fallen and we are travelling very slowly the fog horn sounding constantly about 4 o'clock we got an answer from a passing steamer going our way & we swerved out of our course to avoid her. We were sitting on the opposite deck but two ladies saw her distinctly and said she had two funnels. I think we have also seen something of the Eclipse of the sun. It looked very strange & your

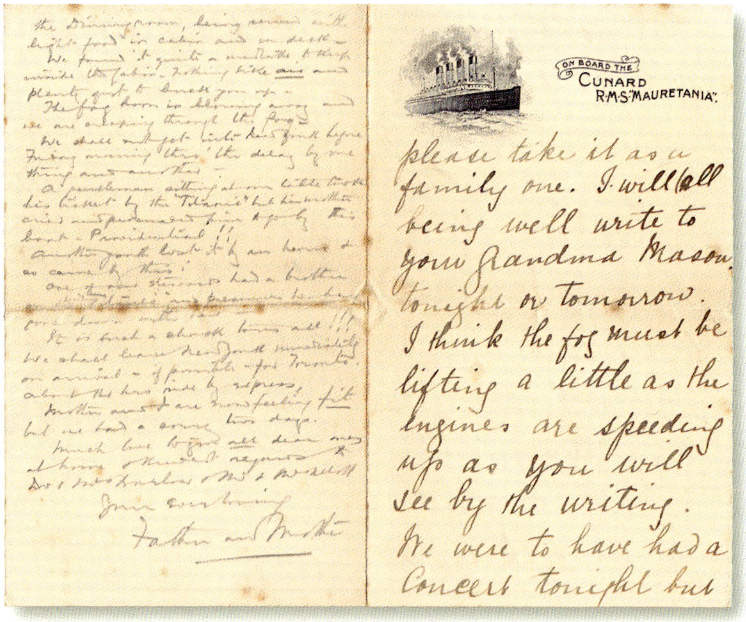

On board the Cunard R.M.S. "Mauretania"

please take it as a family one. I will (all being well) write to your Grandma Mason tonight or tomorrow. I think the fog must be lifting a little as the engines are speeding up as you will see by the writing. We were to have had a Concert tonight but

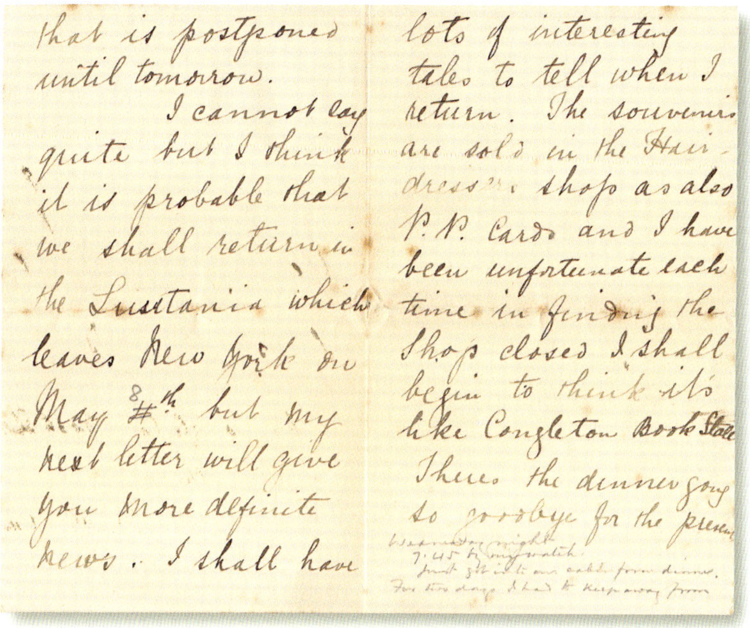

that is postponed until tomorrow. I cannot say quite but I think it is probable that we shall return in the Lusitania which leaves New York on May 8th but my next letter will give you more definite news. I shall have lots of interesting tales to tell when I return. The souvenirs are sold in the Hairdresser's shop as also P.P. Cards and I have been unfortunate each time in finding the shop closed I shall begin to think it's like Congleton Book Stall. There's the dinner gong so goodbye for the present

Wednesday night 7.45 by my watch. Just got into our cabin from dinner. For two days I had to keep away from

▲▶ *Mauretania* Letter

This unique eight-page letter was written on board the *Mauretania* just two days after the *Titanic* sinking. The *Mauretania* was three days behind on the same route *Titanic* was sailing. Passengers Francis and Mary Mason recorded their reactions and those of others on board after they received the news of the sinking. (Mike Beatty collection)

◀ **Letter**

A 21 April 1912 letter written from the Cawthon Hotel in Mobile, Alabama. The author writes: 'Wasn't the sinking of the *Titanic* ship awful – poor little children and babies had to go down like rats – poor little things.' (John Lamoreau collection)

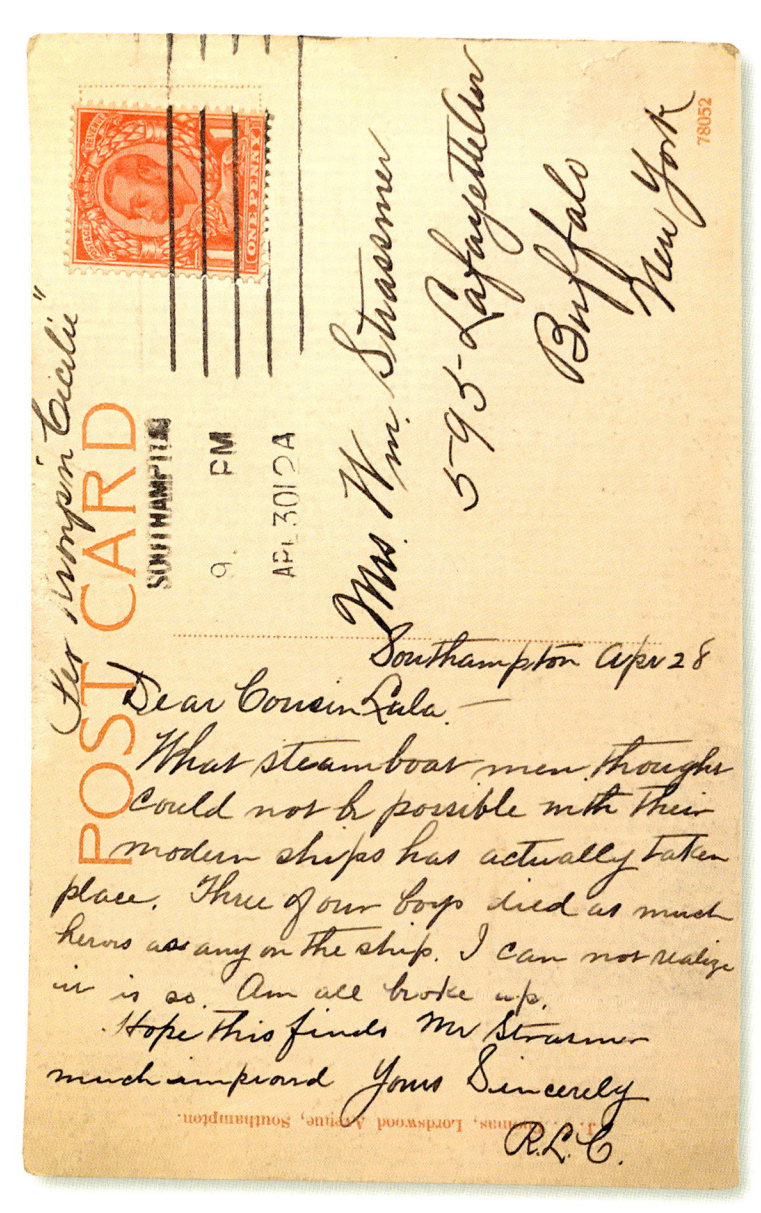

▲ Postcard

Out of *Titanic*'s 891 crew (most of whom were from Southampton), only 213 survived the disaster. On 28 April 1912 an unknown Southampton resident wrote on this pre-sinking postcard lamenting the loss of three family members when the big White Star liner went down: 'Three of our boys died as much heroes as any on the ship. I cannot realize it is so. Am all broke up.' (George Behe collection)

RELIGIOUS MATERIAL

▶ **St Paul's Service Programme**
On 19 April 1912 thousands of people came to the famous London cathedral to mourn the *Titanic*'s victims. An attendee saved this programme from the service. (Mike Beatty collection)

▼ **Religious Pamphlets**
The *Titanic* disaster became the chosen subject of many clergymen, who expounded on the subject from their pulpits. These three pamphlets summarise the types of moral lessons that certain ministers hoped to convey to their flocks. (George Behe collection)

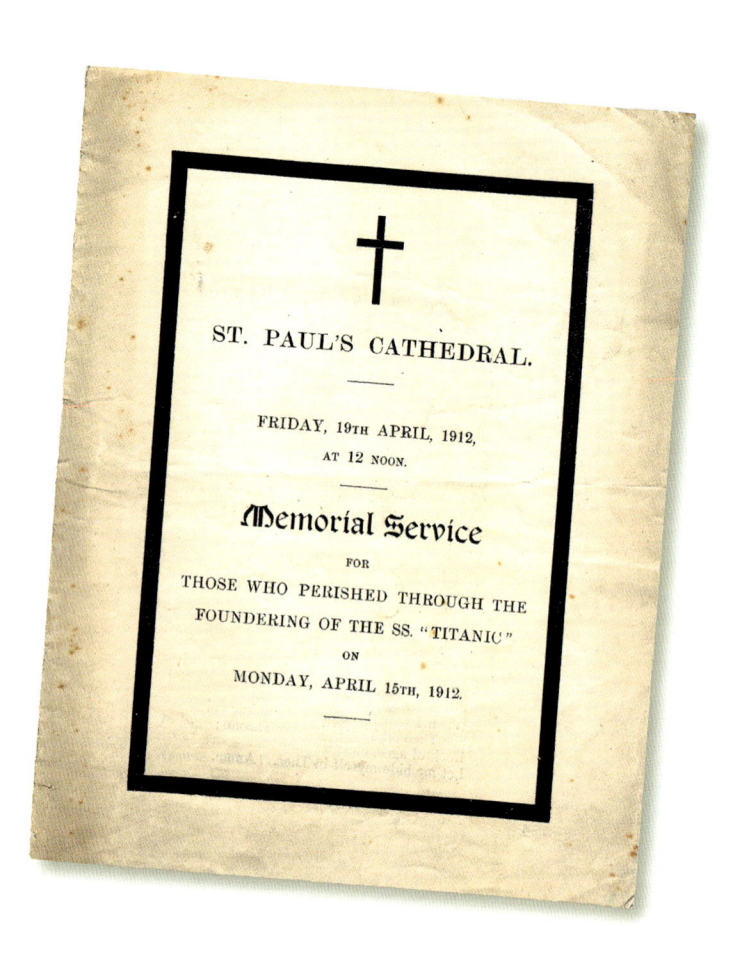

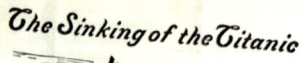

MEMORIAL CARDS

▶ ▼ Memorial Postcards

An American postcard (right) and a French postcard that both utilise the lyrics and published music of the hymn 'Nearer My God, to Thee'. Although the subject has been debated for years, most serious historians now agree that this hymn was the final piece of music played by the *Titanic*'s bandsmen before the great ship went down. (George Behe collection)

▲ Postcard

During the months after the disaster, a multitude of memorial postcards were published in remembrance of *Titanic*'s 1,496 lost passengers and crew. The Bamforth Company published a series of six cards that were especially maudlin in their presentation, with this illustrated card being one of the set. (George Behe collection)

▲ Postcard

A hastily executed memorial postcard showing a primitive depiction of the *Titanic* positioned alongside the lyrics of 'Nearer My God, to Thee'. (George Behe collection)

▶ Postcard

This memorial card honours Captain Edward Smith and Marconi operator Jack Phillips, the latter of whom lost his life after sending out distress calls until just a few minutes before the *Titanic* went down. (George Behe collection)

▲ Postcard

This Danish card memorialises the *Titanic*'s eight bandsmen, although only seven are pictured. These men performed their calming music until shortly before the *Titanic*'s bridge submerged, at which time they concluded their heroic presentation with 'Nearer My God, to Thee', which bandmaster Wallace Hartley had once said he would play if he ever found himself on a sinking ship. (George Behe collection)

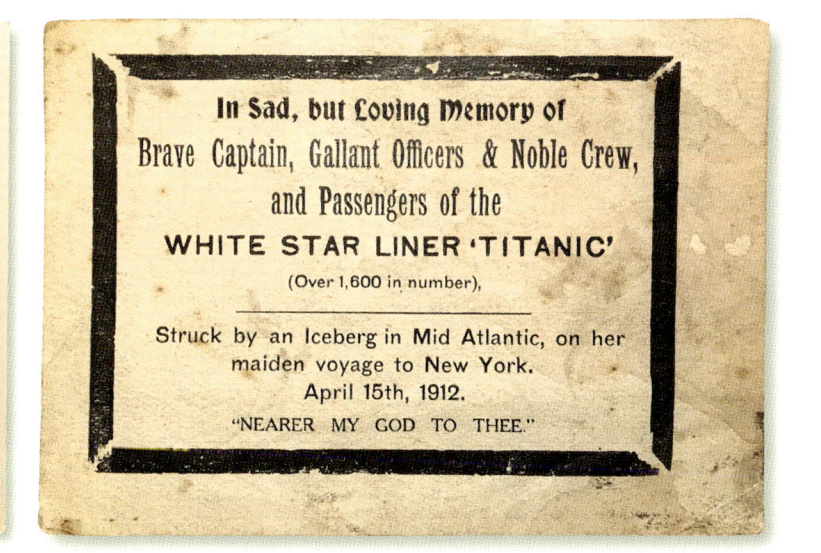

▲ Memorial Card

This card is one of many that were published in the wake of the disaster. It has overstated the death toll slightly, claiming that 'over 1,600 in number' lost their lives. (George Behe collection)

> How short is life, how sure is death,
>   Our days, alas! are few,
> This mortal life 'tis but a breath,
>   'Tis like the morning dew.

▲ ▶ **Memorial Cards**
Small fold-out cards were produced in various designs to pay tribute.
Each card was accompanied with a black-bordered mourning envelope.
(Mike Beatty collection)

In Sacred Memory of

The "TITANIC"

WHICH COLLIDED WITH AN ICEBERG

OFF CAPE RACE, on APRIL 15th, 1912.

The most appalling disaster in Maritime History

with a loss of over 1,000 lives.

▲ ▶ *Titanic* Memorial Posters
Three typical post-disaster posters commemorating the huge loss of life that occurred when the *Titanic* went down. The first poster measures 13½ inches by 22½ inches. (George Behe collection)

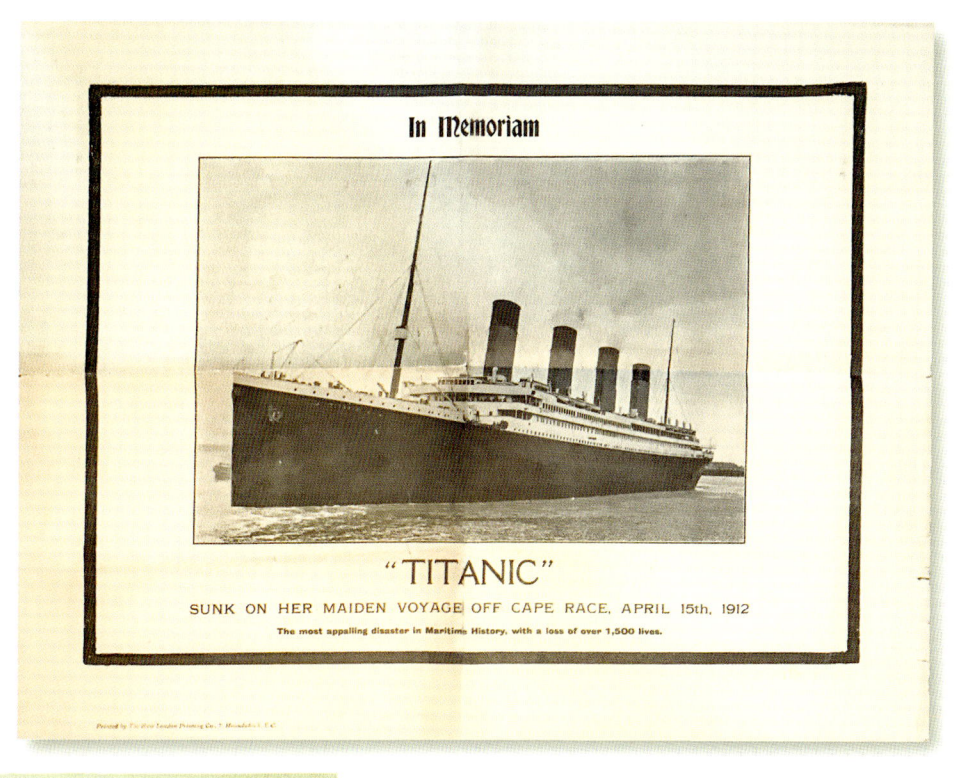

POETRY

Maailman suurin haaksirikko.

Valtamerijättiläisen „TITANIC'in"; upottua Atlannin-merellä 15 p:nä huhtikuuta 1912.

Hukkuneitten siirtolaisten muistoksi sepitti ja kustansi J. T.

THE LOSS OF THE TITANIC

The great Titanic is no more,
  She sank two thousand fathoms deep,
Away t'ords yonder distant shore,
  And leaves a mourning crowd to weep.

The gallant ship was sinking fast
  Into the cold and briny sea ;
The Band struck up a hymn—*the last !*
And played " Nearer, my God, to Thee."

The angry waters swallowed up
  A fated throng of human lives :
Breadwinners drank the bitter cup,
  And left, to mourn, the bairns and wives.

The ocean deep, with all its wealth,
  Cannot give back its plundered store ;
Her victims, gay and in good health,
  Farewelled to Merrie England's shore.

God bless the huge Titanic's dead,
  Console and pity the bereaved ;
Widows and orphans *must* be fed,
  And duty's task be yet achieved.

And when the voyage of life is o'er,
  And sad calamities shall cease,
The sea will then her spoil restore,
  Safe ! In the Harbour—Perfect Peace.

W. W.

The Proceeds to be handed over to the Mayoress for the Mansion House Fund.

▲ Poem
A 1913 Finnish memorial pamphlet, written in poem form by 'J.T.,' published by Otto Andersin's Press in Pori. (Kalman Tanito collection)

▲ Memorial Postcard
A memorial postcard bearing a poem written to commemorate the *Titanic* disaster. (George Behe collection)

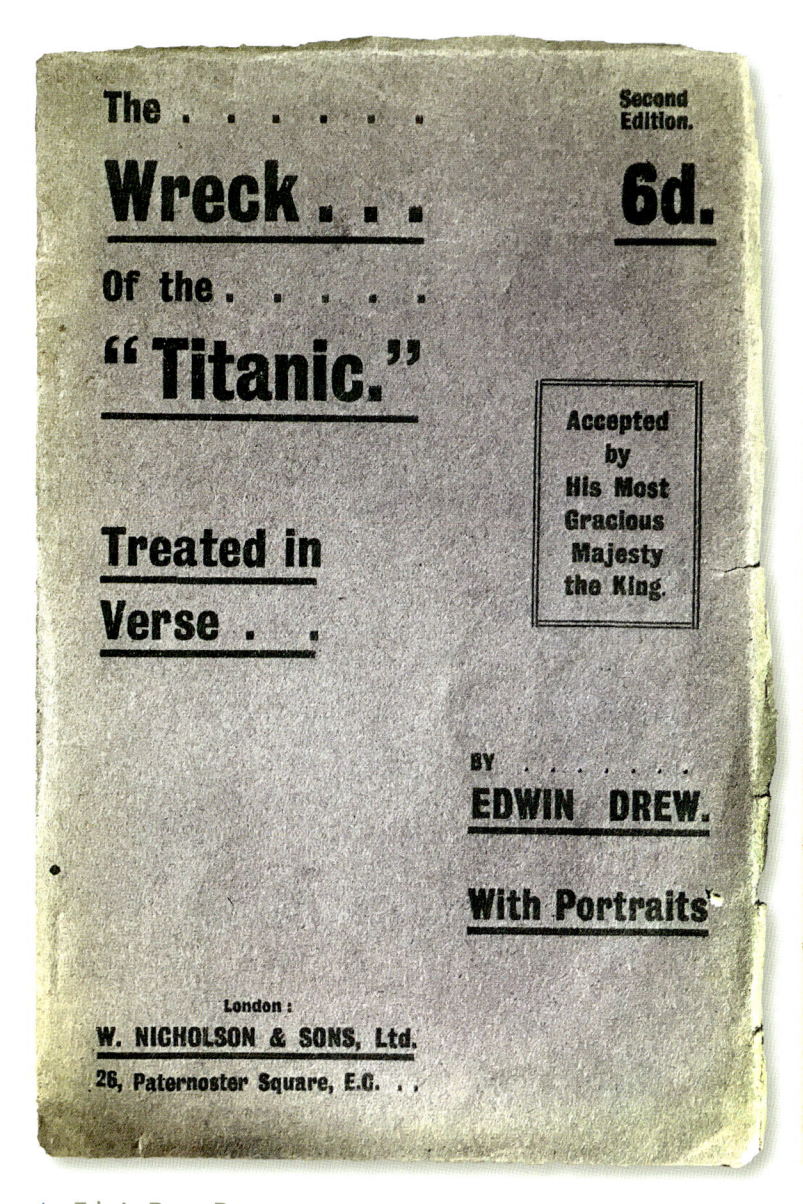

▲ Edwin Drew Poem

In 1912 Edwin Drew published *The Wreck of the Titanic*, a forty-six-page booklet containing a lengthy poem he wrote. (George Behe collection)

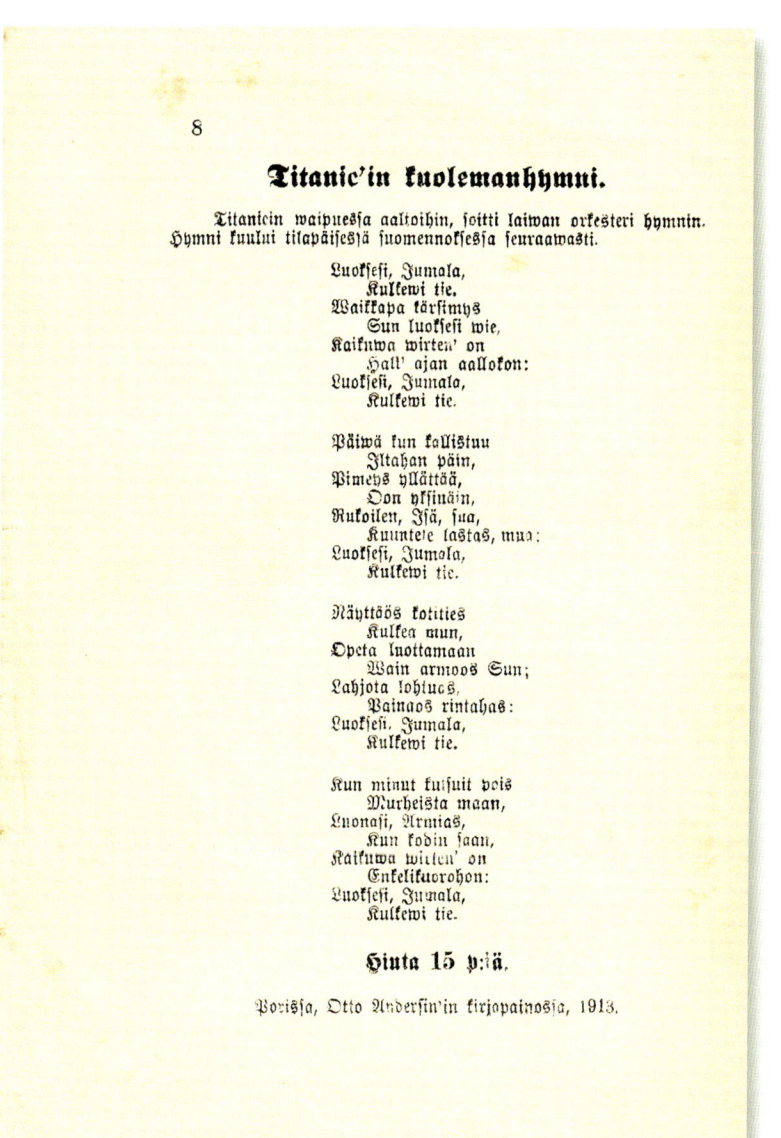

▲ Poetry

A *Titanic* memorial poetry card published in 1913. (Kalman Tanito collection)

MUSIC

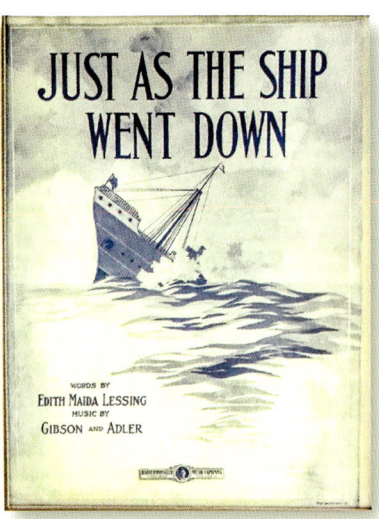
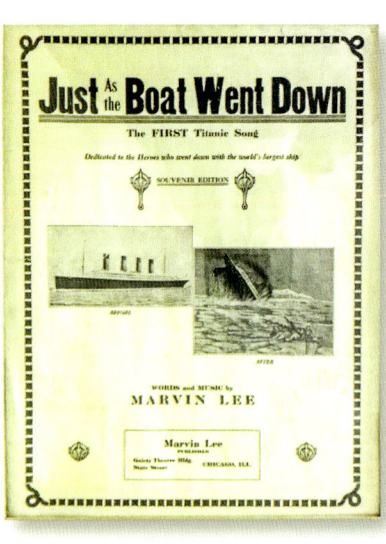

▲ Sheet Music

The disaster inspired all kinds of memorial items, including sheet music containing songs composed especially for that purpose. These pieces of sheet music are just a few examples of many. (George Behe collection)

▶ Sheet Music

A piece of French memorial sheet music containing a French translation of 'Nearer My God, to Thee'. (George Behe collection)

▼ **French Hymns**
The *Titanic* disaster was commemorated worldwide, and items were produced in many countries, like these examples of French hymnal sheet music. (Mike Beatty collection)

MEMORIAL SOUVENIRS

▲ China Memorial Souvenirs

The Carlton China Company manufactured high-quality porcelain vases and urns as souvenirs of the *Titanic* disaster. Here is a small collection of miniature items that were available in many different shapes, which were modelled after ancient Roman pottery. (Kalman Tanito collection)

INVESTIGATION

▶ **Speech**

After the Senate concluded its investigation into the *Titanic* disaster, Michigan Senator William Alden Smith (the driving force behind the inquiry) delivered a closing speech describing his own reaction to the disaster and giving recommendations he felt were desirable. Smith's speech was published by the government as a routine part of the Senate's record-keeping. (George Behe collection)

▼ **Campaign Ribbon**

A pin and ribbon from one of Smith's election campaigns. (Kalman Tanito collection)

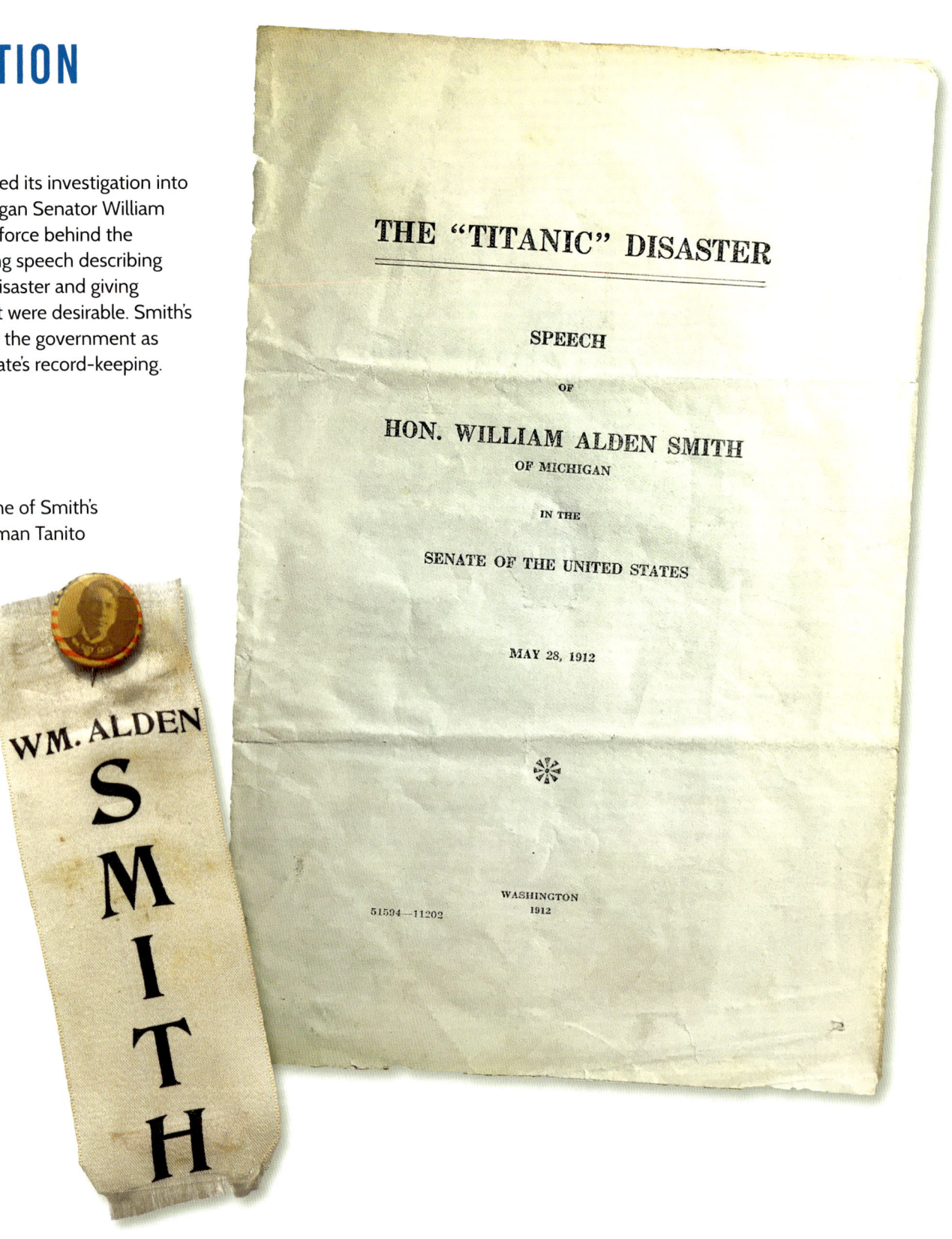

THE "TITANIC" DISASTER

SPEECH

OF

HON. WILLIAM ALDEN SMITH

OF MICHIGAN

IN THE

SENATE OF THE UNITED STATES

MAY 28, 1912

✳

WASHINGTON
1912

51594—11202

RELIEF FUNDS

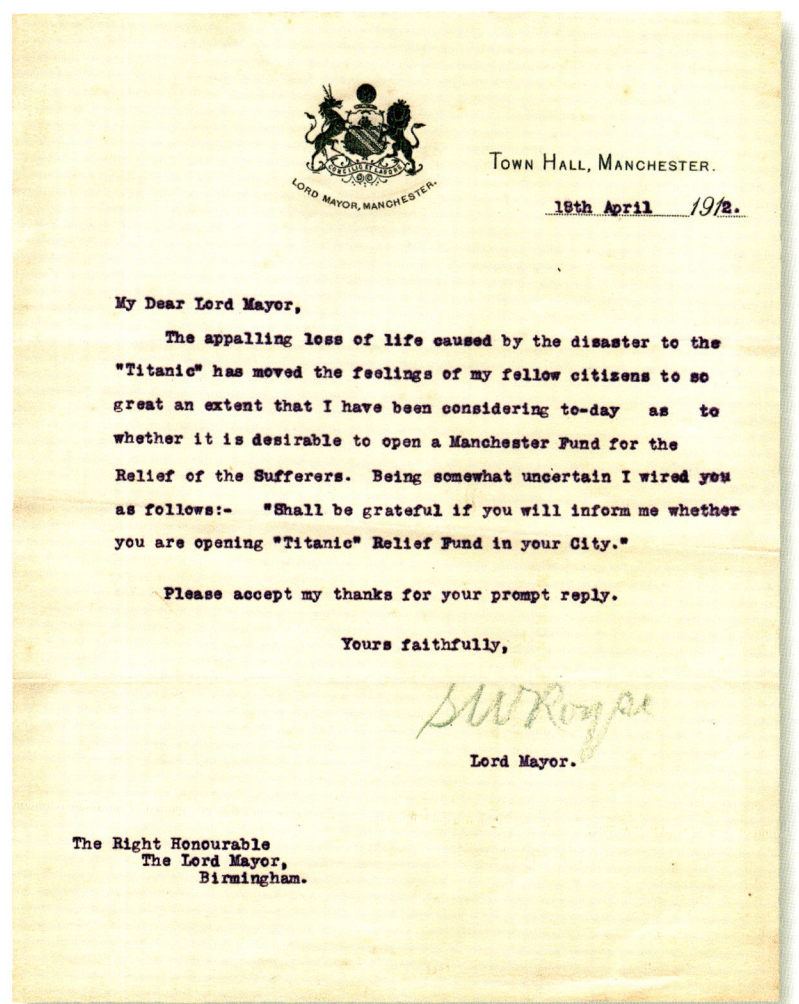

▲ **Relief Fund Letter**
Many relief funds were set up just days after the sinking. On
18 April 1912 the Lord Mayor of Manchester sent a letter to the Lord
Mayor of Birmingham in England to confer about relief fund efforts in
his city. (Mike Beatty collection)

▲ **Royal Albert Hall Concert**
Concerts were held all over England to raise funds for those
affected by the sinking. One of the largest performances
was held at London's Royal Albert Hall on 24 May 1912. (Mike
Beatty collection)

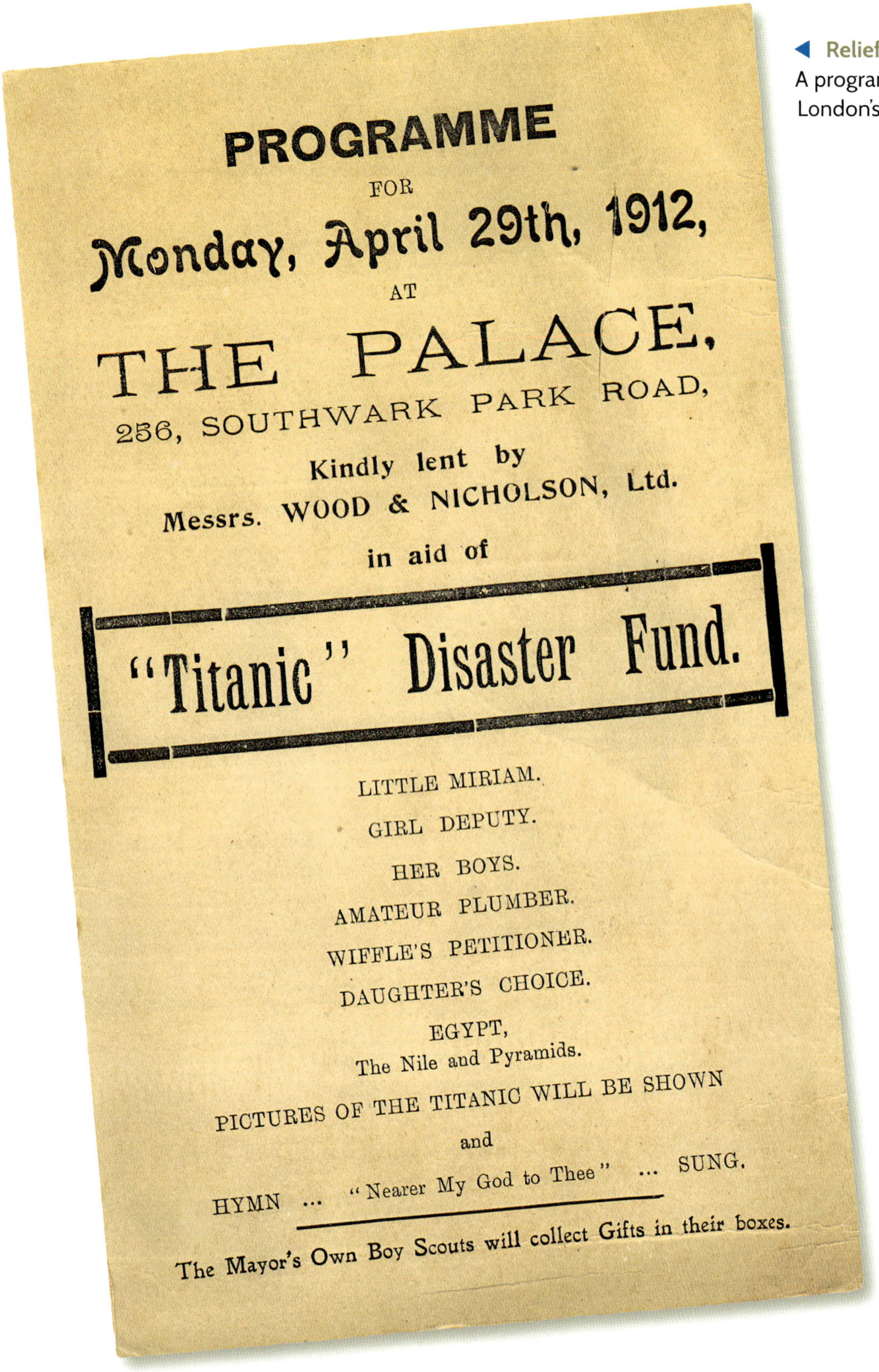

PROGRAMME

FOR

Monday, April 29th, 1912,

AT

THE PALACE,

256, SOUTHWARK PARK ROAD,

Kindly lent by

Messrs. WOOD & NICHOLSON, Ltd.

in aid of

"Titanic" Disaster Fund.

LITTLE MIRIAM.

GIRL DEPUTY.

HER BOYS.

AMATEUR PLUMBER.

WIFFLE'S PETITIONER.

DAUGHTER'S CHOICE.

EGYPT,
The Nile and Pyramids.

PICTURES OF THE TITANIC WILL BE SHOWN

and

HYMN ... "Nearer My God to Thee" ... SUNG.

The Mayor's Own Boy Scouts will collect Gifts in their boxes.

Relief Fund Flyer
A programme from a *Titanic* relief fundraiser held at London's Palace theatre. (Mike Beatty collection)

▶ Women's Memorial Programme

One of the most iconic memorials to the disaster was the Women's Titanic Memorial erected in Washington, DC, as a tribute to the men who gave their lives so the women and children could be saved. Fundraising began soon after the disaster, led by Natalie Harris Hammond. On 23 August 1912, a spectacular garden fête at Lookout Hill, the Gloucester, Massachusetts, the estate of her husband John Hays Hammond, had a prestigious guest list that included President and Mrs Taft. (Mike Beatty collection)

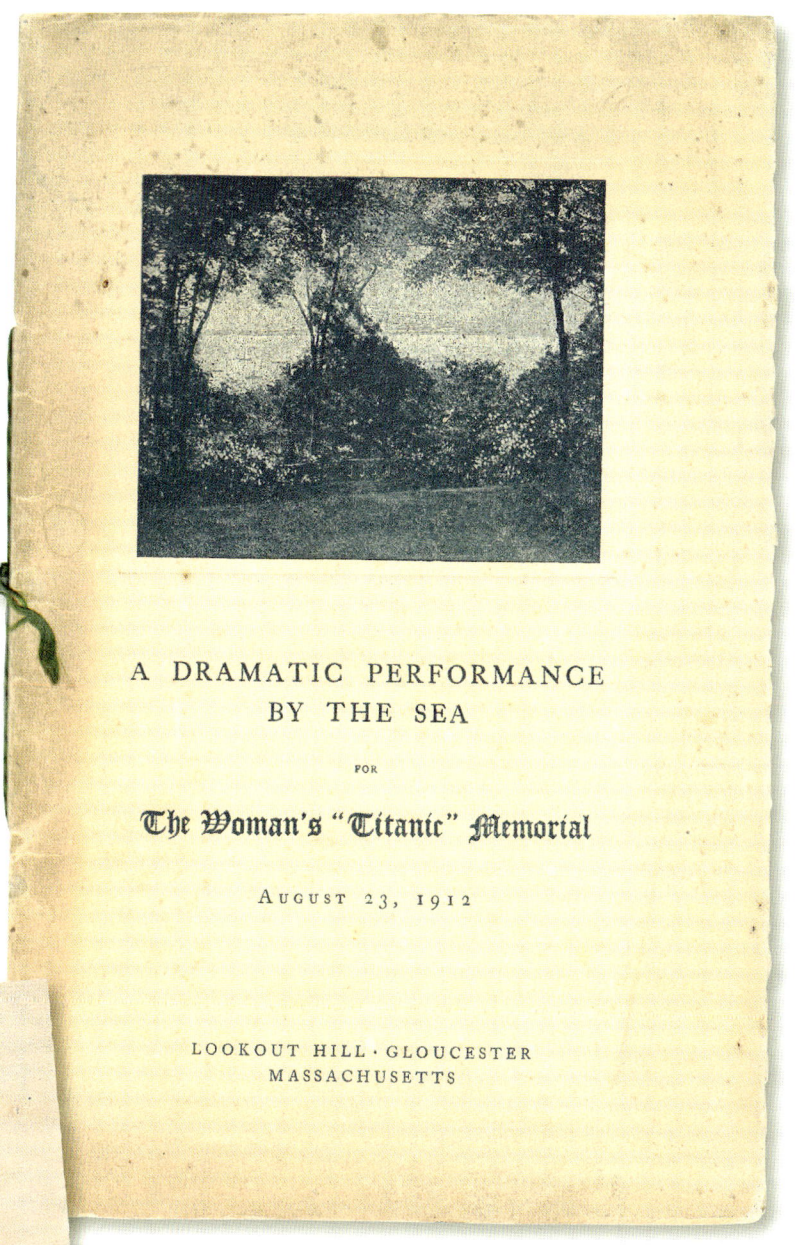

A DRAMATIC PERFORMANCE
BY THE SEA

FOR

The Woman's "Titanic" Memorial

AUGUST 23, 1912

LOOKOUT HILL · GLOUCESTER
MASSACHUSETTS

▼ Women's Memorial Slip

A donation slip given out to solicit funds to build the memorial. (Mike Beatty collection)

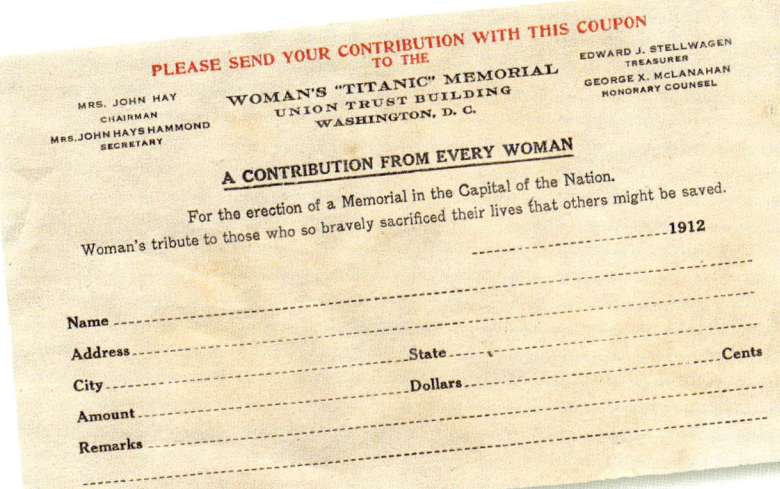

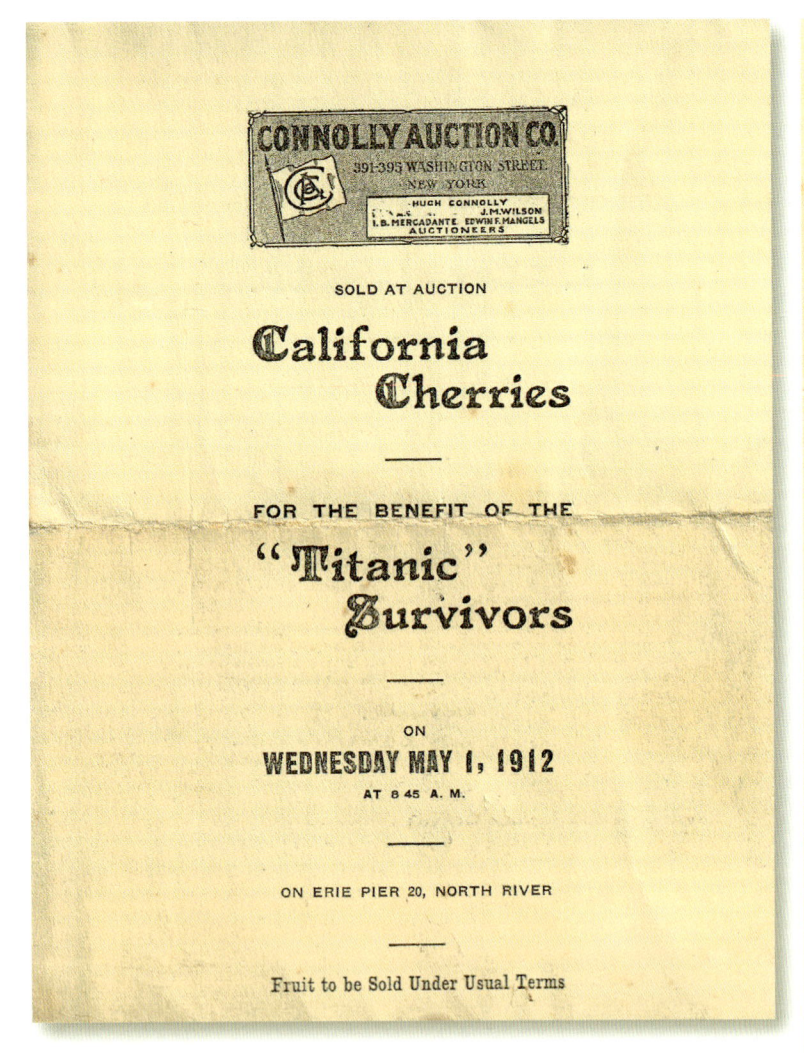

CONNOLLY AUCTION CO.
391-395 WASHINGTON STREET
NEW YORK

HUGH CONNOLLY
J. M. WILSON
I. B. MERCADANTE   EDWIN F. MANGELS
AUCTIONEERS

SOLD AT AUCTION

California Cherries

FOR THE BENEFIT OF THE

"Titanic" Survivors

ON

WEDNESDAY MAY 1, 1912

AT 8.45 A. M.

ON ERIE PIER 20, NORTH RIVER

Fruit to be Sold Under Usual Terms

▲▶ Fundraiser

One of the many fundraising events in the United States was this sale of California Cherries, the proceeds of which were to benefit the *Titanic*'s survivors. (Kalman Tanito collection)

OFFICE OF
D. D. BLACK
NEW YORK CITY

May 2nd, 1912

The Honorable W. J. Gaynor,
   Mayor of New York City,
Dear Sir:-

   Messrs. L. Scatena & Co. of San Francisco forwarded one box of California Cherries to the writer with instructions to have same sold at public auction for the benefit of the "Titanic" survivors. This box of cherries was sold Wednesday through the Connolly Auction Co. and the wholesale fruit trade of New York, together with the various auction companies, are responsible for the very flattering results obtained.

   I take pleasure in transmitting to you herewith the amount realized from the sale $629.88, and would appreciate a written acknowledgment in order that I may acquaint the donors of the box with the fact that the amount in question has been received by you for the purpose above mentioned.

   Very respectfully yours,

      (Signed) D. D. BLACK.

CITY OF NEW YORK
OFFICE OF THE MAYOR

May 2nd, 1912

Dear Sir:-

   I thank you for your letter of May 2nd enclosing check for $629.88, realized from a sale at auction of one box of California cherries sent by Messrs. L. Scatena & Co. of San Francisco, to be sold at public auction for the relief of the survivors of the crew and passengers of the "Titanic" steamship and of the dependents of those who lost their lives in the disaster.

   Please also convey my thanks to the New York trade and Messrs. Scatena & Co. for their generosity.

      Sincerely yours,
      (Signed) W. J. Gaynor,
            Mayor.

Mr. D. D. Black
204 Franklin St.
   New York City.

Century Theatre Fundraiser

Another high-profile fundraising performance was held on 6 December at the Century Theatre in New York City. The performance raised over $10,000 for the Women's Titanic Memorial fund. (Mike Beatty collection)

▼ Palace Theatre Programme

A souvenir from a benefit show performed at the Palace Theatre in Southampton. No town was probably more affected than Southampton, where the majority of *Titanic*'s crew lived. (Mike Beatty collection)

▲ London Hippodrome Performance

On 30 April 1912 a benefit was held at one of London's landmark performance centres, the London Hippodrome. Artists and musicians donated their time to help raise funds for the victims' families. (Mike Beatty collection)

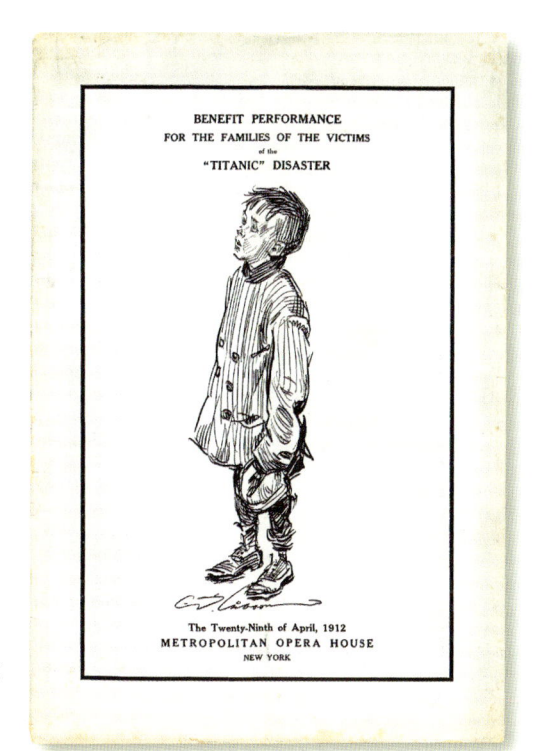

▶ New York Metropolitan Concert

Other countries held fundraising concerts as well. The famous concert hall in New York City held a fantastic event on 29 April 1912 to benefit destitute *Titanic* survivors. (Mike Beatty collection)

▶▶ Mansion House Relief Fund

On 20 April 1912 the Mansion House Relief Fund opened for the benefit of widows and children of lost *Titanic* crewmen. This booklet was from one of their many fundraisers. (Mike Beatty collection)

▶ Postcard

The hastily constructed model in this photograph was probably used to raise money for the Titanic Relief Fund to assist destitute *Titanic* survivors and the families of those who lost their lives in the disaster. (George Behe collection)

MEMORIAL PAINTINGS

▲ Painting

A rendering of the *Titanic* disaster done as a reverse glass painting. Many similar paintings utilising a number of different patterns were sold to the general public in the wake of the sinking. (George Behe collection)

MEMORIAL BOOKS

▶ **Book**

Many memorial books describing the *Titanic* disaster were published soon after the sinking. This paperback volume was published in Dutch in Grand Rapids, Michigan, which has many citizens with roots in the Netherlands. (George Behe collection)

▼ **Memorial Book**

This memorial book, written in Lithuanian, was published in Worcester, Massachusetts. It includes a chapter about Juozapas Montvila, a young priest who was on his way to the United States to become a pastor at the Lithuanian parish in Athol, Massachusetts. Montvila lost his life in the disaster. (Kalman Tanito collection)

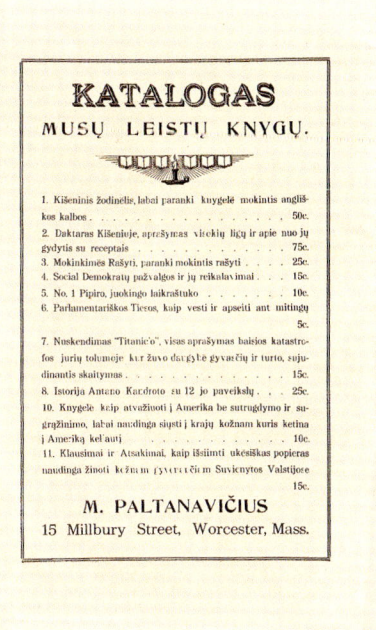

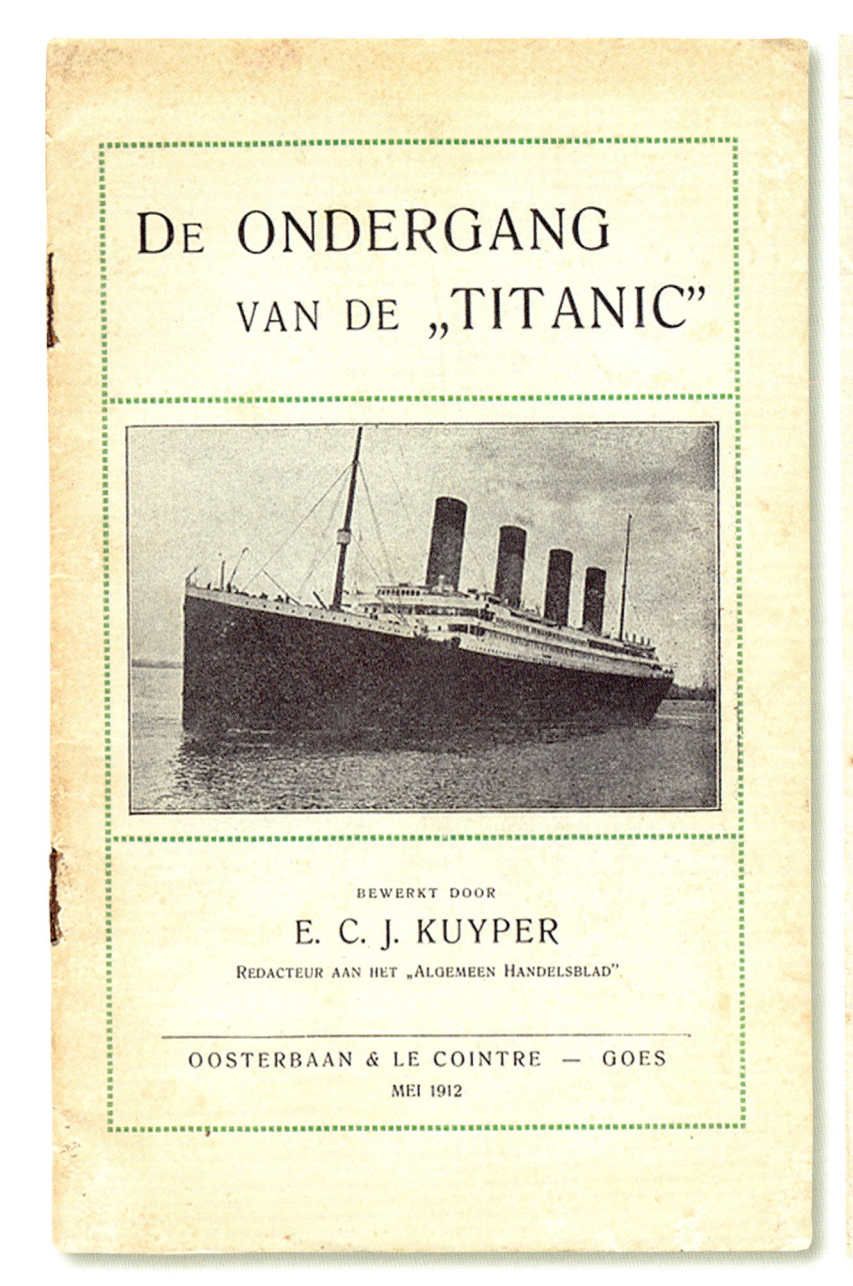

▲ **Dutch Booklet**
This booklet in Dutch was published in May 1912.
(Mike Beatty collection)

▲ **Pamphlet**
A Danish memorial pamphlet about the *Titanic* disaster,
published in Copenhagen. (Kalman Tanito collection)

◄ **Elbert Hubbard Book, 1912**
This first edition copy of Elbert Hubbard's book is signed, and one chapter is titled 'The *Titanic*'. Hubbard wrote of *Titanic* victims Isidor and Ida Straus: 'Mr. and Mrs. Straus, I envy you that legacy of love and loyalty left to your children and grandchildren. The calm courage that was yours all your long and useful career was your possession in death. You knew how to do three great things – you knew how to live, how to love and how to die ... Happy lovers, both. In life they were never separated and in death they are not divided.' Elbert Hubbard and his wife would meet the same fate as the Strauses, as they were victims in the 1915 sinking of the *Lusitania*. (John Lamoreau collection)

► **Elbert Hubbard Book**
In 1923 the Roycroft Shops reprinted the *Titanic* chapter as a separate leatherbound volume. (George Behe collection)

MONUMENTS

◀ **Postcard**
This bronze and granite memorial to the *Titanic*'s heroic engineering staff was unveiled in Southampton on 22 April 1914. The event was attended by an estimated 100,000 residents of the town. (George Behe collection)

▶ **Watch**
A Waltham pocket watch presented to George Catlin for his efforts in co-ordinating the work for the Titanic Engineers' Memorial, Southampton, in 1914. (Kalman Tanito collection)

▲ Postcard

This card depicts the Titanic Memorial in Belfast, Northern Ireland, that was erected to commemorate the lives lost in the disaster. The memorial was funded by contributions from the public, shipyard workers, and victims' families, and was dedicated in June 1920. (George Behe collection)

▲ Postcard

A view of the Titanic Memorial on the roof of the Seamen's Institute in New York City. (George Behe collection)

▲ Postcard

A Southampton memorial to the stewards, sailors and firemen who lost their lives when the *Titanic* went down. (George Behe collection)

VARIOUS

"... mig a hajó bordái között egy új világ-ról álmodozott ezer és ezer ember; addig folyt a bor, pezsgő és csattogott a kártya a tiszturak és legénység között."

◄ Propaganda

'The *Titanic* and Alcohol', published by the Anti-Alcohol League of Gyergyószentmiklós, Hungary (now Romania). 'While in the ship, thousands of people were dreaming of a new world, the officers and the crew drank wine and champagne and played cards.' (Kalman Tanito collection)

▼ Confectionery

The A.M. Merikanto confectionery factory in Tampere, Finland, manufactured sweets with at least three different commemorative wrappers, two of which are depicted here. (Kalman Tanito collection)

▶ Postal Cover

In 1932 a Newfoundland postal cover commemorated the twentieth anniversary of the *Titanic* disaster. (George Behe collection)

▼ *Titanic* Wood Chips

Edward Rowe Snow was a prolific writer on nautical subjects who authored more than forty books, the first being published in 1935. One thing that set Snow's books apart from others was that he would often include wafer-thin slices of wreck wood from famous ships, including the *Titanic*, which made his books highly collectible; how he would do this is demonstrated by the note on the left.

Mr Snow died in 1982, and from his workshop and estate came a paper bag containing the last sixty 1-inch square slices of his *Titanic* wreck wood. (John Lamoreau collection)

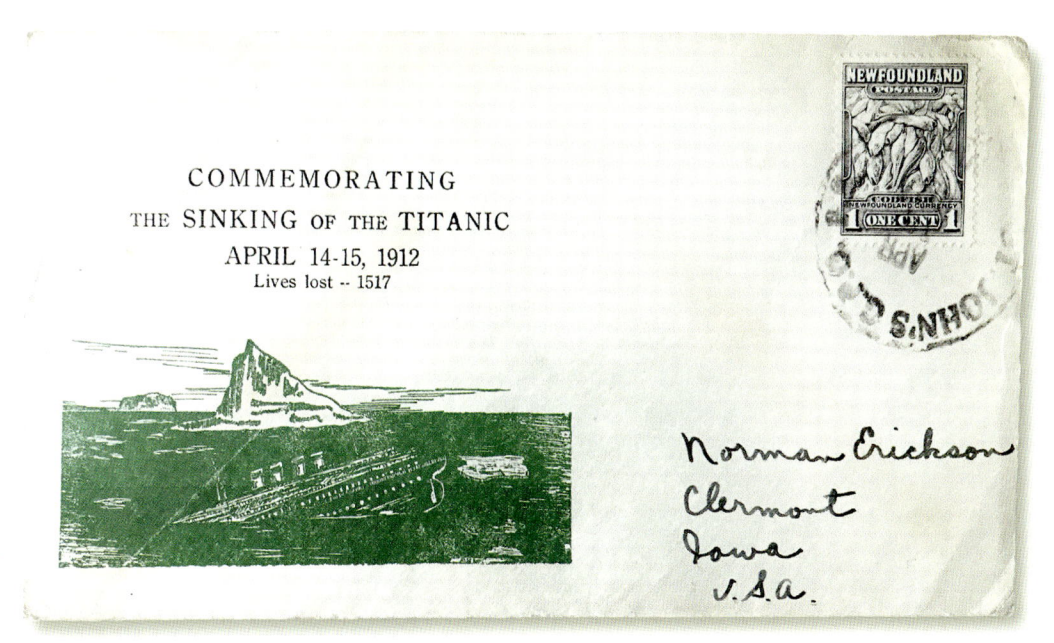

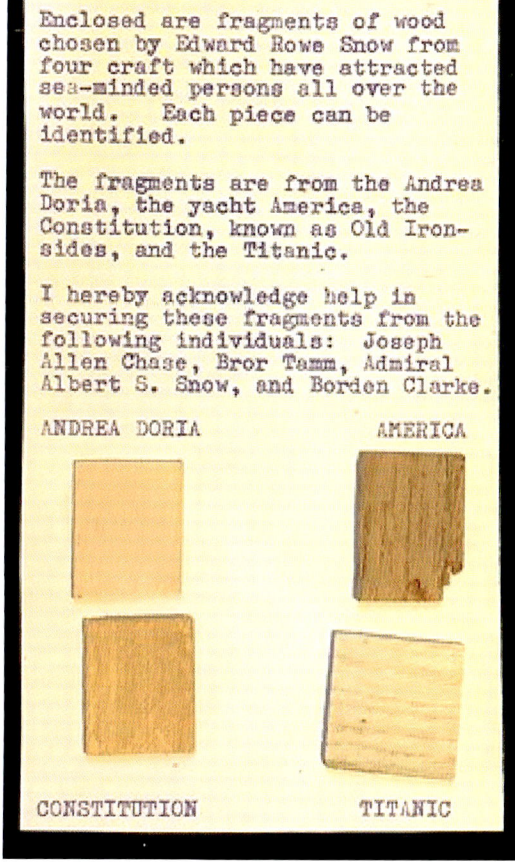

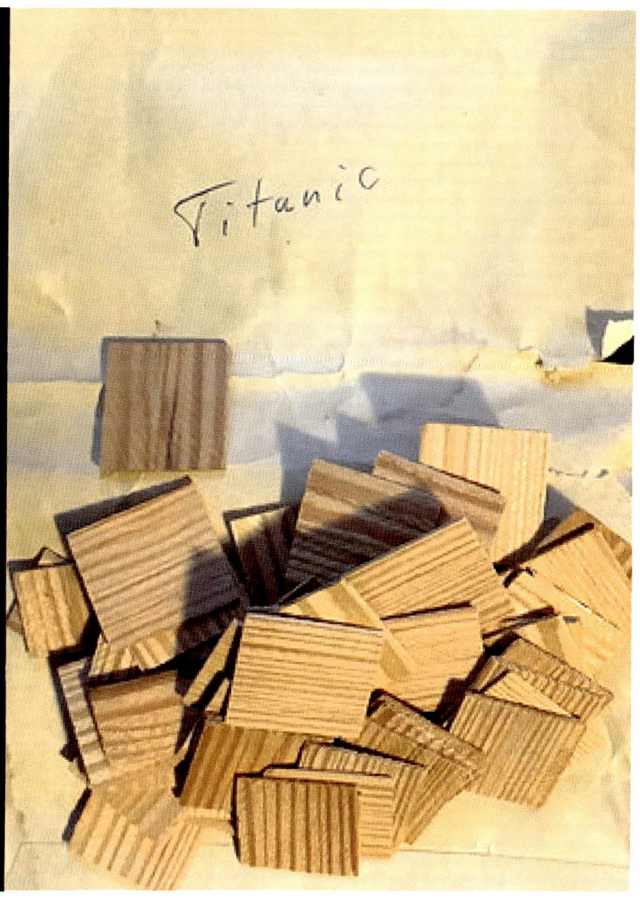

TITANIC PEOPLE

RHODA, ROSSMORE AND EUGENE ABBOTT

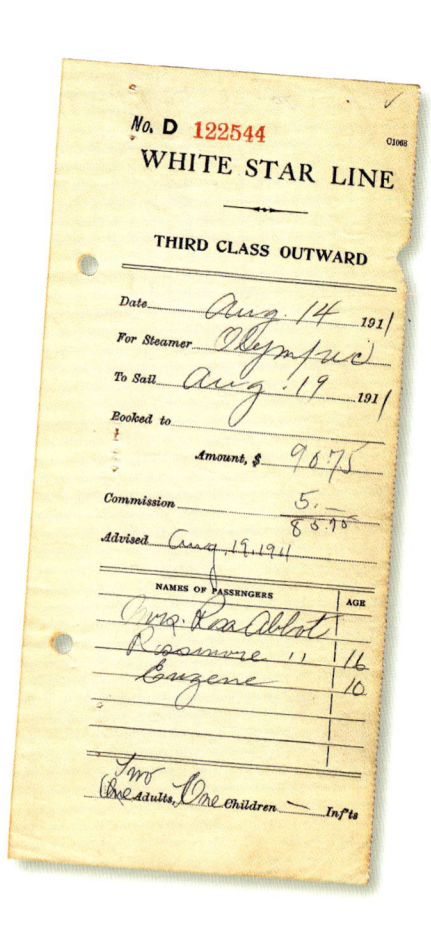

▶ **Rhoda Abbott *Olympic* Ticket**

This is half of a third-class ticket to sail from New York to England on the *Titanic*'s sister *Olympic* on 14 August 1911, this portion of the ticket having been retained by the ticket agent. The ticket was purchased by Rhoda 'Rosa' Abbott, who had immigrated to the US with her sons Rossmore and Eugene early in 1911 following her separation from her husband. A few months later, after deciding to return to England to live with her mother, Rosa and her two boys left New York on the *Olympic* using the other half of this ticket. However, the boys were not happy in England and wanted to return to the US, so in April 1912 Rosa booked three third-class passages to return to the US ... on board *Titanic*.

Five nights after sailing from Southampton, Rosa stood with her arms around her two young sons and watched as the *Titanic*'s forward boat deck began to submerge. The little family was swept into the sea as a big wave surged aft over the slanting deck, but Rosa found herself alone after she fought her way back to the ocean's surface. Rosa Abbott spent the rest of the night standing in the half-submerged lifeboat collapsible A while fellow swimmers who climbed into that same boat died of hypothermia all around her. Rosa barely survived the sinking of the *Titanic*, but she never saw her sons Rossmore and Eugene again. (Mike Beatty collection)

BESS ALLISON

◀ **Allison Letter Reference**

This letter, dated 30 April 1912, has great historical content. The writer was a friend of first-class *Titanic* victim Bess Waldo Daniels Allison, and he writes: 'Wasn't the Titanic disaster the most terrible one could imagine? If you have read the papers, you no doubt read of the little 11-months-old baby boy who was saved by his nurse, his mother, father and sister being drowned. Allison is the name, and it was his mother who used to be Bess Daniels that I knew so well ...' (John Lamoreau collection)

CHARLES EDWARD ANDREWS

▼ **Charles Andrews Discharge Book**

The continuous Certificate of Discharge for Charles Edward Andrews, born in 1893, steward on the *Titanic*. It bears the famous 'Intended New York' remark, and on the first page of the book it is stated: 'Renewal Book. Original lost through shipwreck'. A twist of fate is that in 1920 Andrews served on the *Mauretania* under Captain Arthur Rostron of *Carpathia* fame. (Kalman Tanito collection)

THOMAS ANDREWS

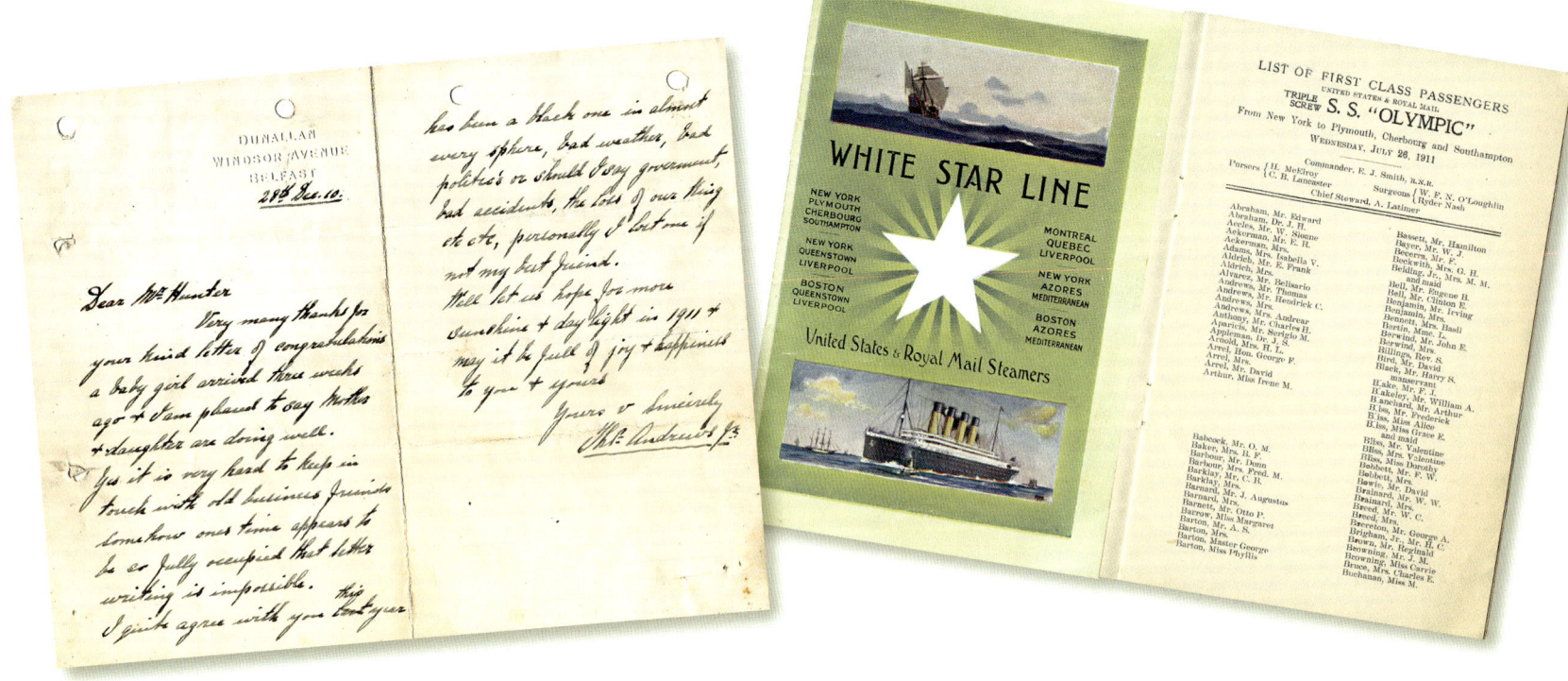

▲ **Thomas Andrews Letter**

C.P. Hunter was a lighting, heating and ventilation engineer at the Harland & Wolff shipyard and worked under Thomas Andrews from 1902 to 1905. He was also a personal friend of Andrews, who took time from his busy schedule to write to Hunter just before New Year 1910. He had just celebrated the birth of his daughter Elizabeth and was in the final months of *Olympic*'s build and well into the building of *Titanic*. (Mike Beatty collection)

▲ *Olympic* **Passenger List**

A 26 July 1911 first-class passenger list for the *Olympic*, which was under the command of *Titanic*'s future commander, Captain Edward Smith; *Titanic*'s future chief purser Hugh McElroy, surgeon William O'Loughlin and chief steward Andrew Latimer were also on board. Passengers on this voyage included Thomas Andrews and professional gambler George Brereton, both of whom were destined to sail on the *Titanic*'s maiden voyage. Out of these six people, only Brereton would survive the sinking. (Don Lynch collection)

◀ **Door Sign**

This simple sign was on the door of Thomas Andrews' office at the Harland & Wolff shipyard in Belfast. (Kalman Tanito collection, originally from the Phillip A. Gowan collection)

CARL ASPLUND

▶ **Letter**

A water-stained letter recovered from the body of third-class victim Carl Asplund, who, together with his wife and five children, was en route to Worcester, Massachusetts, from Sweden. The sender, corresponding in Swedish, writes: 'I am glad you are coming to Worcester again. I will keep the work for you until you arrive; don't worry the position is reserved for you. Write me a few lines when you leave Sweden so I have time to have it arranged.' Only Mrs Asplund and two of her five children would survive the sinking. (Trevor Powell collection)

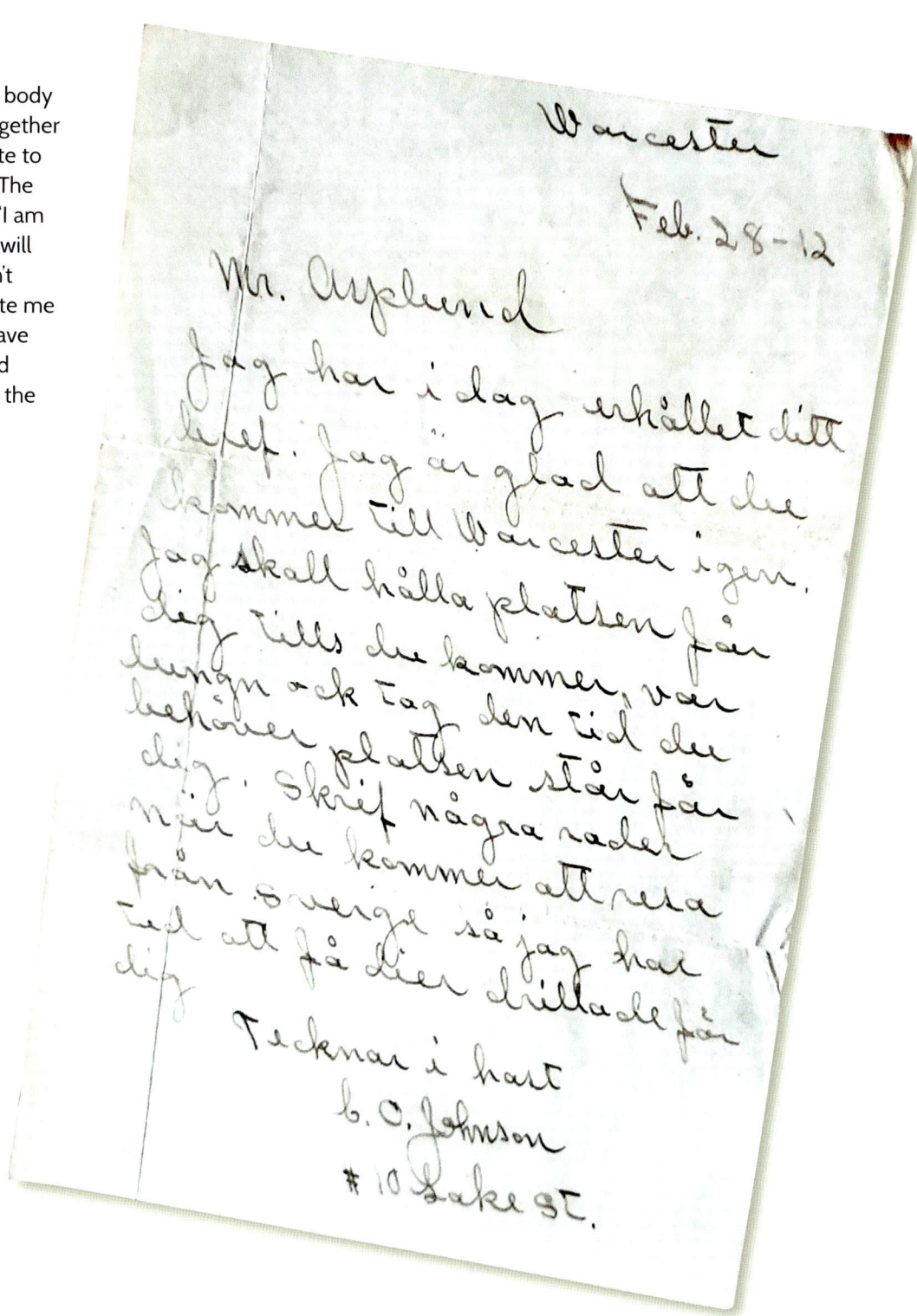

SELMA ASPLUND

CLARENCE J. SHEARN
NASSAU-BEEKMAN BUILDING
140 NASSAU STREET
NEW YORK

December 16, 1912.

Mrs. Selma Asplund.

151 Vernon St.,

Worcester, Mass.

Dear Madam:-

I have your letter of December 11, 1912, in reference to an award made for the benefit of your children by the New York American Titanic Fund Committee. In reply thereto I beg to advise you that the trust is now being arranged and in a short time I shall be able to notify you just how this money is to be paid.

Yours very truly,

C. J. Shearn

JPS/V

CLARENCE J. SHEARN
NASSAU-BEEKMAN BUILDING
140 NASSAU STREET
NEW YORK

February 8, 1913.

Mrs. Selma Asplund.
No. 151 Vernon St.,
Worcester, Mass.

Dear Madam:-

I am the attorney for the New York American which has made an award from its Titanic Fund for the benefit of your children.

Please send me the names and ages of each of your children with the dates of their births.

Yours very truly,

C. J. Shearn

CLARENCE J. SHEARN
NASSAU-BEEKMAN BUILDING
140 NASSAU STREET
NEW YORK

April 26, 1913.

Mrs. Selma Asplund,
151 Vernon St.,
Worcester, Mass.

Dear Madam:

I am in receipt of a letter dated April 25, 1913, from Victor E. Runo an attorney in your city inquiring about the disposition of the fund awarded by the New York American Titanic Committee for the benefit of your children.

In reply thereto I beg to advise you that the sum of $1522.41 has been deposited with the Equitable Trust Co. of New York City who will act as Trustee thereof and pay the income thereon to you until your older child becomes 16 years old when one-half the principal will be delivered to her general guardian. The income on the balance will then be paid to you as before until Felix becomes 16 when the balance will be delivered to his general guardian.

JPS/E

Yours very truly,

C. J. Shearn.

▲ Relief Fund Correspondence

Letters received by survivor Selma Asplund relating to relief fund money her children, Lillian and Felix, were awarded by the *New York American* Titanic Fund Committee. Lillian (5) and Felix (3) survived the disaster with their mother, but Selma lost her husband Carl and three sons, Clarence, Oscar and Carl, when the *Titanic* went down. (Mike Beatty collection)

JOHN JACOB ASTOR IV

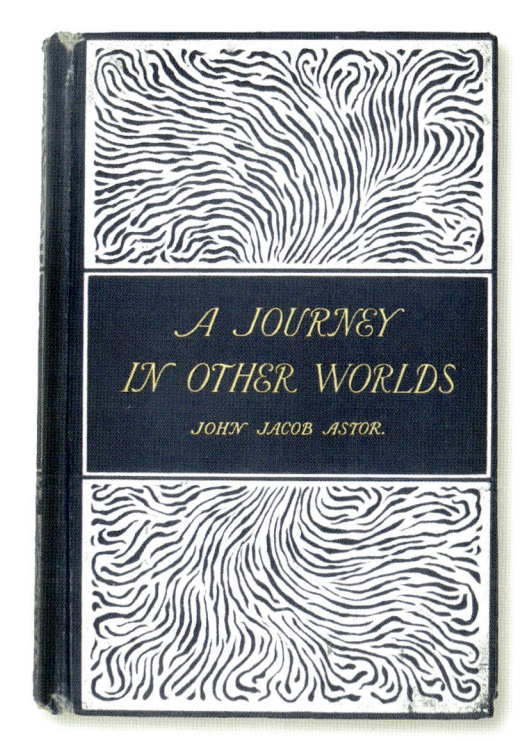

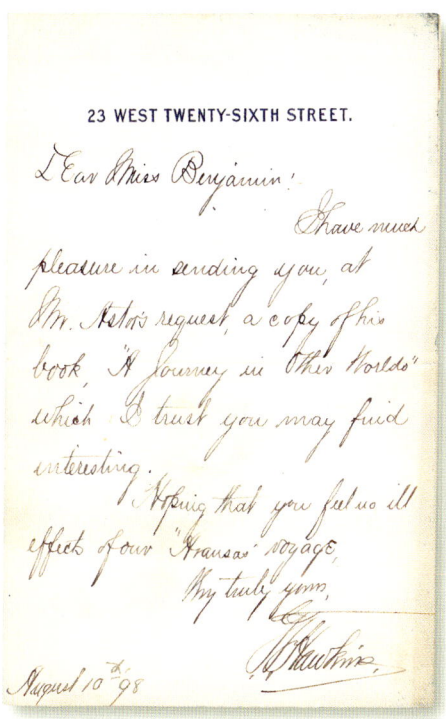

▲ Letter
An 1895 letter written by John Jacob Astor IV to a secretary at Trinity Church in Manhattan, where the Astors were prominent members of the congregation. After his body was recovered by the crew of the *Mackay-Bennett*, it was interred in the church's cemetery. (Trevor Powell collection)

▶ *A Journey in Other Worlds*
Astor published this fanciful book of future space travel in 1898, the same year he served in the Spanish–American War. This particular copy he signed to Anna Northend Benjamin, America's first female war correspondent, and Astor's personal secretary penned a note when he sent the book to her. Astor met Benjamin when they were both travelling home on the *Arkansas*; the journey home was a rough one, the ship being filled with illness and only minimum provisions. (Mike Beatty collection)

▶ ▼ **Binoculars**
Astor's Carl Zeiss Jagdglas binoculars, serial number 1674, produced in 1898, distributed by Theo Mundorff, New York. (Kalman Tanito collection)

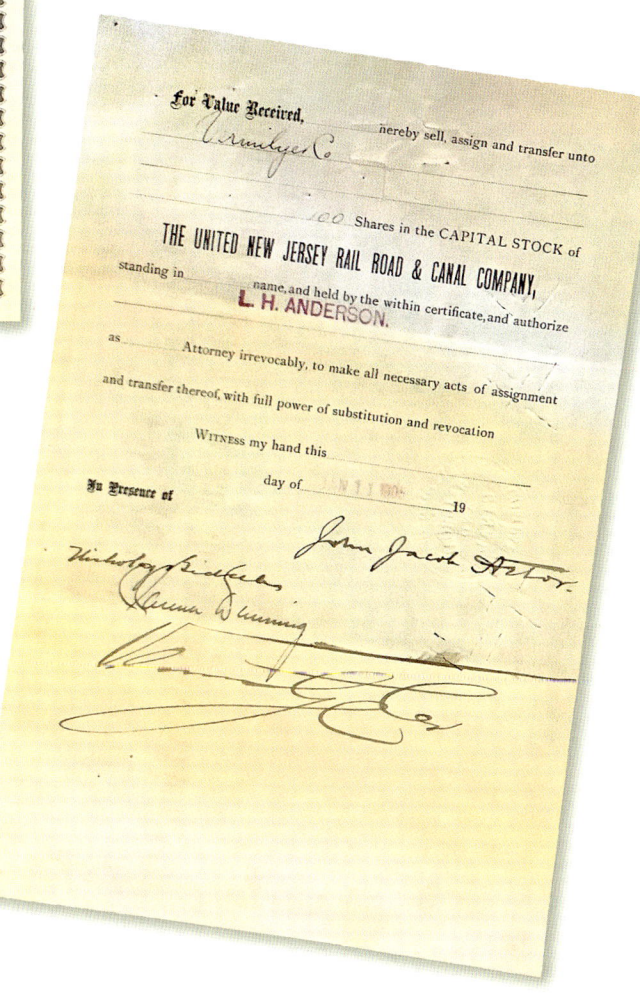

◀▼ Astor Stock Certificate

This certificate for 100 shares of the United New Jersey Rail Road & Canal Company was sold by Astor on 11 January 1905. At the time of his death, Astor was considered to be one of the richest men in America. (John Lamoreau collection)

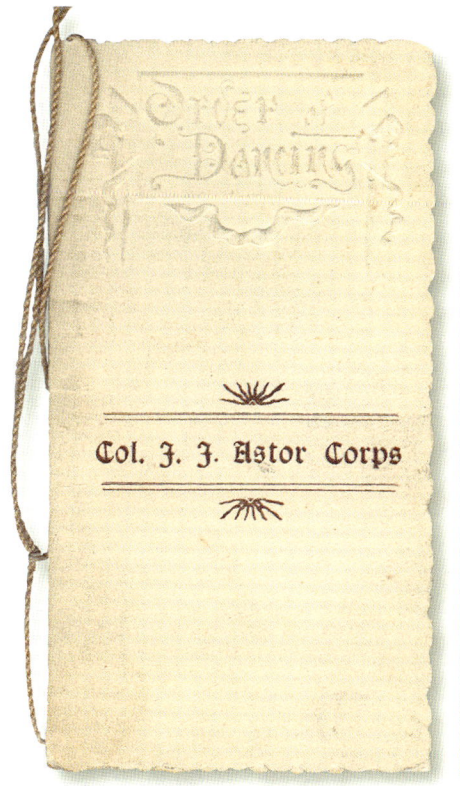

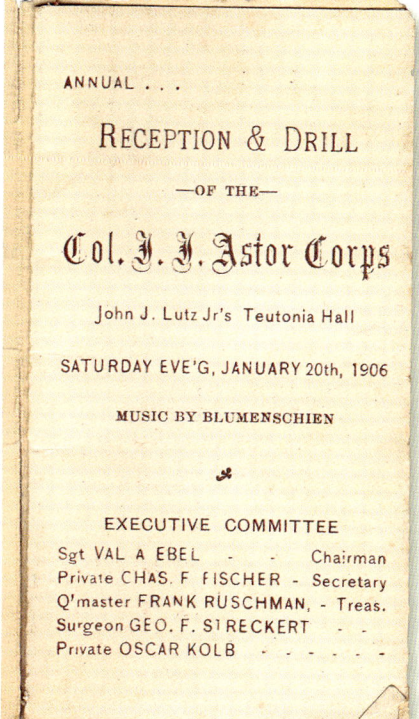

◀ Announcement

A 1906 announcement for the annual reception and drill of the Col. J. J. Astor Corps, which may have been associated with Astor's military service during the Spanish–American War. (Mike Beatty collection)

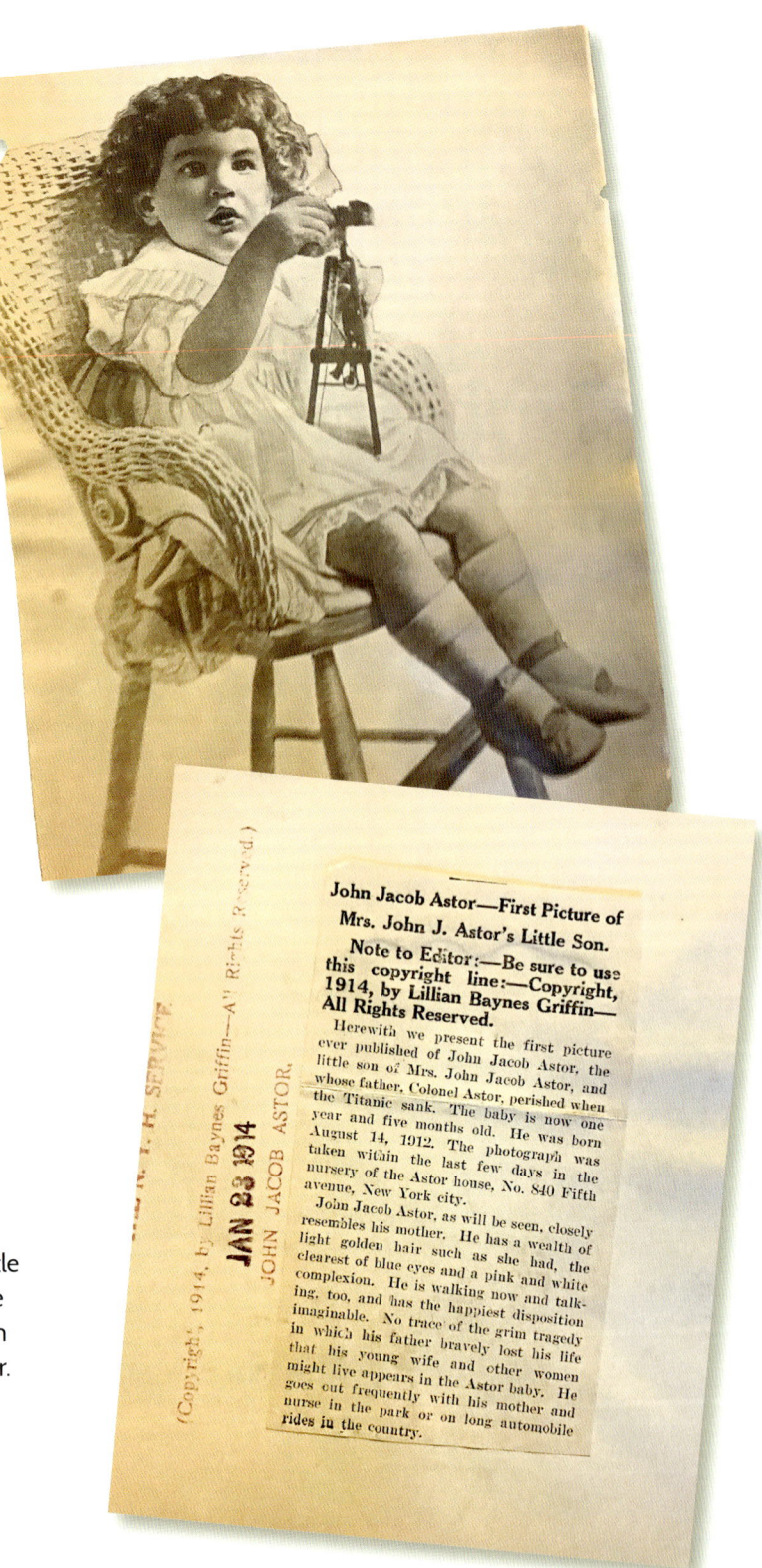

▲ **Astor Press Photo**

A press photo often used to portray Astor after the sinking of the *Titanic*. (John Lamoreau collection)

▶ **John Jacob Astor V Press Photo**

This photo is dated 23 January 1914, with the caption, 'First Picture of Mrs. John J. Astor's Little Son'. Madeleine Astor was pregnant when she entered a *Titanic* lifeboat; her son was born on 14 August 1912 and was named after his father. (John Lamoreau collection)

John Jacob Astor—First Picture of Mrs. John J. Astor's Little Son.

Note to Editor:—Be sure to use this copyright line:—Copyright, 1914, by Lillian Baynes Griffin— All Rights Reserved.

Herewith we present the first picture ever published of John Jacob Astor, the little son of Mrs. John Jacob Astor, and whose father, Colonel Astor, perished when the Titanic sank. The baby is now one year and five months old. He was born August 14, 1912. The photograph was taken within the last few days in the nursery of the Astor house, No. 840 Fifth avenue, New York city.

John Jacob Astor, as will be seen, closely resembles his mother. He has a wealth of light golden hair such as she had, the clearest of blue eyes and a pink and white complexion. He is walking now and talking, too, and has the happiest disposition imaginable. No trace of the grim tragedy in which his father bravely lost his life that his young wife and other women might live appears in the Astor baby. He goes out frequently with his mother and nurse in the park or on long automobile rides in the country.

EDWARD BARROWS

S.S. CAMPANIA.

◀ Postcard

A pre-sinking postcard sent by *Titanic* crewman and victim Will Barrows. Edward William Peter Barrows, better known as 'Will', was a saloon steward on the *Titanic*. This postcard of SS *Campania* dates to 1906, at which time Barrows was working as a waiter on board that vessel, and is addressed to 'Miss Ada Alford' in London. The card is signed on the reverse 'Love and Best Wishes, Will'. (John Lamoreau collection)

NELLIE BECKER

▶ Becker Scrapbook

Mrs Allen O. Nellie Becker and her three children were second-class passengers aboard the *Titanic*. All survived, although the two younger children, 4-year-old Marion and 1-year-old Richard, carried no memories of the sinking. Mrs Becker and her husband later had this scrapbook inscribed with 'Titanic and Other Personal Items' on the spine, and pasted memorabilia and newspaper clippings into it. They later presented it to their older daughter, Ruth, who had clear memories of the disaster. (Don Lynch collection)

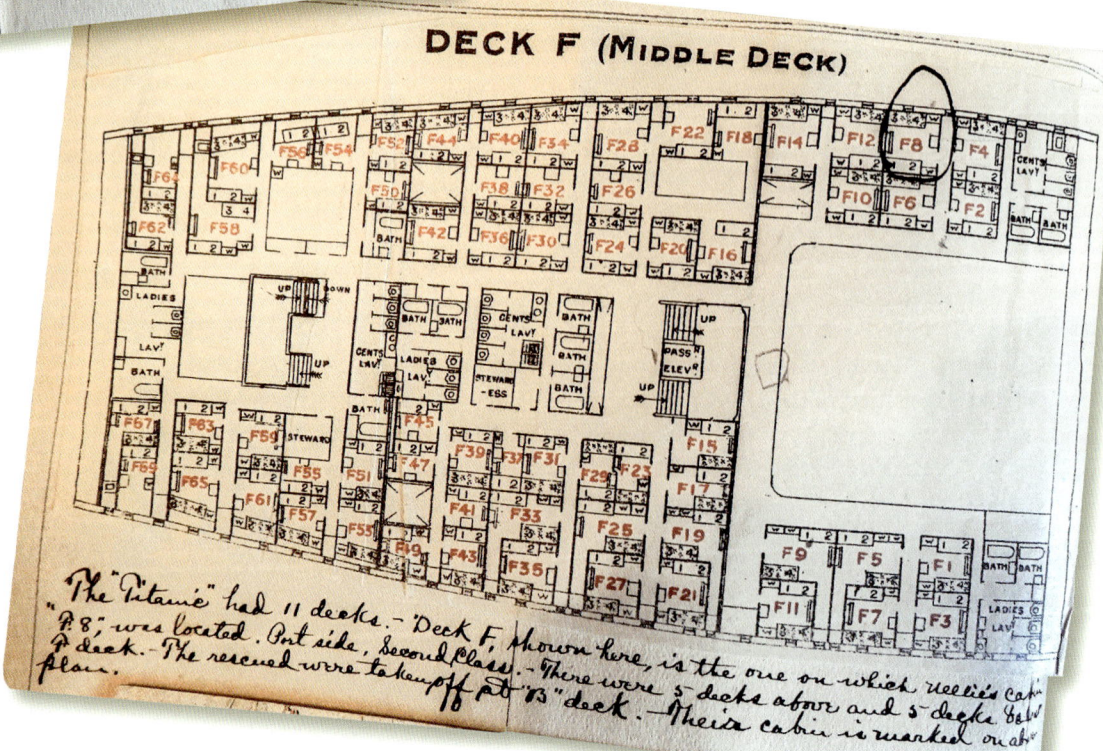

Titanic Deck Plan

The Beckers were in possession of a second-class *Titanic* deck plan. This was later cut up, and only the name of the ship, an image of the liner, its dimensions and the portion showing F-deck were placed in the scrapbook. The rest was apparently discarded. Reverend Becker has written a brief description of where his family's stateroom was, and circled the room itself. He believed that the family escaped from the ship on B-deck. (Don Lynch collection)

WOVEN IN SILK.

R.M.S. CARPATHIA.

▲ Silk *Carpathia* Postcard

While on board the *Carpathia* Nellie Becker apparently obtained this very rare silk postcard of the Cunard liner. Across the top she has written 'The Good Ship which saved us!' (Don Lynch collection)

Clockwise from top left: **Marconigram** On 17 April friends of the Beckers sent this wordy wireless message to Nellie on board the *Carpathia*. It is addressed to her as a 'survivor'. The senders clearly did not appreciate the volume of radio messages going to and from the *Carpathia*, for, although the message is comforting, it's rather lengthy and did nothing to provide immediate assistance for when they reached New York. (Don Lynch collection); **Marconigram** On 18 April, while still aboard the *Carpathia*, Nellie Becker received this wireless message from Dr L.B. Wolf, a representative of the Lutheran Church. Nellie was thrilled to receive this, as she had been told that survivors would not be allowed off the *Carpathia* unless they had someone waiting to receive them. This would act as the ticket for her and her children to disembark. (Don Lynch collection); **Telegram** Dr Wolf had told Nellie in his wireless message that he had cabled her husband. This is the message Rev. Becker received in India, having gone to the mountains for his health. The news had not yet reached him of the *Titanic* disaster, and the message made no mention of it. Seeing that it had been sent on 17 April, he assumed his family's transatlantic voyage must have been completed, and that they had been saved from a train accident of some kind on their way to South Bend, Indiana. (Don Lynch collection); **Telegram** After leaving the *Carpathia*, Nellie and her children were escorted to the Hotel Avon on Lexington Avenue in New York City. It was there that Nellie received this telegram from her mother. According to her granddaughter, Nellie and her mother did not have a good relationship. This is apparent in that, although Mrs Baumgardner is pleased with her daughter's rescue, she obviously has no consideration for what Nellie has been through, nor does she even know if Nellie has so much as a penny to her name, yet she states that she 'will expect [a] wire in [the] morning'. (Don Lynch collection)

RICHARD BECKWITH

▶ **Richard L. Beckwith Business Correspondence**
Survivor Richard Beckwith worked in investment and real estate. This collection of correspondence pertains to an investment in the US Adding Machine Company that Richard was handling between two other parties in 1916. Some misunderstandings, tempers, and maybe even some deceit on the part of one of the parties ensued over the course of several months, but the parties were made whole after Richard had his final say on matters (although he probably didn't do business with them again!). Richard would go on to become second vice president of the company under the new partnership of Ruland & Benjamin Co. (Mike Beatty collection)

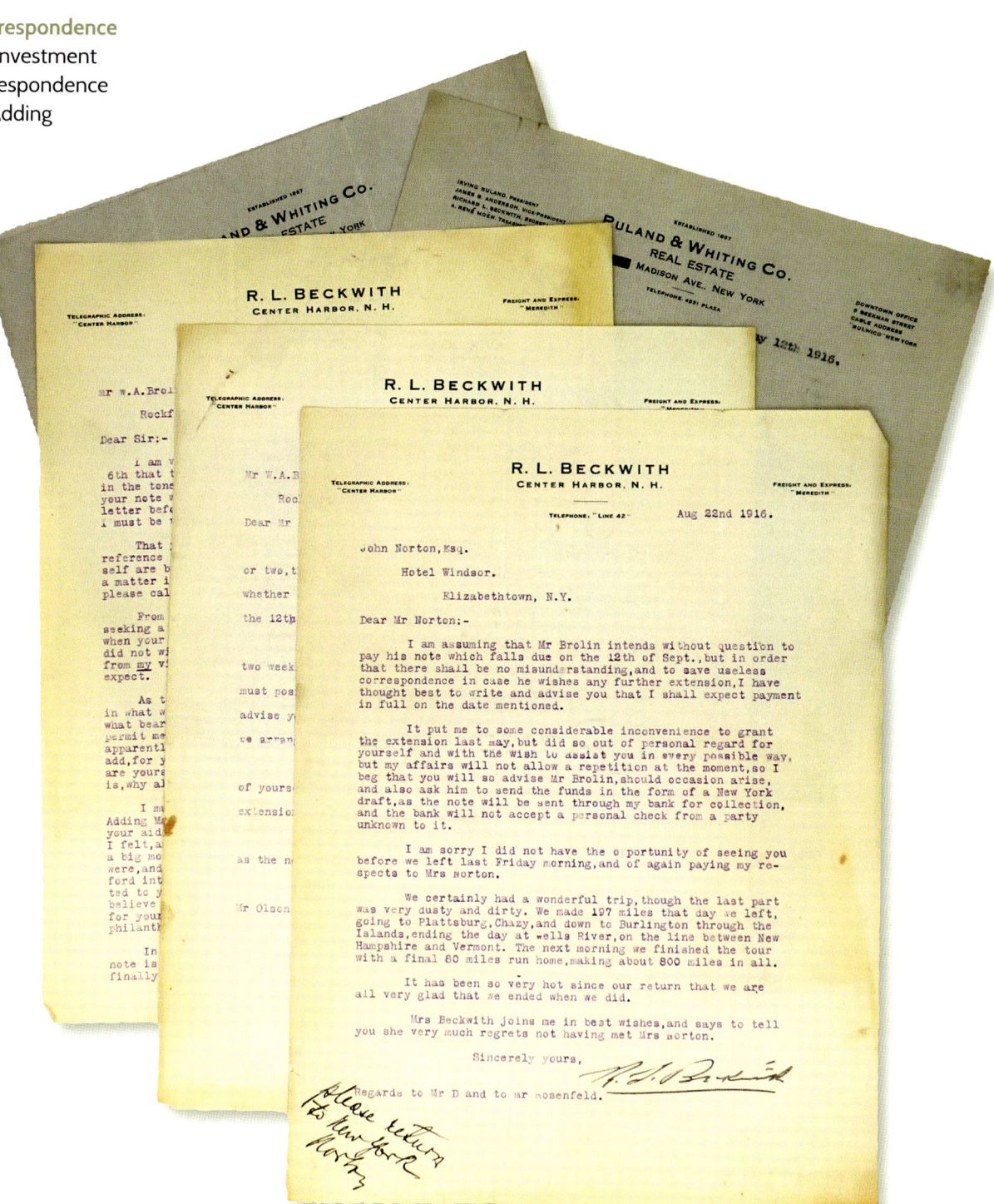

LAWRENCE BEESLEY

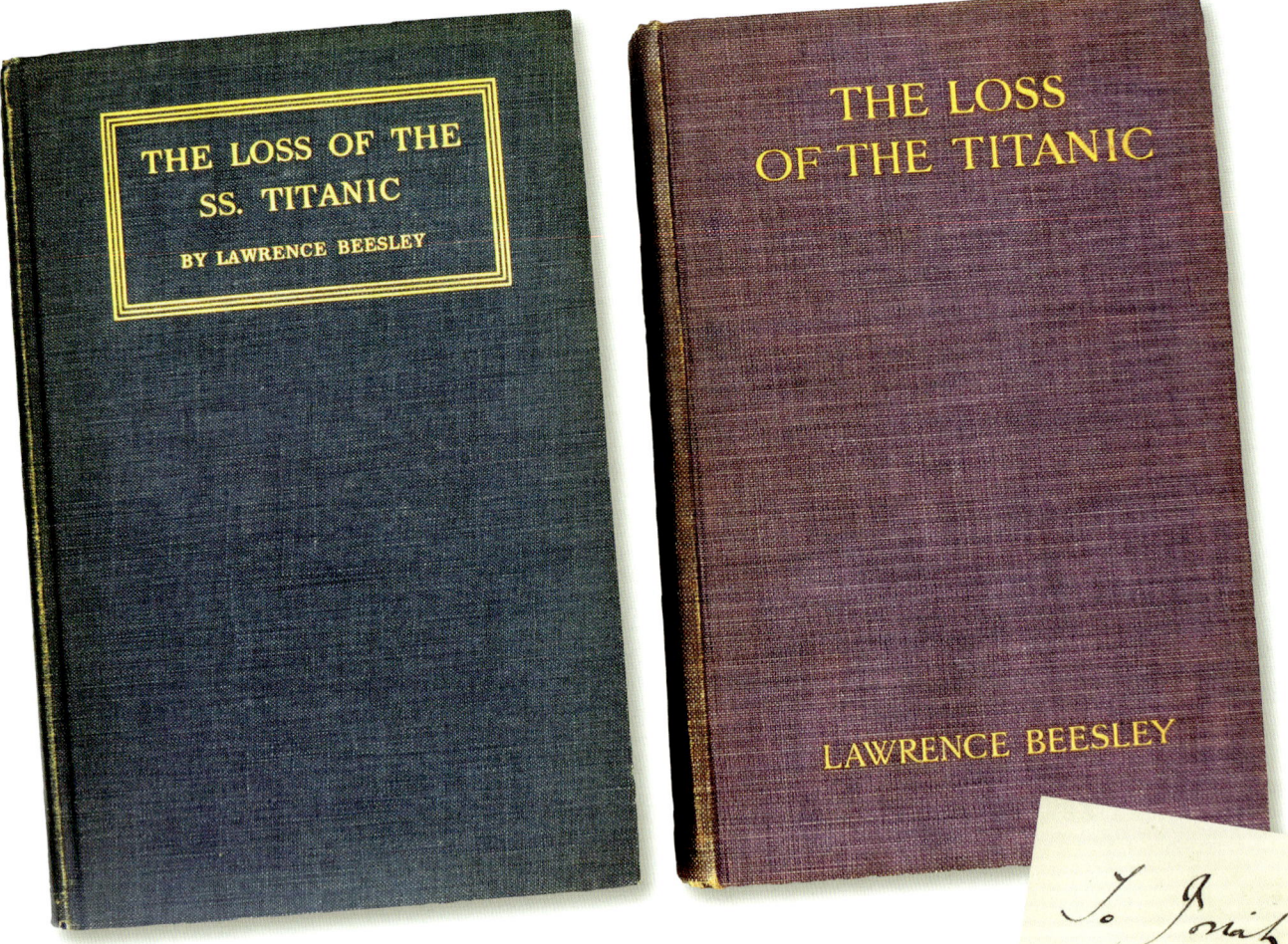

▲▶ Book
Second-class passenger Lawrence Beesley wrote one of the most well-known accounts published about the disaster. He wasted no time in doing so, and his book was initially released in July 1912. Shown here are the first US (left) and UK (right) editions of his book. In a 1914 edition, Beesley signed a copy for a friend. (Mike Beatty collection)

KARL BEHR

▶ **Karl Behr Press Photo**

Karl Behr is caught fielding a serve in this 1914 Underwood & Underwood press photo. Karl was on board the *Titanic* in pursuit of his love interest, Helen Newsom. Both managed to escape in lifeboat 5 and were married a year later. Karl was not the only tennis player on board. Up-and-coming star Richard Williams was also a passenger and barely escaped, almost losing both legs from exposure. The two players would meet on the court three months later in a tournament at Longwood. Williams lost to Behr in five sets. (Mike Beatty collection)

MABEL BENNETT

▶ **Marconigram**

Mabel Kate Bennett was a stewardess on the *Titanic* and was one of the last people ushered into a lifeboat by Bruce Ismay. While on the rescue ship *Carpathia*, she managed to send a two-word message to her sister: 'Mabel Saved'. Her message was dated 18 April 1912. (John Lamoreau collection)

WILLIAM BERRIMAN

◀ **Relief Cheque**

Second-class passenger William John Berriman was immigrating to Calumet, Michigan, where he intended to be a miner. However, he died in the sinking and his body was never recovered. His family received compensation for his loss, as shown in this relief cheque made out to his father, John. (Mike Beatty collection)

PERCIVAL ALBERT BLAKE

▶ **Discharge Book**

This British Board of Trade discharge book was issued to Percival Albert Blake and records his career at sea. Blake was one of the few trimmers aboard the *Titanic* to survive and his original discharge book was lost in the sinking. Written in the opening pages of this book is 'Renewal of book. Original lost through shipwreck'. (Trevor Powell collection)

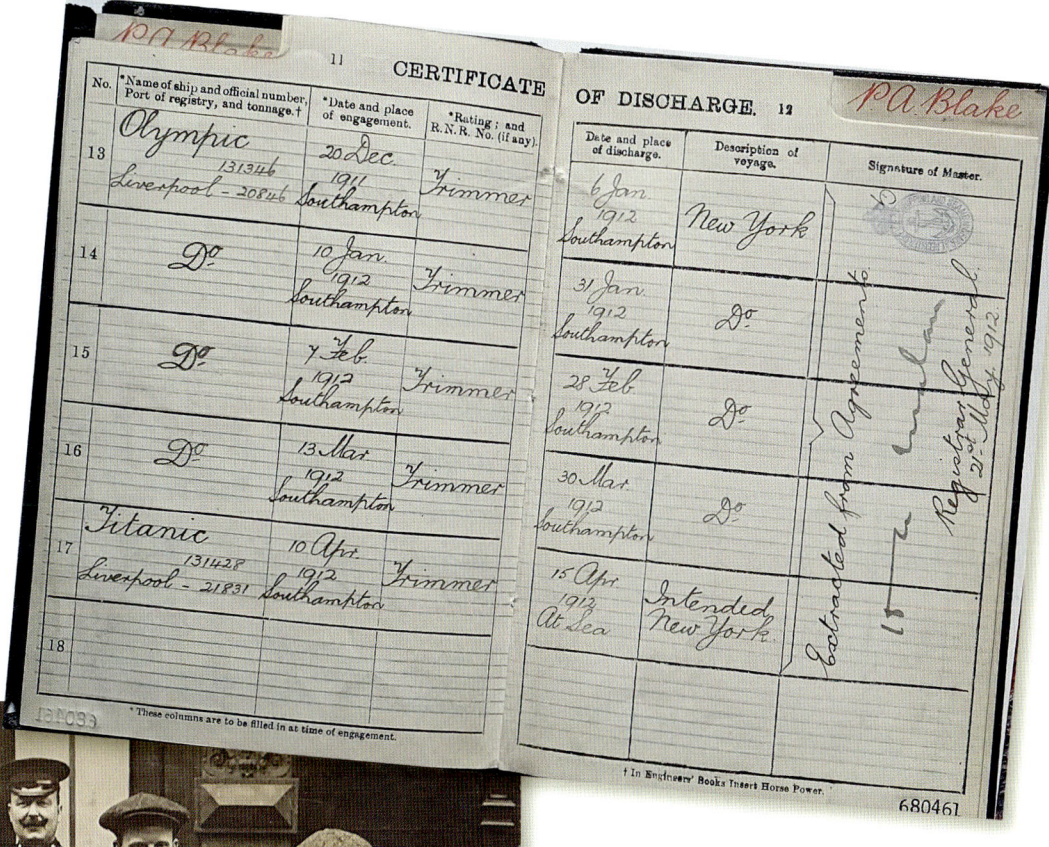

◀ **Survivors' Photo**

This photograph depicts Percival Albert Blake, second from the left, posing with three other surviving crewmen upon arrival in Plymouth. (Trevor Powell collection)

HAROLD BRIDE

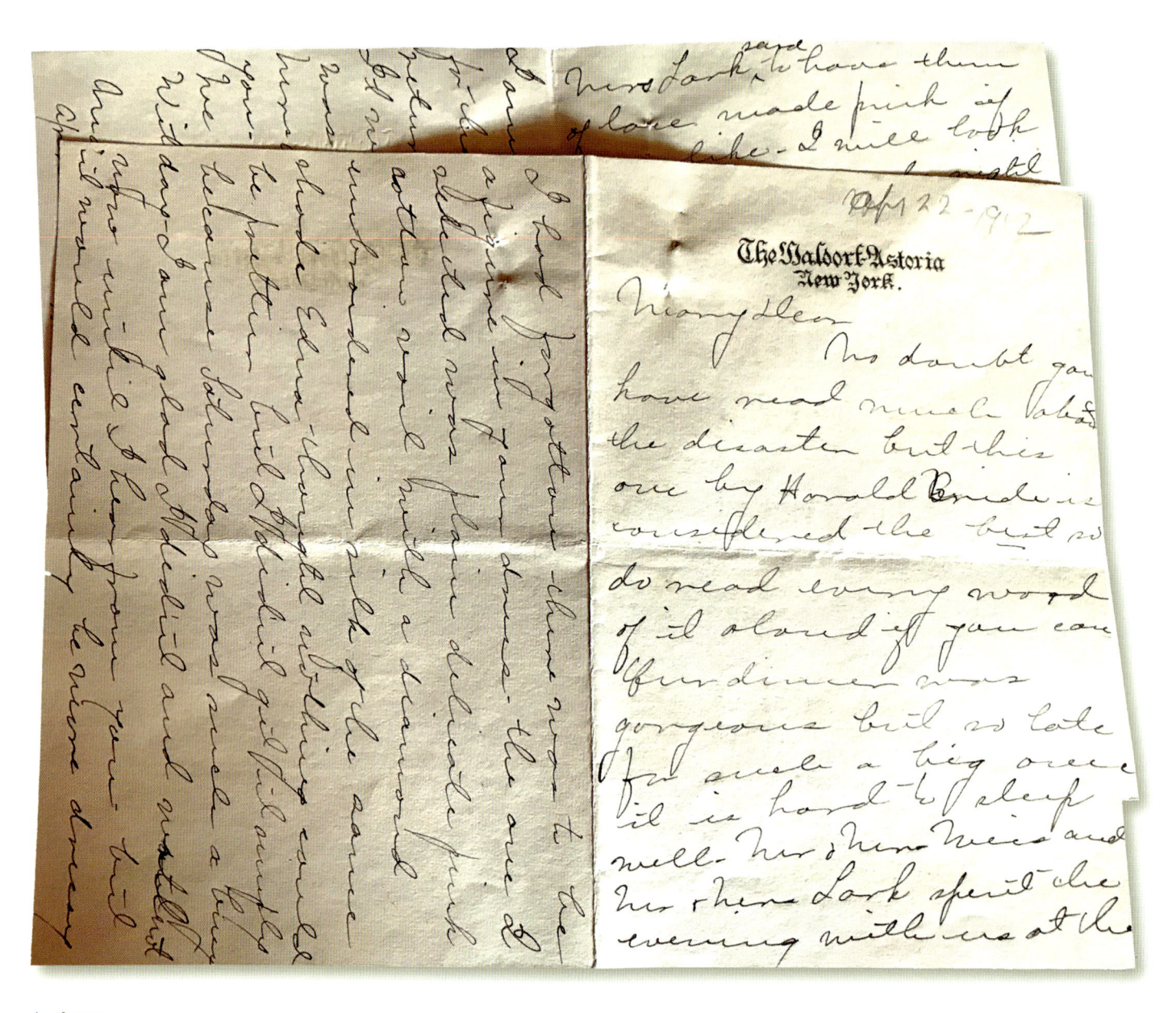

▲ **Letter**
A 22 April 1912 letter sent from the Waldorf-Astoria Hotel, where many of the *Titanic* survivors sought refuge. A mother writes to her daughter: 'Mary Dear, No doubt you have read much about the disaster but this one by Harold Bride is considered the <u>best</u> so do read every word of it aloud if you can … The Larks had expected to sail to Europe on the Titanic but gave up going as soon as they heard of the disaster. They expect to go this summer on the Olympic but want to wait until there are plenty of life boats on board …' (John Lamoreau collection)

EMMA BUCKNELL

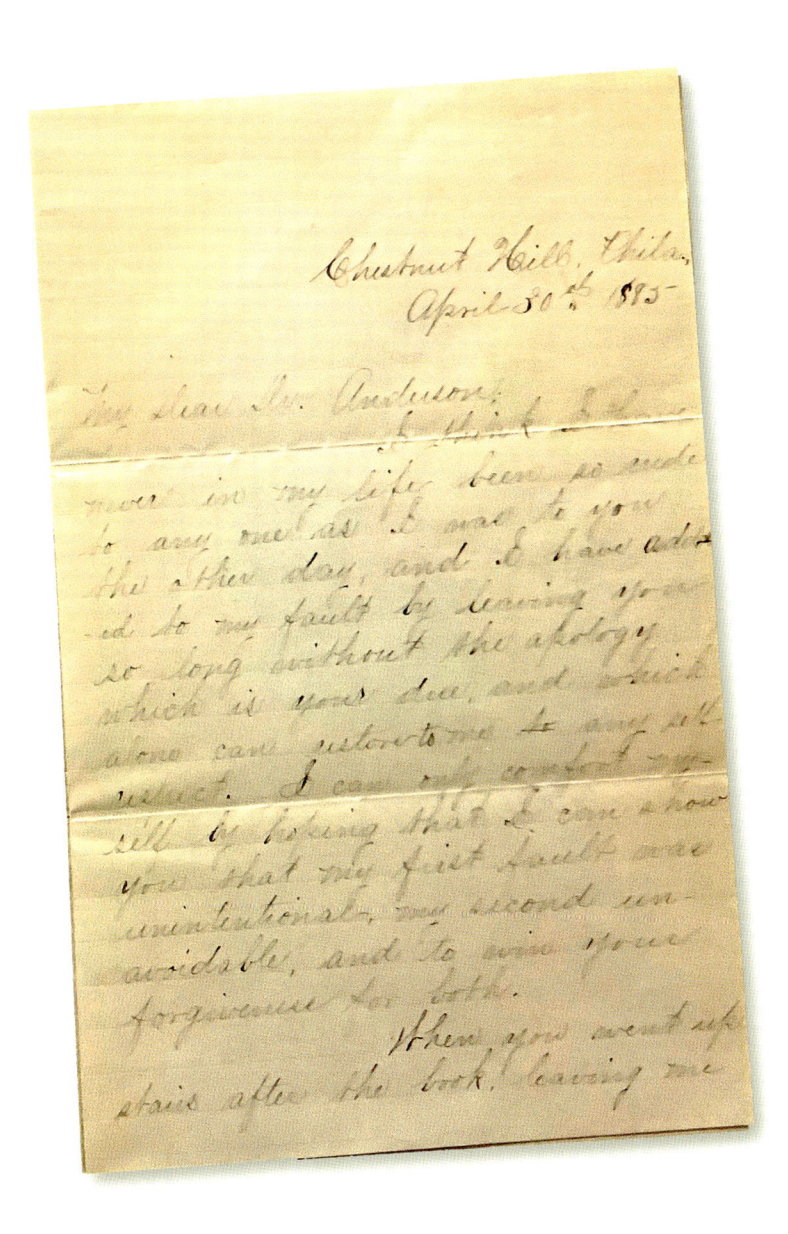

▲ 1885 Letter

Emma Bucknell was a Philadelphia heiress, first-class *Titanic* passenger and a survivor of the disaster who left the sinking ship in lifeboat 8. Bucknell College in Pennsylvania is named for her husband. This eight-page letter is faded but readable, offering wonderful insight into her world. (John Lamoreau collection)

ARCHIBALD BUTT

▲ Signed Portrait

Victim Archibald Butt signed and gifted a portrait on 14 May 1909. That day he attended a May party held at the White House hosted by the First Lady, and later he had dinner with the French ambassador and his wife. His day concluded with some late-night socialising with members of the 'Night Riders' (Alice Roosevelt Longworth and her friends), who paid an unannounced visit to his residence to invite him to join them in making mischief. (Mike Beatty collection)

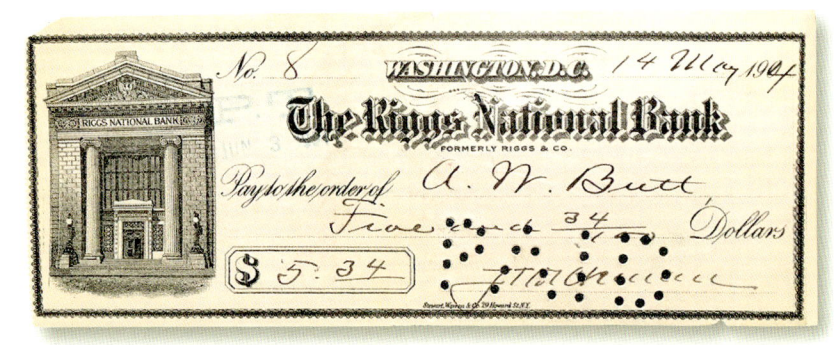

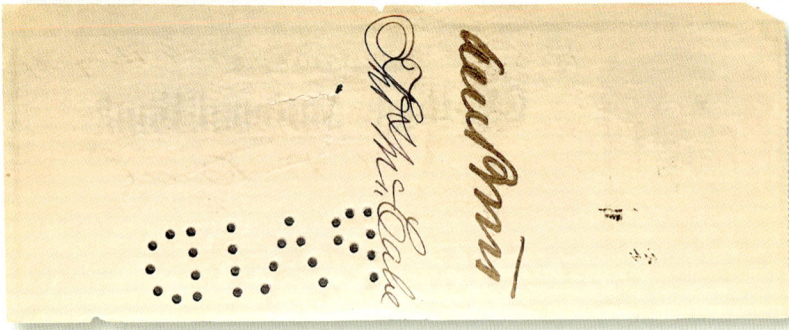

▲ **Cheque**

A cheque made out to Captain Butt on 14 May 1904. 'Archie' endorsed the cheque on its reverse side. (George Behe collection)

▲ **Bookplate**

An example of Captain Butt's personal bookplate. This specimen is affixed inside the army-issue book *Index to Special Orders Issued from the Adjutant General's Office, 1890*. (George Behe collection)

◄ **Stereopticon Slide**

A 3D slide showing President Taft formally opening the Gunnison Tunnel in Montrose, Colorado, on 23 September 1909. Captain Butt (wearing a campaign hat) is standing directly behind Taft. This stereopticon slide is very likely the only 3D view we'll ever have of a *Titanic* passenger or crew. (George Behe collection)

Presidents William H. Taft and Porfirio Diaz, occasion of their meeting in C. Juarez, Mexico, Oct. 16th, 1909.

◀ **Postcard**
In October 1909 Captain Butt (left) accompanied President Taft to Ciudad Juárez, Mexico, where Taft met Mexican President Porfirio Díaz. (George Behe collection)

▶ **Photograph**
In March 1910 Captain Butt (right) escorted President Taft and his party back to Washington, DC, after completing a brief excursion elsewhere. (George Behe collection)

◀ Photograph

In this candid photo, most likely taken on 3 or 4 June 1910, when they visited Michigan, Captain Butt (second from right) is seen in uniform with President Taft. The man in the top hat to the right of Taft is Senator William Alden Smith, who would head the US Inquiry into the *Titanic* disaster two years later. (Mike Beatty collection)

▶ Photograph

In November 1910 Captain Butt accompanied President Taft to Panama to inspect the ongoing construction of the canal. (George Behe collection)

Clockwise from top left:

Postcard
On 11 February 1911 President Taft and Captain Butt reviewed the military cadets at the University of Illinois. (George Behe collection)

Photograph
President Taft and now Major Butt during a trip to Brooklyn, New York, on 8 June 1911. (George Behe collection)

Postcard
Here Major Butt (far left) is seated in front of President Taft during his visit to Rochester, New York, on 23 August 1911. (George Behe collection)

Postcard
Another view of Major Butt (foreground) and President Taft in Rochester, New York. (George Behe collection)

◄ Photograph

On 16 September 1911 President Taft and Major Butt (centre rear) were at the Syracuse Fair in New York. (George Behe collection)

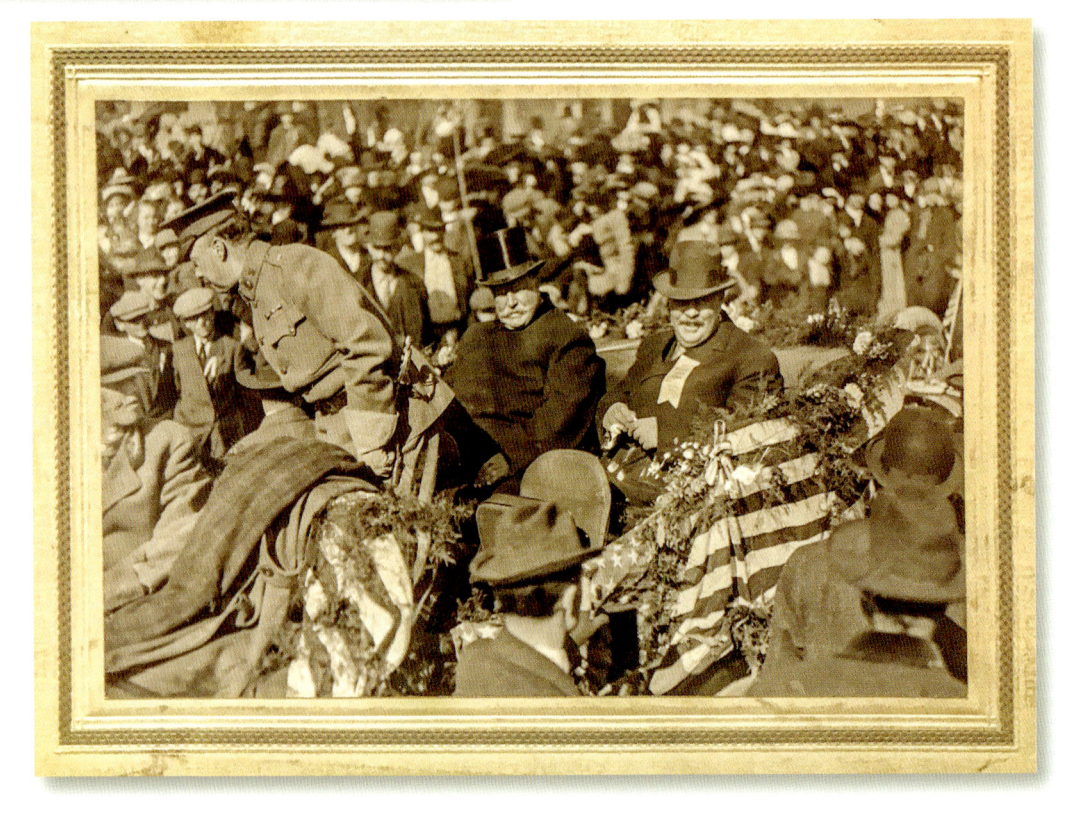

► Photograph

On 19 October 1911 President Taft and Major Butt were in Butte, Montana, during Taft's cross-country railroad tour. Major Butt may have been the world's most photographed *Titanic* passenger prior to April 1912. (Original Floyd Bushnell photograph, George Behe collection)

Major Butt Gift to Niece

A 1910 copy of Nathaniel Hawthorne's *A Wonder Book and Tanglewood Tales*, illustrated by Maxfield Parrish. Major Butt gave this book to his niece, 8-year-old Julia Brailsford Butt, for Christmas 1911, just a few months before his trip to Europe with Frank Millet. Inside the book he pasted his 'Aide de camp to the President' calling card with a pencilled-in note: 'To Julia with love from her Uncle Archie.' In a 21 December 1911 letter to his sister-in-law Clara he writes: 'I am sending Julia a book. It treats of fairies. I hope Bessie is teaching her to believe in these persons of imagery, for they certainly people a child's world with delightful companions. I am always sorry for children who don't believe in fairies. To you I am sending a cheque. There is hardly anything as insulting, but somehow I think it might be more useful than some piece of jewellery or even a set of books this year.' (Mike Beatty collection)

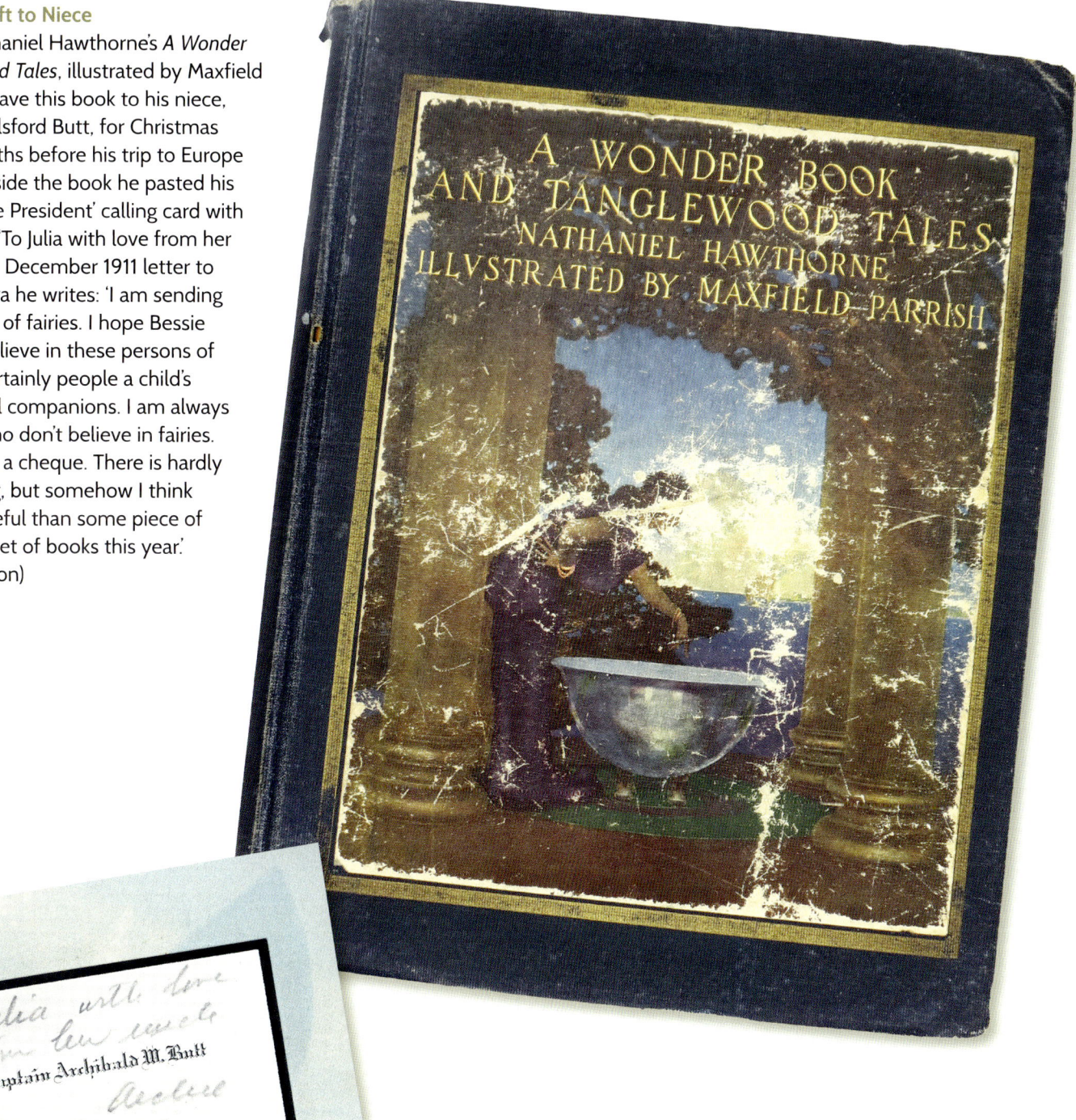

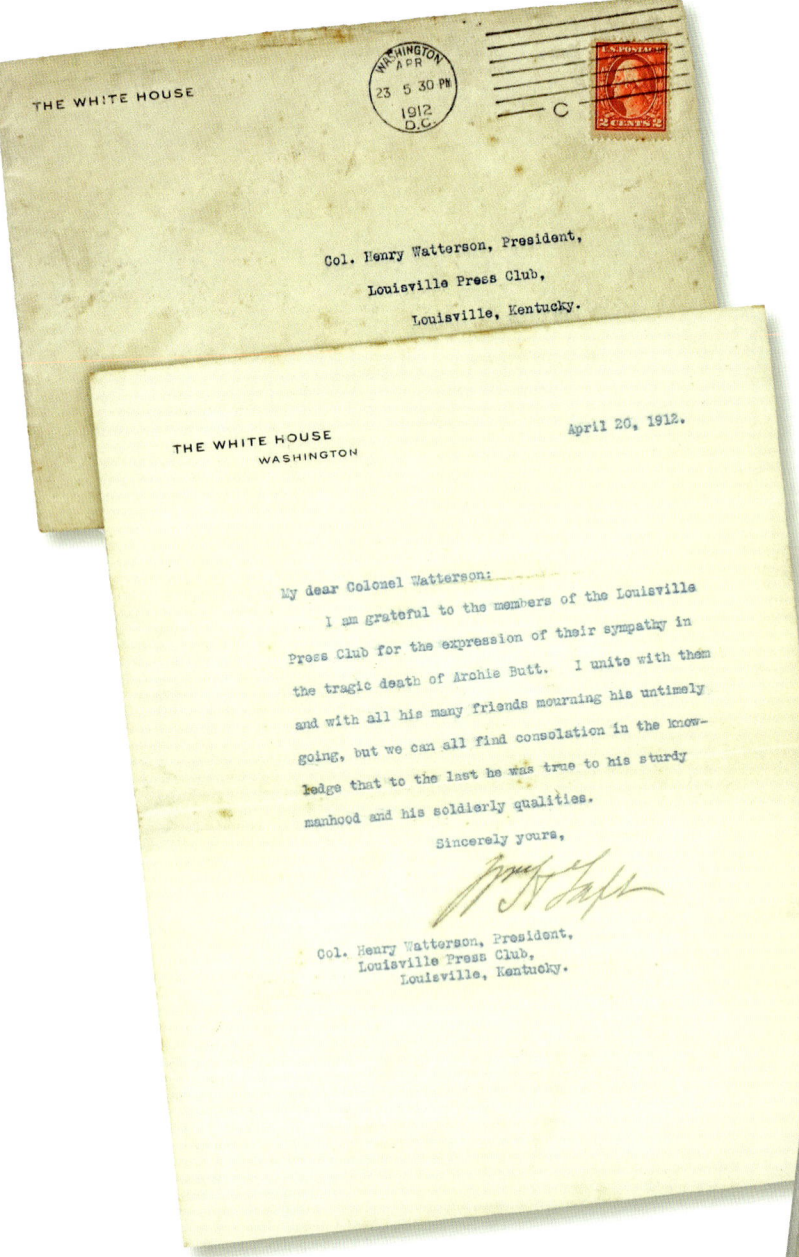

▼   **Book**

Although Major Butt's story *Both Sides of the Shield* was originally published in serial form in *Lippincott's* magazine in 1905, it wasn't until after his death on the *Titanic* that it appeared in book form. President Taft wrote a foreword for the book to honour his late aide-de-camp. (George Behe collection)

▲   **President Taft Letter**

President Taft sent a reply to Henry Watterson in response to Archie's death. Watterson was a friend of Major Butt's and had offered him a place on the *Louisville Courier Journal* to cover the police beat, thus starting his journalism career. (Mike Beatty collection)

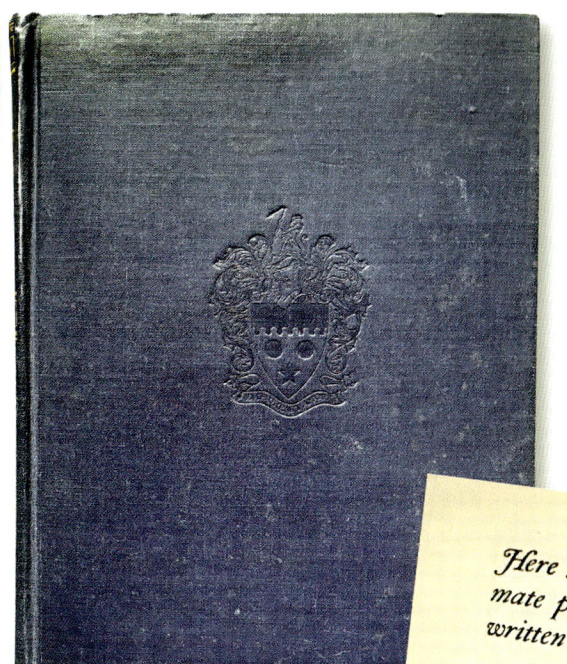

▲ Books

The Letters of Archie Butt (1924) and *Taft and Roosevelt: The Intimate Letters of Archie Butt* (two volumes, 1930) were published posthumously and consist of excerpts from letters Major Butt wrote to his mother and sister-in-law during his lifetime. These particular letters deal with the years Archie spent as chief military aide to Presidents Theodore Roosevelt and William Howard Taft from 1908 to 1912, and the front cover of each volume contains an impressed depiction of Major Butt's personal bookplate. The complete collection of original letters now resides in the Georgia Archive. (George Behe collection)

▶ Major Butt Book Advertisement

A magazine advertisement for the 1924 edition of *The Letters of Archie Butt*, which detailed his official activities during Theodore Roosevelt's presidential administration. (George Behe collection)

CLEAR CAMERON

▼ Clear Cameron Postcard
Second-class survivor Clear Cameron sent this postcard to her sister Janet 'Gert' Dowding. (Mike Beatty collection)

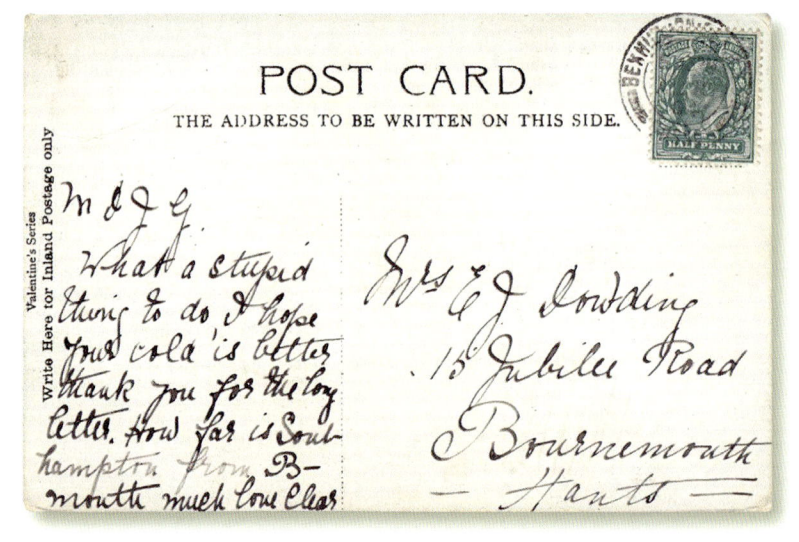

HELEN CANDEE

▼ Helen Churchill Candee Inscription
Helen Churchill Candee wrote this dedication on a page that most likely was removed from a copy of her first book, *How Women May Earn a Living*, published in January 1900. In 1912 she was doing research in Europe for a new book when she received word that her son Harold was seriously hurt in an accident. She booked a first-class passage on the next available ship for New York, and left on 10 April on board the *Titanic*. (Mike Beatty collection)

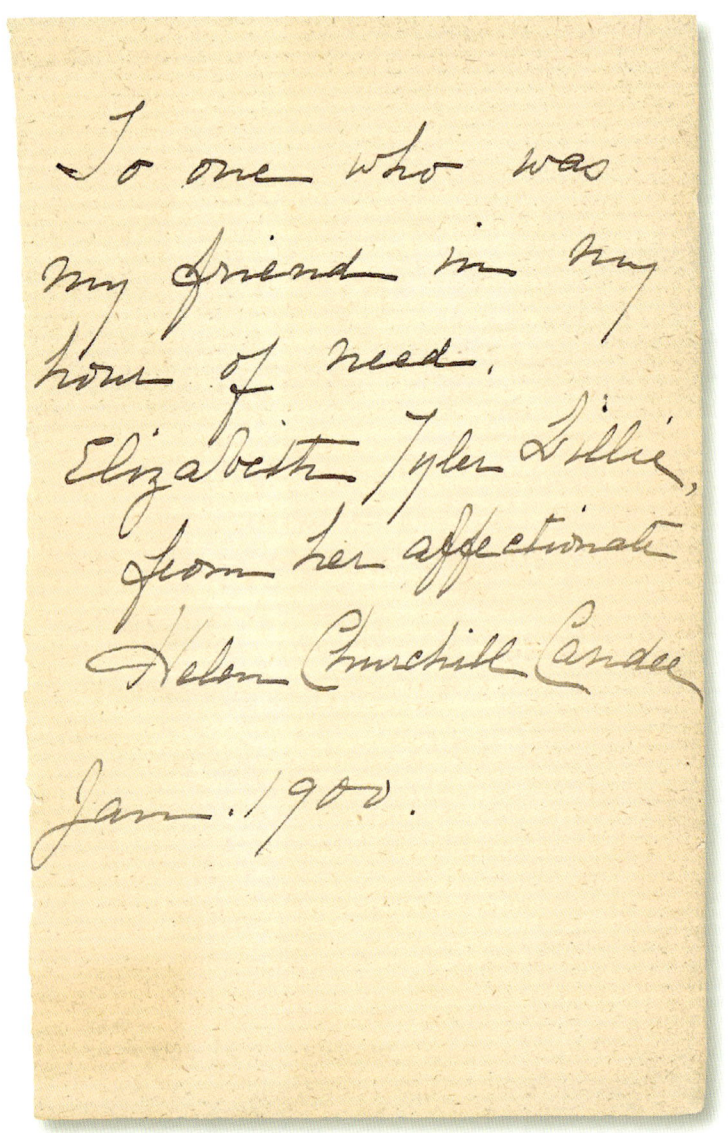

ELEANOR CASSEBEER

◄▼ Eleanor Cassebeer Christmas Card
Many survivors stayed in contact with each other long after the disaster, and Eleanor Cassebeer was no exception. When she mailed out Christmas cards in 1913, she sent this one to *Titanic*'s third officer Herbert Pitman. (Mike Beatty collection)

With every Good Wish

With Heartiest Greetings and Good Wishes for a happy Christmas and the Brightest of New Years.

from

Mrs. Eleanor Genevieve Cassebeer.

Christmas 1913.

◄ Bottles
A set of bottles and a mould for producing them for the New York apothecary of Henry Arthur Cassebeer, Eleanor's husband. (Kalman Tanito collection)

PAUL CHEVRÉ

◀ Paul Chevré Marconigram

Artist Paul Chevré was sailing on *Titanic* for his yearly work trip to Canada. He was first headed to Ottawa for the grand opening of the Grand Trunk Railway's new Château Laurier Hotel, for whose lobby fellow *Titanic* passenger Charles Hays commissioned him to create a bust of Canadian prime minister Sir Wilfrid Laurier. Chevré was playing cards when *Titanic* struck the iceberg, and he quickly got into lifeboat 7 and was rescued. He sent four Marconigrams ashore from the *Carpathia*, including this one, sent in French: 'Saved by *Carpathia*, headed to New York.' (Mike Beatty collection)

▶ Paul Chevré Letter

Chevré remained in Quebec for six months before returning to Paris. Four weeks after the sinking he sent this letter in French:

14 May 1912

Dear Mr Bance,

Before leaving Ottawa, I want to thank you for the friendly welcome by Mrs Bance and yourself.

Please pass along my respects to Madame, your wonderful brother and your father-in-law the Colonel.

One day soon I hope to have the pleasure of seeing you in Paris. Until that lucky day keep in touch and write.

Best regards,
Yours truly
P. Chevré

(Mike Beatty collection)

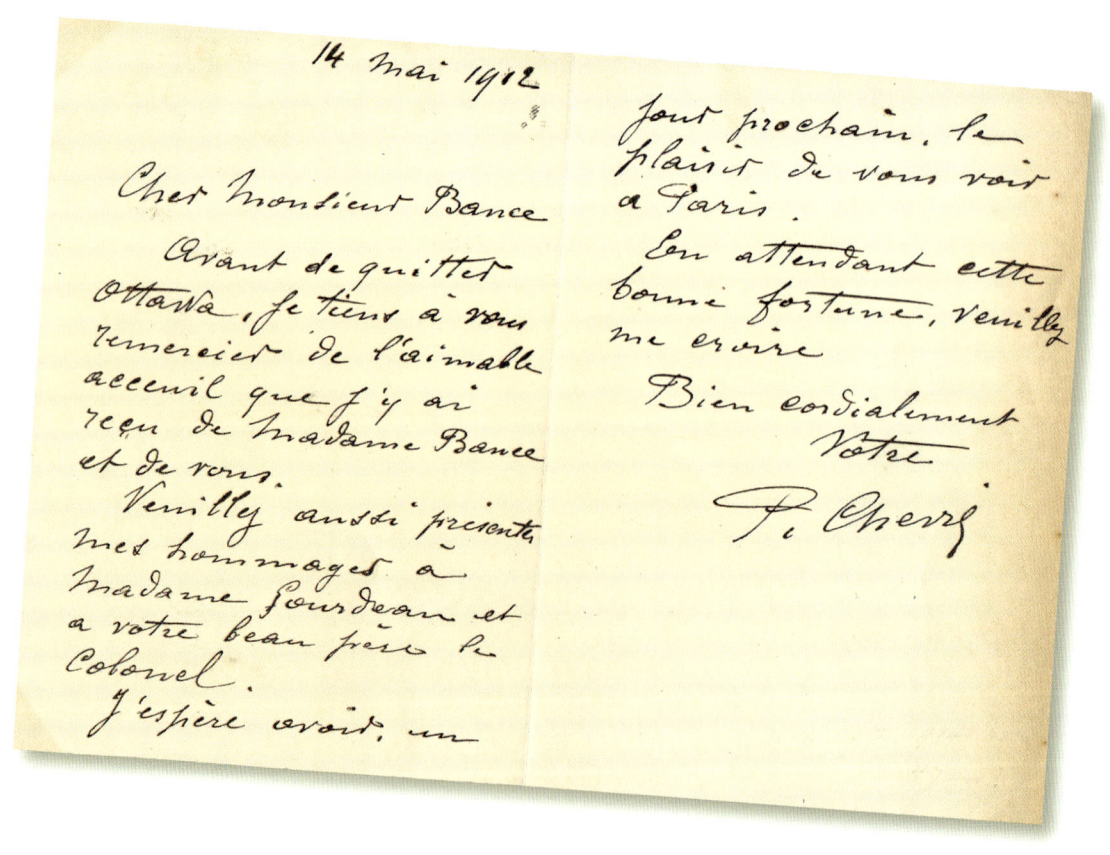

ALICE CHRISTY

▶ **Alice Christy Marconigram**

The twice-widowed Alice Christy was travelling second class on *Titanic* along with her daughters Juli and Amy, as well as Amy's husband Sydney Jacobson. Their destination was Quebec. After she and her daughters were rescued, Alice sent this Marconigram from the *Carpathia*. Sydney lost his life on the *Titanic*. (Mike Beatty collection)

WALTER CLARK

◀ **Brush**

A silver monogrammed brush that once belonged to first-class victim Walter Miller Clark. The brush was kept by his wife Virginia, who survived the sinking in lifeboat 4. (Trevor Powell collection)

ROBERT DANIEL

▶ **Robert W. Daniel Scrapbook**

Ruth C. Lynn was a neighbour and family friend of Robert Daniel's mother in Richmond, Virginia. When she heard the news of the sinking and Daniel being on board, she assembled this scrapbook of clippings, most of them mentioning Daniel, and ended up amassing forty-five pages. Later she gave this scrapbook to Daniel's mother. Daniel survived the sinking and would go on to marry fellow survivor Eloise Smith, who lost her first husband in the sinking. (Mike Beatty collection)

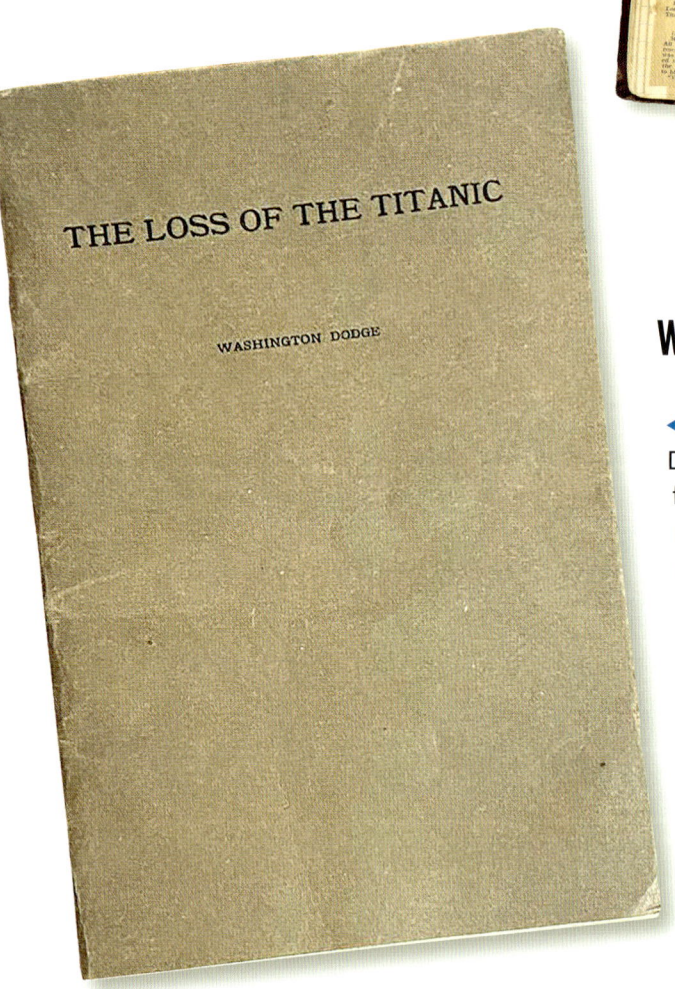

WASHINGTON DODGE

◀ **Dr Henry Washington Dodge Booklet**

Dr Washington Dodge, his wife Ruth and son Washington Jr were returning from France when they boarded the *Titanic* in Cherbourg. All three first-class passengers were fortunate to survive the sinking. On 11 May 1912, Dr Dodge gave an account of his ordeal at a luncheon of the Commonwealth Club in San Francisco. This booklet was one of a few printed for the occasion and is just like the one from which Dr Dodge read. (Mike Beatty collection)

LUCY DUFF GORDON

◄ **Lady Duff Gordon**
Two original photos from the liquidated Brown Brothers archive. The first was taken outside the ballroom at the Waldorf Astoria Hotel in New York City in December 1909. The second was taken at her store Lucile Ltd in New York City when she opened her US branch in 1910. (Mike Beatty collection)

▶ **Booklet**
A 1917 booklet from *Titanic* survivor and fashion designer Lady Duff Gordon. (John Lamoreau collection)

▲ **Catalogue**

A catalogue featuring a line of Lady Duff Gordon's clothing that was available from Sears, Roebuck & Co. for the 1917 season. (Mike Beatty collection)

▲ **Lady Duff Gordon Dress Design Sketch**

Survivor Lady Duff Gordon was a well-known fashion designer during the early twentieth century. Her design process involved dressing up live models with fabrics while one of her assistants sketched out the design. This original sketch, featuring a green silk dress over white and silver lace, was drawn by one of her assistants at her Paris studio around 1917. (Mike Beatty collection)

▶ **Book Inscription**

Inscription in Lucy Duff Gordon's personal copy of her autobiography, *Discretions and Indiscretions*. She was a first-class passenger on the *Titanic*, and the book covers her long and successful career as a fashion designer. (Kalman Tanito collection)

▼ **Autobiography**

In 1932 Lady Duff Gordon published her memoirs titled *Discretions and Indiscretions*, and committed one chapter to describing her *Titanic* experience. Shown here are UK (left) and USA (right) first editions of her book, including the rare original dust jackets. (Mike Beatty collection)

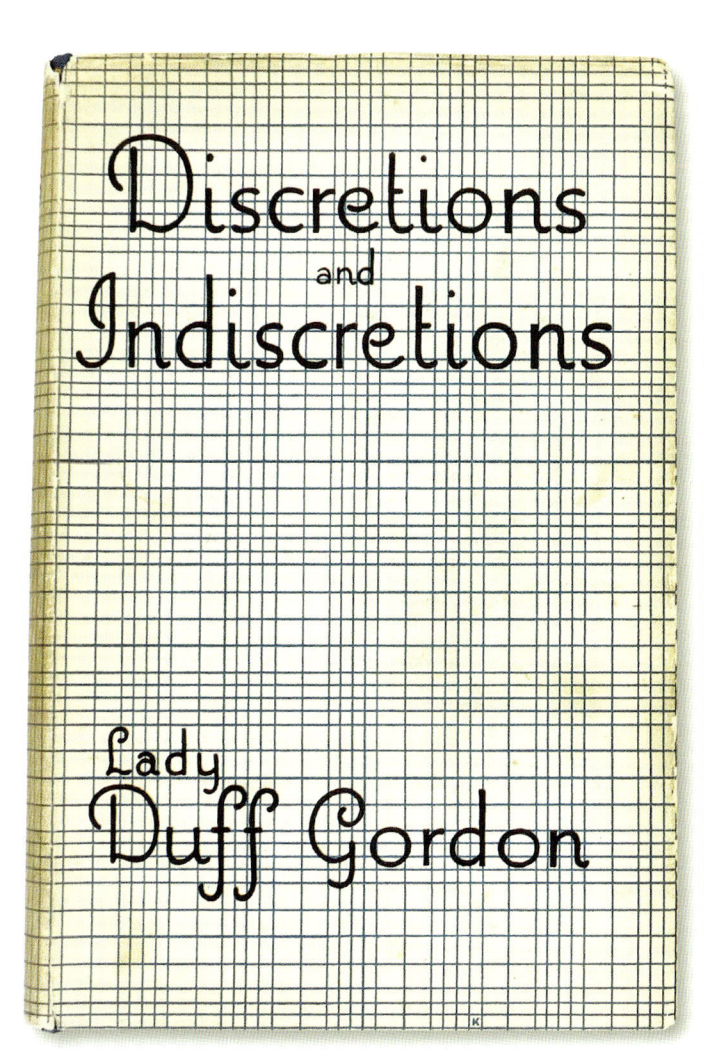

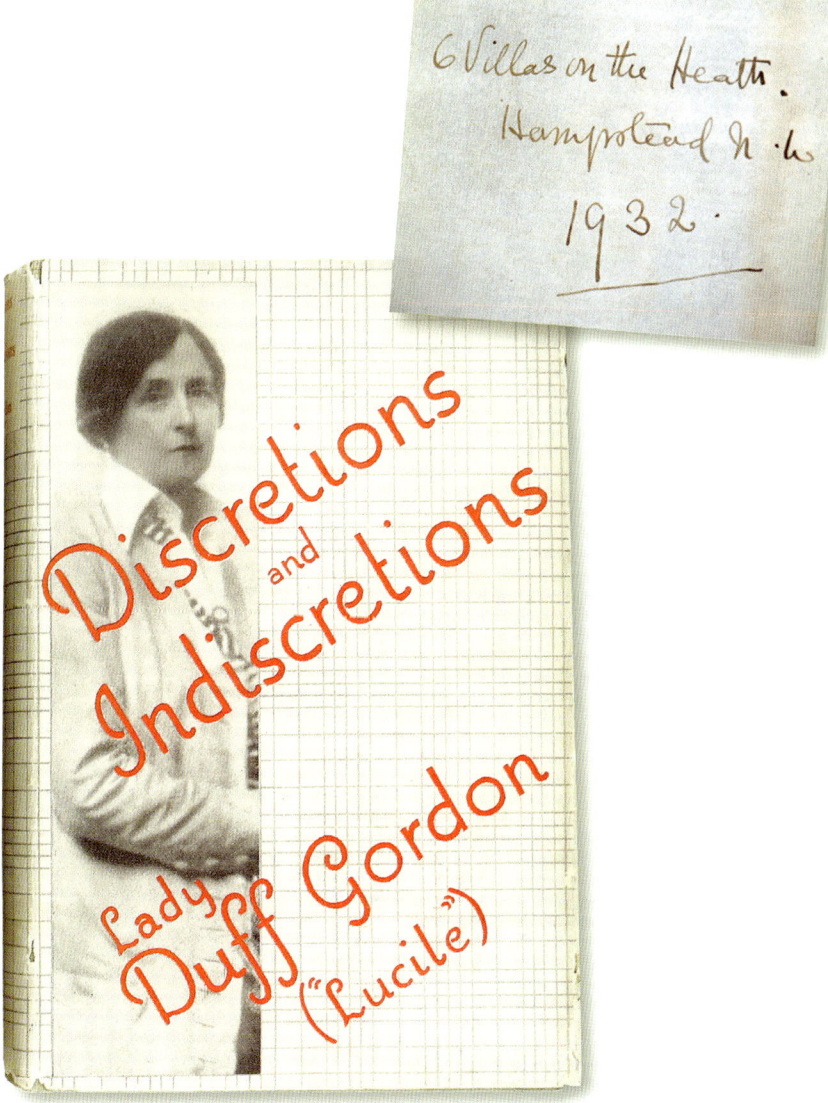

LUCY NOËL MARTHA DYER-EDWARDS

▶ *Carpathia* **Message**

First-class survivor Lucy Noël Dyer-Edwards, the Countess of Rothes, was travelling with her husband's cousin, Gladys Cherry. Both were rescued, and the countess became famous for taking charge of the tiller in lifeboat 8. On board the *Carpathia* she wrote out this simple message, but it was never transmitted. (Mike Beatty collection)

THOMAS EVERETT

▼ **Relief Fund Cheque**

Thomas Everett boarded the *Titanic* in Southampton travelling third class with his destination being Troy, New York. He did not survive the sinking, but his body was recovered and buried in Halifax, Nova Scotia. He left behind a wife, Fanny, who was the recipient of this cheque from the Titanic Relief Fund. (Mike Beatty collection)

JACQUES FUTRELLE

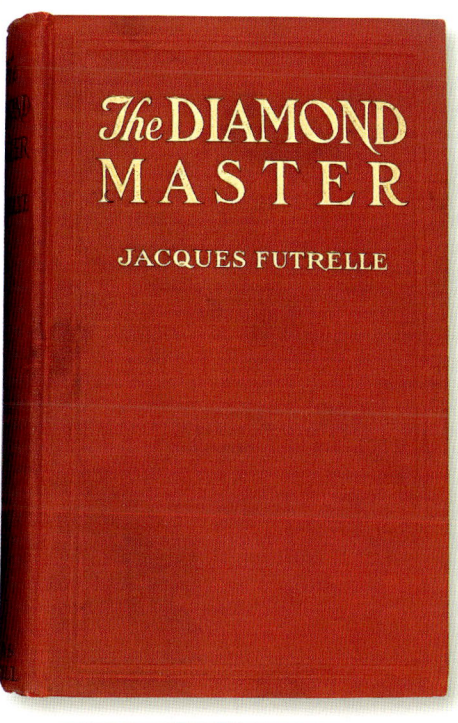

◄ **Books**

Jacques Futrelle was a world-renowned writer of detective mystery novels, among which was *The Diamond Master* in 1909. Jacques was holidaying in Europe with his wife May and boarded *Titanic* in Cherbourg. May Futrelle survived in lifeboat 9, but Jacques didn't make it. His book *My Lady's Garter* was released posthumously later that same year, and inside the volume May wrote a dedication: 'To The Heroes of the Titanic I dedicate this my husband's book.' (Mike Beatty collection)

▶ *The High Hand*

Jacques Futrelle's 1911 novel *The High Hand*, with an interesting tipped-in letter handwritten by the author. Maybe the message explains why Futrelle's signature is so hard to find today!

N.Y. City
1/1/1909

My dear Sir:
   I have made it an absolute rule never to give my autograph to anyone – unless they ask for it.
   Sincerely,
   Jacques Futrelle

(Mike Beatty collection)

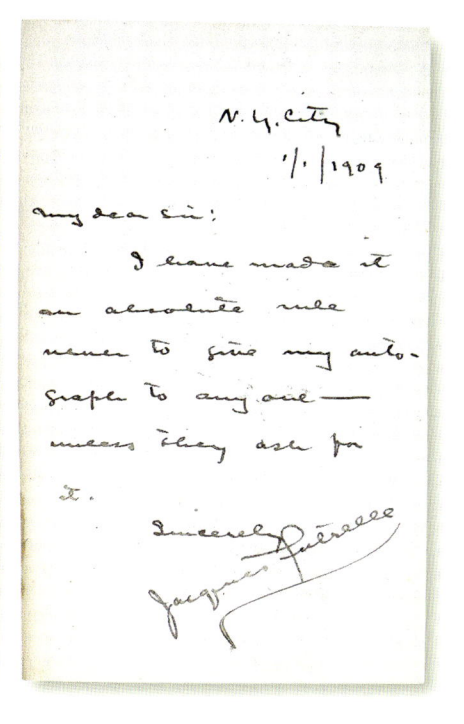

MAY FUTRELLE

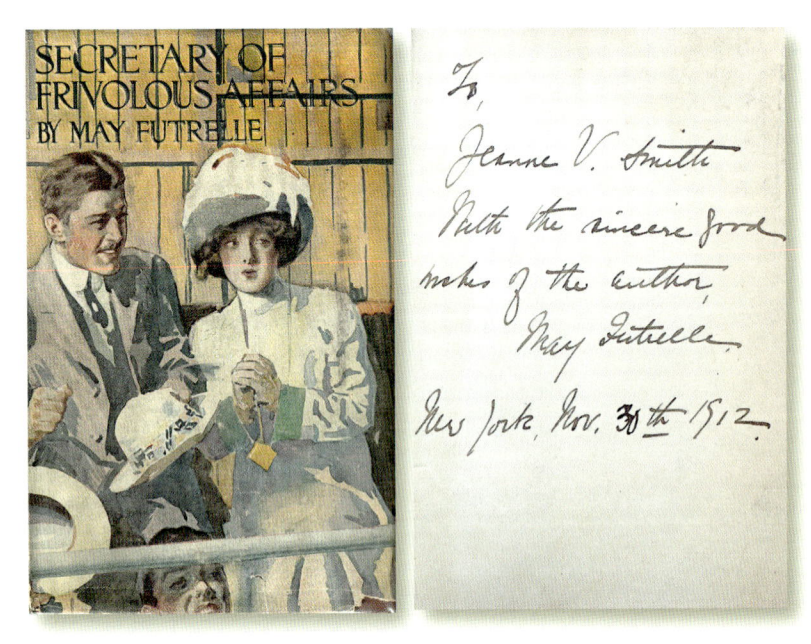

◀ **Book**
May Futrelle's own book, *Secretary of Frivolous Affairs*, was published in 1911 and was the basis of a 1915 film of the same title. This copy of the book is inscribed by her. (Kalman Tanito collection)

JOHN GILL

▶ **John Gill Hunting Licences**
Englishman John 'Will' Gill immigrated to the US in 1907, first to Michigan and later settling in Wisconsin, where he spent a few years as a farm labourer before returning to England sometime in late 1911. These state hunting licences from 1910 and 1911 are a small fragment remaining from his time living in Wisconsin. (Trevor Powell collection)

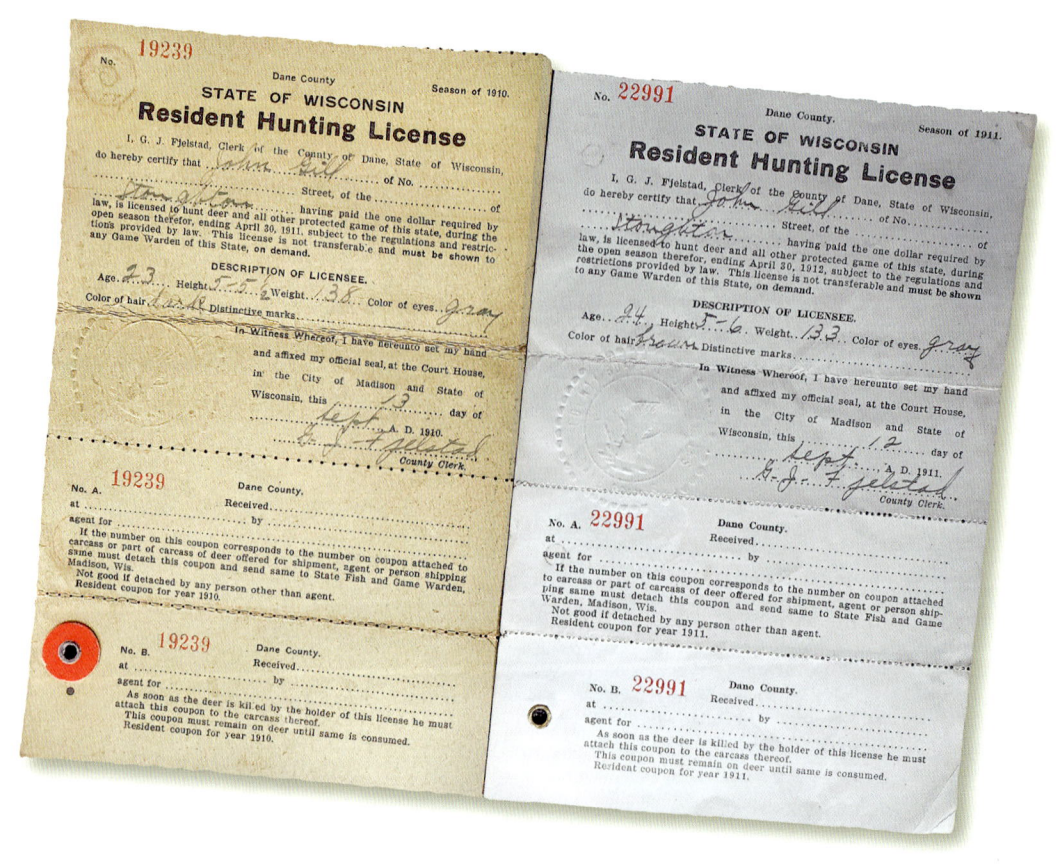

▲ (and overleaf) John Gill 1911 Postcards
In 1911 John Gill was courting Sarah Elizabeth Wilton and regularly sent her postcards letting her know he was thinking of her. They would be married on Valentine's Day in 1912. (Mike Beatty collection)

▶ **John Gill 1912 Postcard**

A month after their wedding and a few weeks before sailing on *Titanic*, John sent Sarah this postcard dated 12 March 1912. It reads: 'My Dear Mrs Gill, Many thanks for P.C. [postcard] sorry not to have written before but hope Dear you had a good time. Well [?] shall be down ... tomorrow night. If I do not see you will come round to meet you. Trusting you are well. Much love from Will.' It's believed John was headed to America to set up a home for himself and his new bride, but he never made it, being one of many second-class victims. (Mike Beatty collection)

THE SWEETS OF LIFE.

SAMUEL GOLDENBERG

▶ Caricature

Samuel Goldenberg sat for a caricature sketch while staying at the Royal Hotel in Nice, France. The artwork was by Louis Hels, who spent the years 1909–11 creating these portraits for guests at the hotel, where they were possibly displayed. This example, dated 'Nice, July 28/11,' is signed 'Your naughtical [sic] friend S.L. Goldenberg' and is also signed by Hels. The following year Goldenberg and his wife Nella boarded the *Titanic* at Cherbourg, travelling first class. Both escaped the sinking ship in lifeboat 5. (Mike Beatty collection)

FRANK GOLDSMITH

▼ Memorial Booklet

Toolmaker Frank Goldsmith, his wife Emily and their 9-year-old son Frankie Jr were third-class passengers who were immigrating to Detroit. On the night of the sinking, Frank put Emily and Frankie into collapsible C, patted his son on the head and said, 'So long, Frankie, I'll see you later.' That was the last time Emily and Frankie ever saw their husband and father. This booklet is from Frank's memorial service, and someone has glued a 1912 threepence coin inside. (Mike Beatty collection)

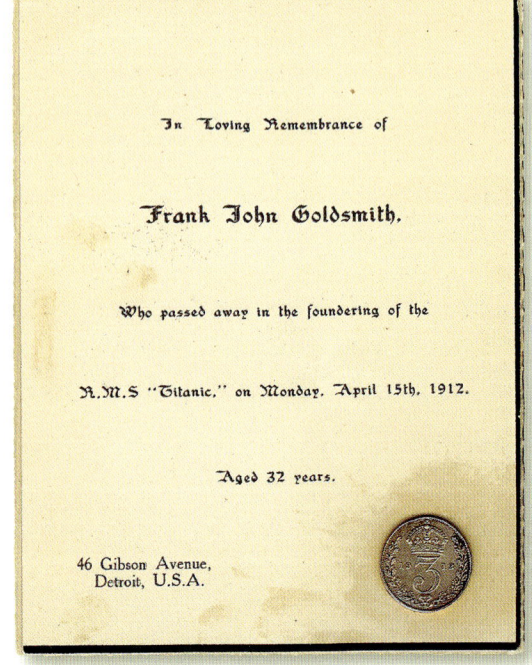

In Loving Remembrance of

Frank John Goldsmith.

Who passed away in the foundering of the

R.M.S "Titanic," on Monday, April 15th, 1912.

Aged 32 years.

46 Gibson Avenue,
Detroit, U.S.A.

ARCHIBALD GRACIE

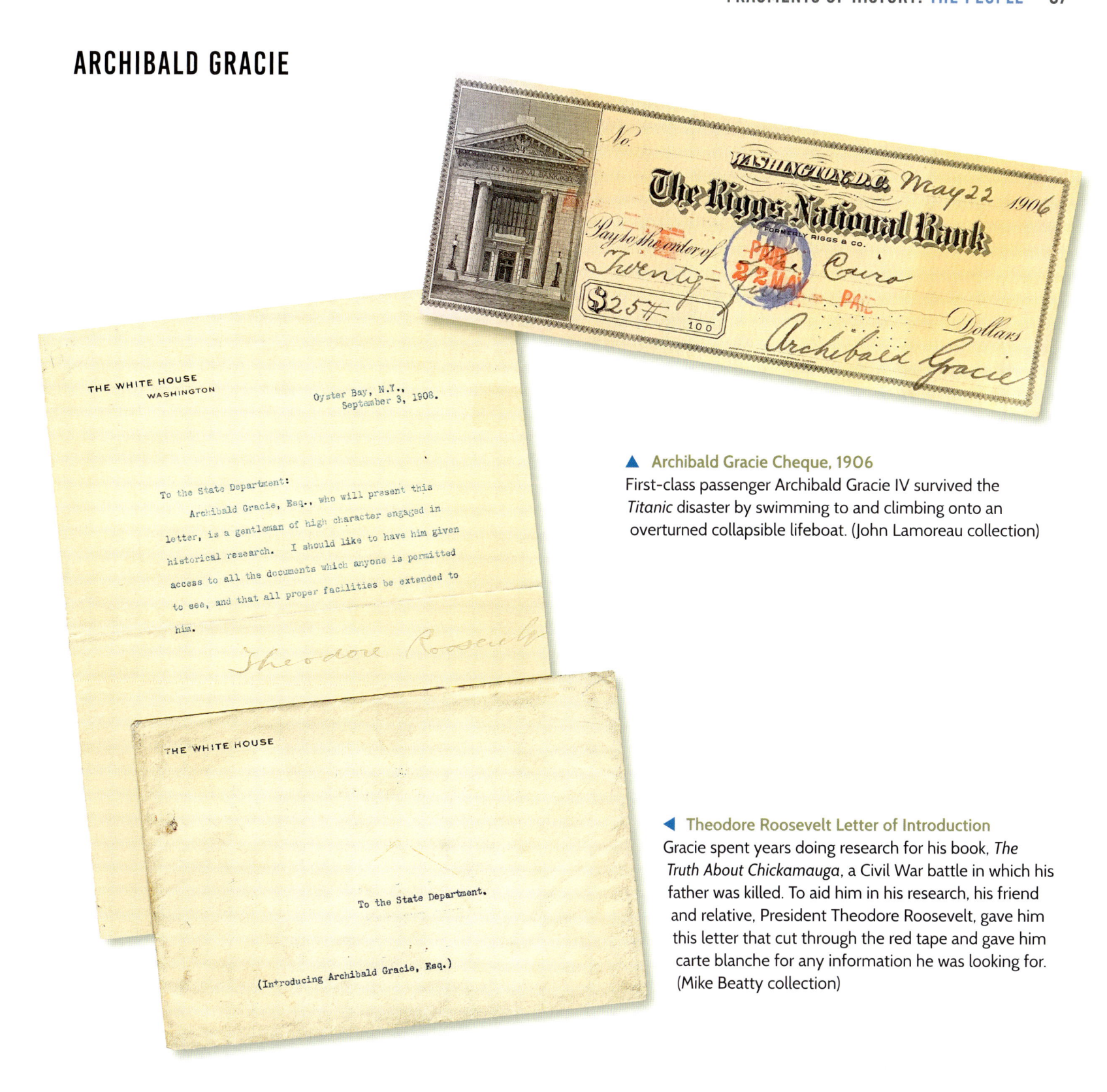

▲ Archibald Gracie Cheque, 1906
First-class passenger Archibald Gracie IV survived the
Titanic disaster by swimming to and climbing onto an
overturned collapsible lifeboat. (John Lamoreau collection)

◄ Theodore Roosevelt Letter of Introduction
Gracie spent years doing research for his book, *The
Truth About Chickamauga*, a Civil War battle in which his
father was killed. To aid him in his research, his friend
and relative, President Theodore Roosevelt, gave him
this letter that cut through the red tape and gave him
carte blanche for any information he was looking for.
(*Mike Beatty collection*)

▼ Gracie Letter to Luther Hopkins

On 17 June 1912, just two months after surviving the sinking, Gracie wrote this lengthy handwritten letter to fellow author and Civil War veteran Luther Hopkins, who was planning on reviewing Gracie's book, *The Truth About Chickamauga*, in the *Baltimore Sun*. The letter suggests Hopkins highly praised the book, and Gracie mentions he will lend him a large collection of news clippings about its release. Gracie's publisher gave him the clippings 'when they learned that my more complete collection contained in my scrap-book, had been lost with my other effects in the ship-wrecked *Titanic*'. (Mike Beatty collection)

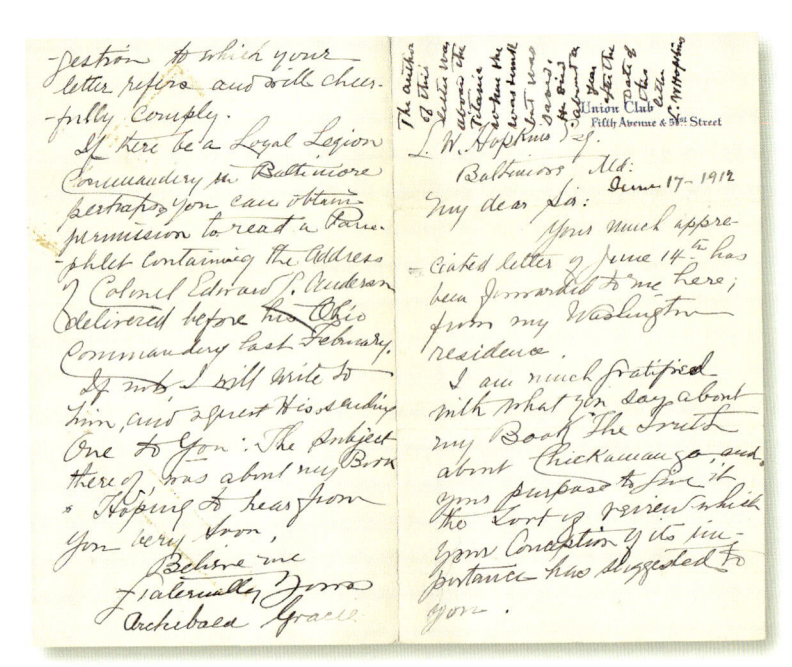
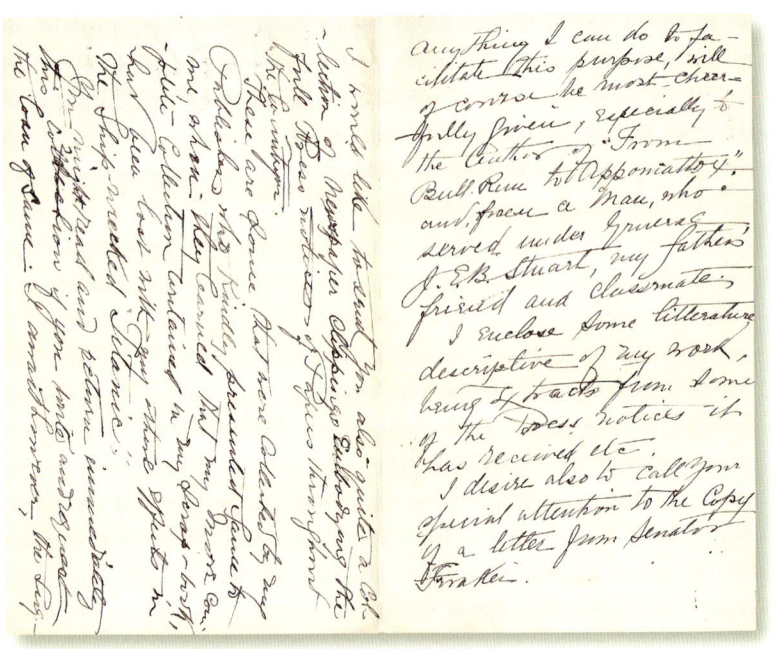

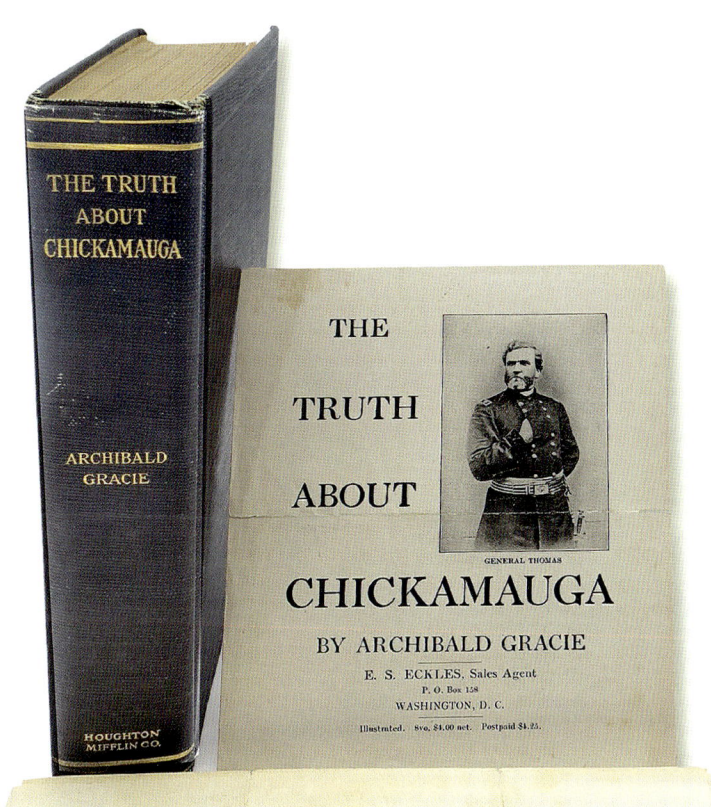

◄ Gracie's *The Truth About Chickamauga*
The culmination of years of gruelling research, Archibald Gracie's *The Truth About Chickamauga* was finally published in 1911. In July 1912 this copy, along with extremely rare publisher advertising, was given to Luther Hopkins, a Civil War veteran and reviewer for the *Baltimore Sun*. (Mike Beatty collection)

E. S. ECKLES, Sales Agent, Box 158, WASHINGTON, D. C.

"THE TRUTH ABOUT CHICKAMAUGA"
By ARCHIBALD GRACIE
BOSTON: HOUGHTON-MIFFLIN CO.

Testimonials from Federal and Confederate Sources

Some seven years ago the author of this carefully constructed work paid his first visit to the Chickamauga battlefield.

The term "carefully constructed" is purposely employed, for the author, without previous knowledge or prejudice regarding the events of that engagement, found so many discrepancies and contradictions in the descriptions given him that he determined to make a study of the official reports, of federals and confederates, as the basis upon which the truth of the whole matter might be reached by carefully examining every statement of record in endeavoring to reconcile the conflicting recitals, which he "believed, for the most part, to have been intentionally" fair, and supplementing them where necessary with the personal reminiscences of trustworthy soldiers of every grade who had participated in a conflict second in importance to no other great battle of the civil war except Petersburg.

In this task the author has studied every report available from both sides and has had communications from hundreds of officers and men of nearly every command, a continuous and faithful labor extending over a period of six years.

Whether one agrees or disagrees with Colonel Gracie's deductions, his sincerity can hardly be doubted, for throughout it is apparent that he is desirous of arriving at unquestionable truths without fear or favor.

order, and when Thomas was shortly told of the position McCook had taken he sent word that it was a fortunate event for the protection of his left and rear and that the brigade should remain and hold the position. Thomas reports that McCook's brigade, "in a commanding position, kept a large force of the enemy's cavalry at bay while hovering on Baird's left and with his battery materially aided Turchin's handsome charge on the enemy, who had closed in on our left."

The author gives in many places the highest encomiums to General Thomas for a display of "leonine strength and tenacity of purpose" under the most trying ordeals, and no praise could be higher than that enthusiastically bestowed upon Steedman; Harker, that hero who held Horseshoe Ridge for more than four hours against a succession of formidable, fierce charges; Hazen, who aided Harker when the latter was forced to fall back to the hill on which is the Snodgrass house; Van Derveer, Opdycke, and many other paladins of all ranks, who proved their worth in that terrific struggle.

Nor is the author satisfied with giving credit to those whom all of us have recognized as having done their whole duty, for he takes up the gage in behalf of those whose actions have been unjustly attacked or misrepresented by critics, who through spite, envy, or ignorance have unjustly spread stains on the character of brave men who were gallantly and intelligently

ARCHIBALD GRACIE
1527 SIXTEENTH STREET
WASHINGTON, D. C.
September 26, 1912.

Mr. Louis M. Ogden,

Tuxedo, N. Y.

My dear Friend:

I have returned to my residence in Washington, after convalescing during the summer at Long Beach, Long Island. I have been neglectful in not having written to you, but I hope under the circumstances, you will not take it amiss.

I am now trying to write a book and to straighten out much neglected affairs. In connection with the book, remember I want your assistance in the matter of illustrations. What have you done with the films of the pictures you took? I would like to have them that I might put them into the hands of some expert to be enlarged for the purpose, if possible, of identifying some of the passengers in each boat. Prints which I have cannot be developed for this purpose.

I have done considerable research work and may be able to identify, better perhaps than others, the pictures which you took. What I have found out I think will interest you. Perhaps you also have obtained information which may add to my store. In my book, you will find that I have done justice to what your dear wife and yourself did for us unfortunates while on the CARPATHIA, especially what you did for me. I am writing this more to get in touch with you as soon as possible, as I want to publish my book at an early date. My manuscript is nearly completed, and I want to hand it to my publisher within a month. If you or your wife could write me your recollections of that awful morning, April 15th, and what you saw as the TITANIC's lifeboats came in sight and their contents unloaded aboard the CARPATHIA, I might be able to use the same. My book will differ from others that have been written, presenting almost entirely the human side, and giving my personal experience. The title of it will be, "The Truth About the TITANIC."

Mrs. Gracie joins me in best wishes to you both and we hope to see you sometime during the coming winter. She was very appreciative of your kindness to me.

Faithfully yours,

Archibald Gracie

P.S. - I promised Third Officer H. J. Pitman, formerly of the TITANIC, now on board the OCEANIC, White Star Line, that I would call your attention to the fact that he had not received the promised prints from you of the TITANIC'S lifeboats. You can address him either in New York, or at Southampton, c/o White Star Line.

ARCHIBALD GRACIE
1527 SIXTEENTH STREET
WASHINGTON, D. C.
October 1, 1912.

Mr. Louis M. Ogden,
123 Pall Mall,
London, England.

My dear Friend:

I wonder if my various letters have reached you? I am anxious that I may have the best copies possible of your pictures illustrating my coming book.

I wrote you on the 26th ult., and your Mr. Keale replied that he was forwarding my letter to you, and that you would not return until December 4th next.

Your name will, of course, appear in my book as having taken these pictures, each of which being properly accredited. It is a mortification to me that the New York HERALD did not put your name and properly accredit the pictures to you and copyright same. Mr. Bennett was very angry with his employes for not having done so. I hope it is not too late to obtain the films in order to enlarge the pictures so as to establish the identity of persons in each boat.

I feel quite sure that my book will be read with great interest, as many facts are established not hitherto brought to light.

Pardon my haste, but I want to get this on tomorrow's steamer.

Faithfully yours,

Archibald Gracie

▲ **Letters**

In late September 1912, Gracie wrote a letter to his friend and relative Louis Ogden, who – along with his wife – just happened to have been on the *Carpathia* on a Mediterranean trip and witnessed the rescue of *Titanic*'s survivors. Louis used his camera to capture some of *Titanic*'s lifeboats being rescued by the *Carpathia*, and Gracie was eager to get copies of those photos for his upcoming book about his experiences. Apparently he received no reply, since in October he sent a second letter repeating his request. Sadly, Colonel Gracie would not see his book published, because he died of complications from diabetes just two months after writing his second letter to Ogden. During his final hours of life, Gracie was delirious and was heard to murmur, 'We must get them into the boats. We must get them into the boats.' Archibald Gracie was the first adult survivor to die after the *Titanic* disaster. (Mike Beatty collection)

▶ **Letter to Gracie from Senator Foraker**
Civil War veteran Senator Joseph B. Foraker writes to
Gracie in praise of *The Truth About Chickamauga*. (Mike
Beatty collection)

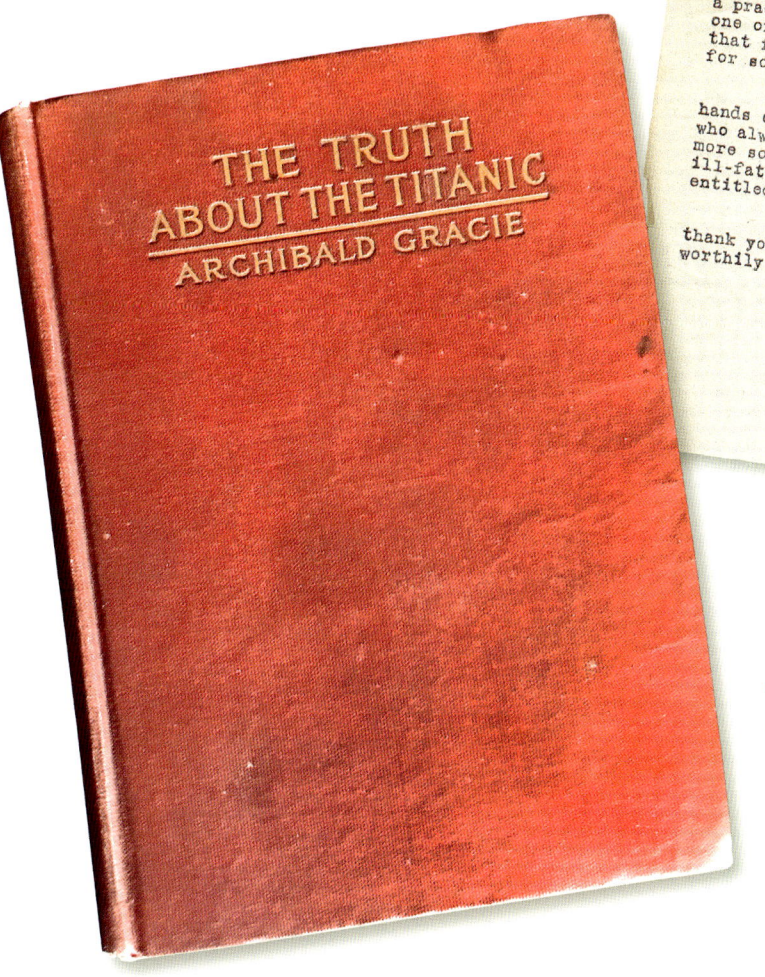

Senator J. B. Foraker's tribute to "THE TRUTH ABOUT CHICKAMAUGA."

(COPY)

Col. Archibald Gracie,   Cincinnati, Ohio.
     Washington, D. C.   December 23, 1911.

Dear Colonel:

     I have just finished reading your book, "The Truth About
Chickamauga." I congratulate you upon the great work you have done.

     I know something of the painstaking care with which you
have labored for so many years to establish the truth about this
great battle in which you had exceptional reason for having the
deepest interest.

     For what you have said about my unfortunate comrades of
the 89th, I thank you more in my heart than I know how to express
with words. You are the first author to do justice to that devoted
band, the 22nd Michigan and the 21st and 89th Ohio regiments.

     You have established the right of the three captured
regiments to the credit to which they are entitled. The officers of
these regiments having been captured and held in prison many months,
there were no proper reports showing the fierce struggle they made,
undertaking to hold "at all hazards" the position to which they were
assigned.

     Some of the warmest and dearest friends I ever had lost
their lives in that engagement; others perished later at Anderson-
ville. The sacrifice was greater than anybody, unacquainted through
a practical experience with the horrors of war, can realize, but no
one of the regiment has ever complained because of the great burdens
that fell upon them on that day. All the survivors have felt that
for some reason, justice has never been accorded.

     It seems strange that now after all these years, at the
hands of the son of a Brigadier-General of the Confederate army,
who always distinguished himself by his gallantry in battle, and never
more so than at Chickamauga, the truth should be uncovered and these
ill-fated regiments should be accorded the praise to which they are
entitled for the valor they displayed on that day.

     On behalf of all my comrades, both living and dead, I
thank you from the bottom of my heart for the great, unexpected, but
worthily deserved service you have rendered them.

     With sentiments of high regard, I remain,

          Very truly yours,

          J. B. Foraker,

◀ **Book**
A 1913 first edition of Gracie's posthumous book *The Truth About the
Titanic*. Gracie survived by swimming to an overturned lifeboat, from
where he was rescued. (John Lamoreau collection)

◄ **Book**
A Swedish edition of *The Truth About the Titanic*. (Kalman Tanito collection)

▶ *The Truth About the Titanic*
This dramatic cover is the 1930 Swedish edition of *The Truth About the Titanic*. (Mike Beatty collection)

WILLIAM GWINN

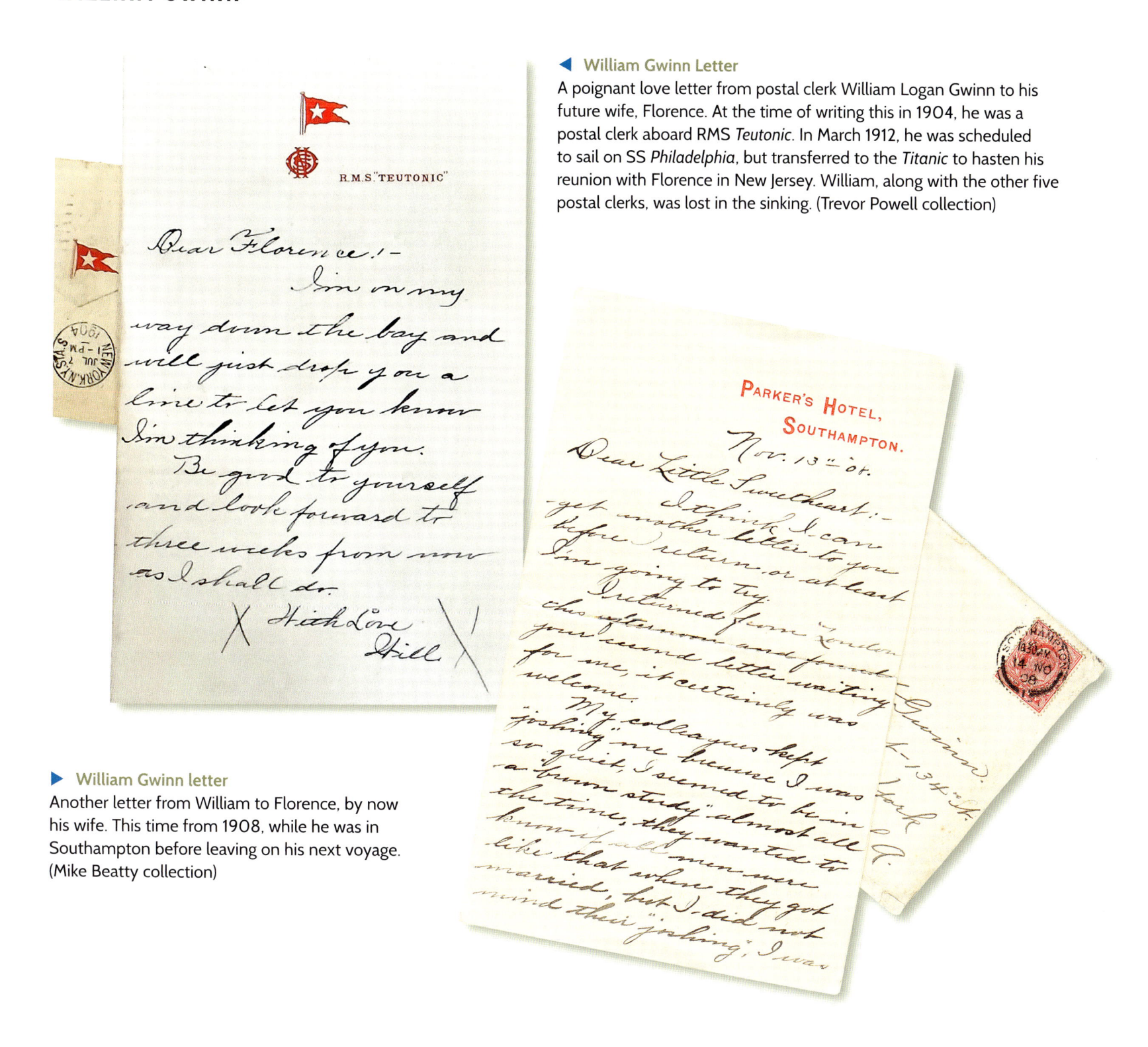

R.M.S. "TEUTONIC"

Dear Florence :-
I'm on my
way down the bay and
will just drop you a
line to let you know
I'm thinking of you.
Be good to yourself
and look forward to
three weeks from now
as I shall do.
X With Love
Will

PARKER'S HOTEL, SOUTHAMPTON.
Nov. 13" '04.
Dear Little Sweetheart :-

▲ William Gwinn Letter
A poignant love letter from postal clerk William Logan Gwinn to his future wife, Florence. At the time of writing this in 1904, he was a postal clerk aboard RMS *Teutonic*. In March 1912, he was scheduled to sail on SS *Philadelphia*, but transferred to the *Titanic* to hasten his reunion with Florence in New Jersey. William, along with the other five postal clerks, was lost in the sinking. (Trevor Powell collection)

▶ William Gwinn letter
Another letter from William to Florence, by now his wife. This time from 1908, while he was in Southampton before leaving on his next voyage. (Mike Beatty collection)

JOHN HARPER

▼ **Book**

This little volume of testimonials was probably published in 1912 and honoured the memory of the Rev. John Harper, a second-class passenger who saved his little daughter but lost his own life when the *Titanic* went down. Rev. Harper was beloved by his friends and associates, who contributed fond personal memories of the man for publication in this book. (George Behe collection)

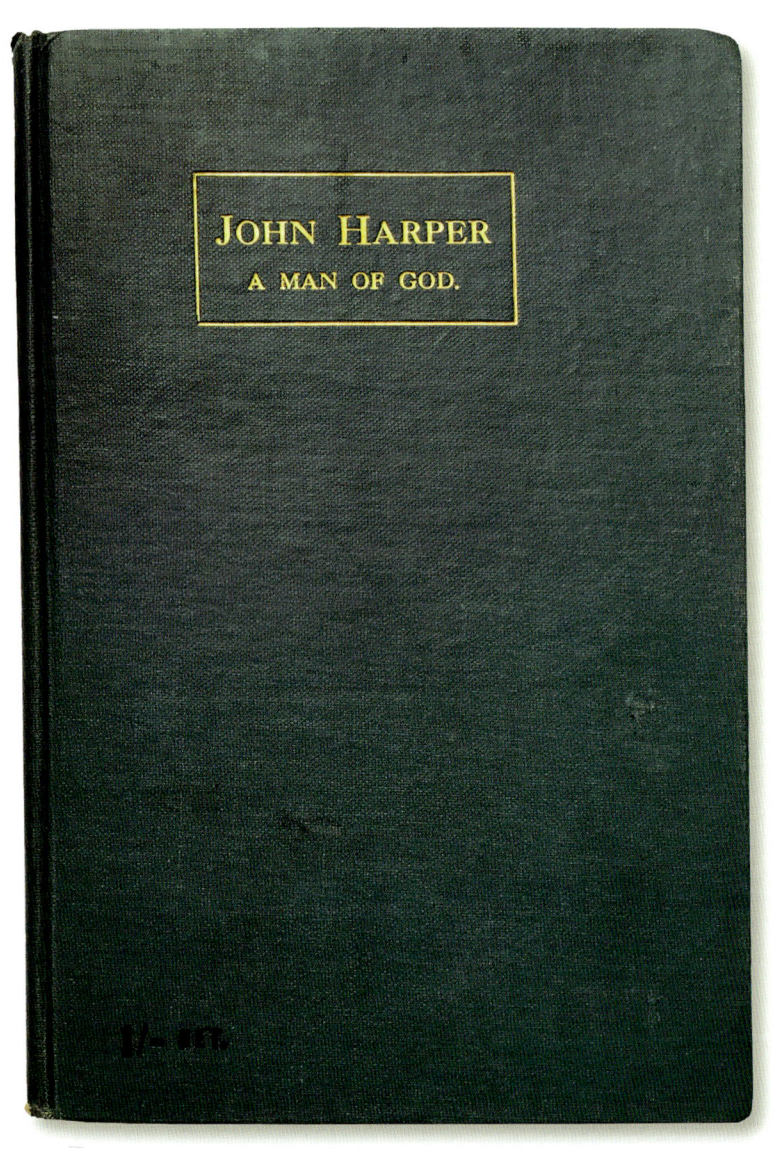

HENRY B. HARRIS

▼ **Letter**

On 18 May 1905, Henry B. Harris sent a letter to Carrie Shubert on behalf of the Association of Theatre Managers of Greater New York in response to the death of her son. Harris was a celebrated Broadway producer who owned multiple New York theatres. (Mike Beatty collection)

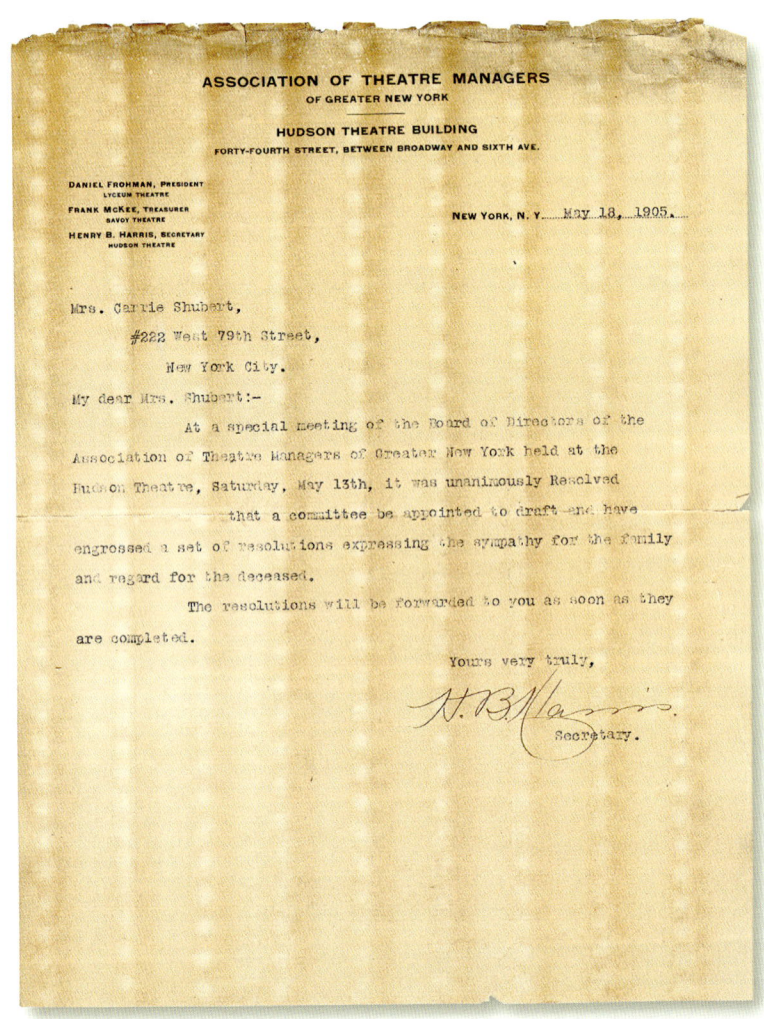

◀ **Poster**

A poster advertising *The Country Boy*, which was staged in theatres from 30 August 1910 until January 1911. (George Behe collection)

▼ **Telegram**

In 1910 Harris sent Christmas greetings to friend and business partner Will J. Davis, manager of the Illinois Theatre in Chicago. (Mike Beatty collection)

▲ **Park Theatre Programme**

The Harris play *The Quaker Girl* was showing in New York the week Henry and his wife Irene left France to return home on the *Titanic*. This programme for the show at the Park Theatre is for the week of 8 April 1912, the week he died in the sinking. (Mike Beatty collection)

IRENE HARRIS

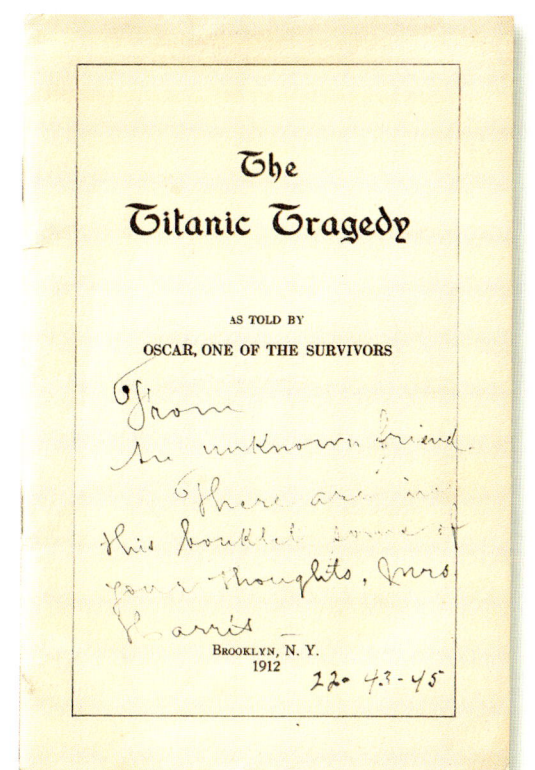

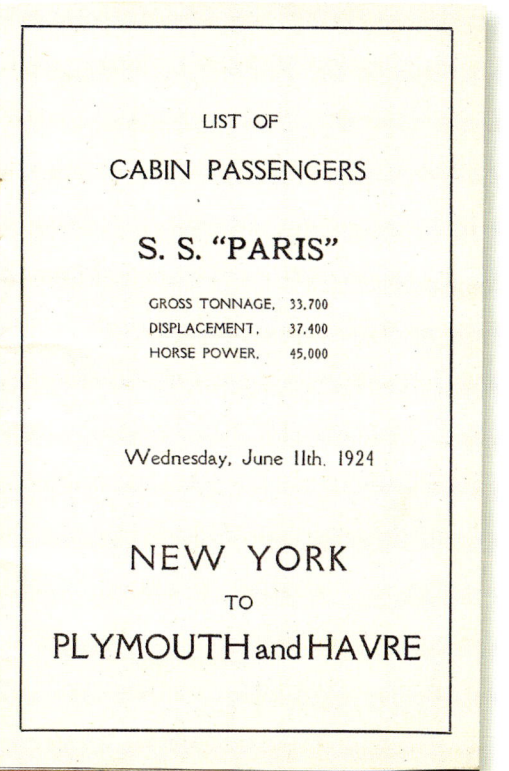

▲ **Memorial Pamphlet**

One of the rarest *Titanic* memorial publications, this was the personal copy of survivor Irene Harris. According to the 'unknown friend' inscribing this copy to her, there are several passages in the booklet that refer to her. (Kalman Tanito collection)

▲ **Passenger List**

A first-class passenger list for the 11 June 1924 crossing of the liner *Paris*. On board the vessel were two *Titanic* survivors – Mrs Henry B. Harris and Amelie Icard – and it's possible that the 'Frank Dwyer' on the list may have been professional gambler 'Frankie' Dwyer. (Don Lynch collection)

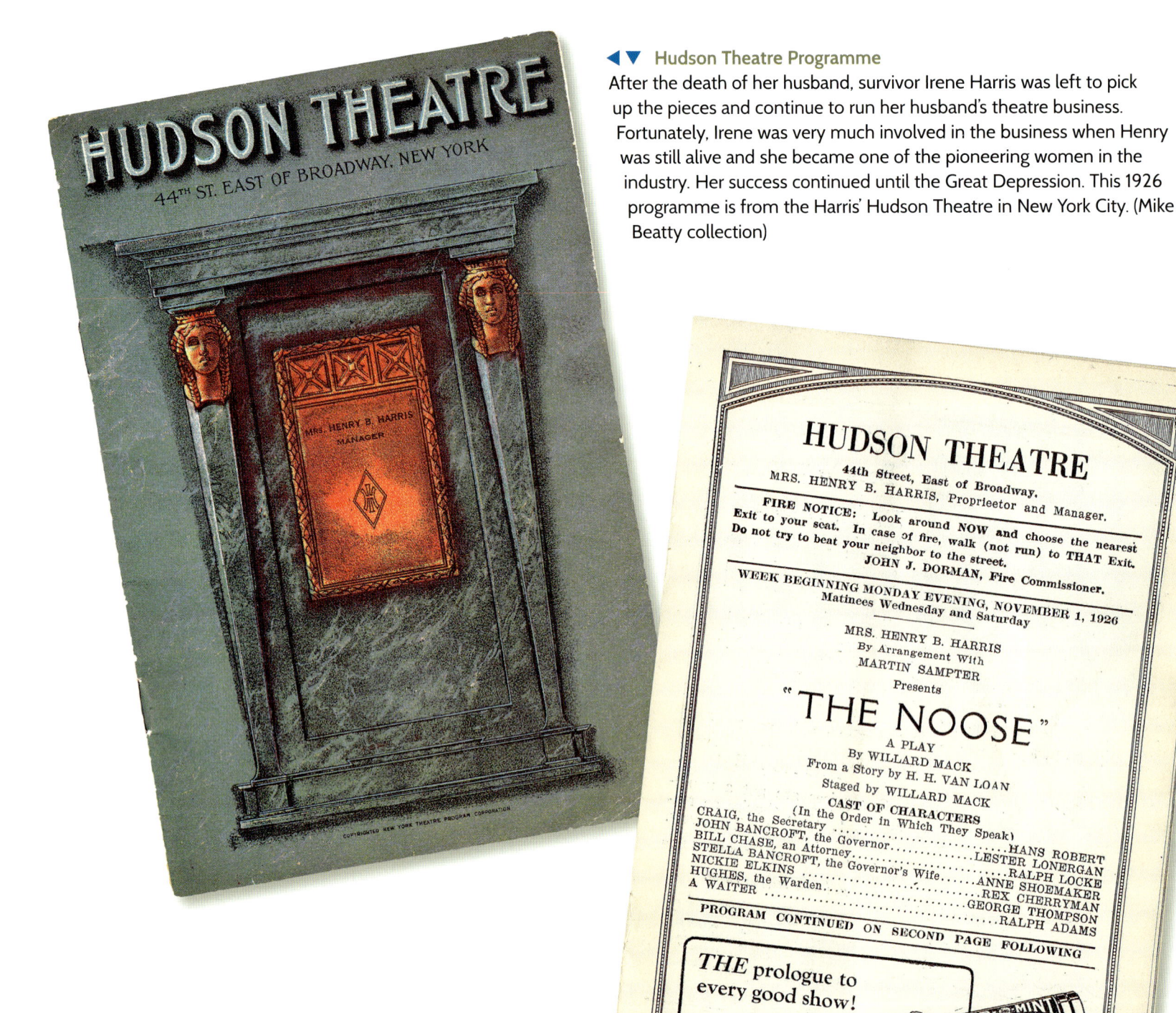

◀▼ Hudson Theatre Programme

After the death of her husband, survivor Irene Harris was left to pick up the pieces and continue to run her husband's theatre business. Fortunately, Irene was very much involved in the business when Henry was still alive and she became one of the pioneering women in the industry. Her success continued until the Great Depression. This 1926 programme is from the Harris' Hudson Theatre in New York City. (Mike Beatty collection)

▶ **White House Letter**

It appears Irene even dabbled in politics in the 1930s. She received this letter after applying for a position in the administration of President Franklin D. Roosevelt, who would be sworn in a month after this letter was written. (Mike Beatty collection)

FRANKLIN D. ROOSEVELT
HYDE PARK, DUTCHESS COUNTY
NEW YORK

February 1, 1933

Mrs. Henry B. Harris
54 Riverside Drive
New York, New York

My dear Mrs. Harris:

This will acknowledge your letter of application. When Mr. Roosevelt gives consideration to the question of appointments this will be brought to his attention again.

Very sincerely yours,

Louis M. H. Howe

Secretary to Mr. Roosevelt

PASSENGER PORTRAITS

Rhoda, Rossmore and Eugene Abbott

Bess Allison

Charles Andrews

Thomas Andrews

Carl Asplund

Selma Asplund

John Jacob Astor

William Barrows

Nellie Becker

Richard Beckwith

Lawrence Beesley

Karl Behr

James Bisset

Harold Bride

Emma Bucknell

Major Archibald Butt

Clear Cameron

Helen Candee

Eleanor Cassebeer

Paul Chevré

Walter Clark

Harold Cottam

Robert Daniel

Washington Dodge

Lucy Duff Gordon

Lucy Noël Dyer-Edwards

Jacques Futrelle

Samuel Goldenberg

Frank Goldsmith

Archibald Gracie

William Gwinn

John Harper

Henry Harris

Irene Harris

Wallace Hartley

Charles Hays

Robert Hichens

Bruce Ismay

Alice Johnson

Henry Julian

Edward Kent

Árpád Lengyel

Courtesy of Katalin Szikors

Charles Lightoller

Harold Lowe

Hugh McElroy

Francis Millet

Juozas Montvila

Clarence Moore

Helen Newsom

William O'Loughlin

Engelhart Østby

Helen Østby

Courtesy of Phil Gowan

John Phillips

Herbert Pitman

Jane Quick

Elisabeth Robert

Courtesy of Phil Gowan

Edith Rosenbaum

Courtesy of Randy Bigham

Arthur Rostron

Adolphe Saalfeld

William Sloper

Captain Edward J. Smith

Lucien Smith

Senator William Alden Smith

Margaretta Spedden

Samuel Stanton

William T. Stead

Charles Stengel

Ida Straus

Isidor Straus

Jack Thayer

John B. Thayer

Marian Thayer

Edwina Troutt

Augustus Weikman

Edwy West

George Widener

Harry Widener

Henry Wilde

Arthur Williams

Richard Williams

Courtesy of Phil Gowan

WALLACE HARTLEY

▶ **Sheet Music**

A piece of sheet music said to have been found inside a music case that was strapped to the recovered body of *Titanic* band leader Wallace Hartley. It seems more plausible that the sheet music was actually part of Hartley's estate, since no mention of a music case is made in the official records listing the items that were recovered with Hartley's body. (John Lamoreau collection)

▼ **Hartley Memorial Programme**

Wallace Hartley's memorial service conducted at Bethel Chapel, Colne. The burial service address was by Thomas Worthington. At the cemetery, they sang 'Nearer My God, to Thee' and the buglers played the 'Last Post'. (Kalman Tanito collection)

◀ **Wallace Hartley Pin**

A small celluloid memorial pin paying tribute to Hartley. (Mike Beatty collection)

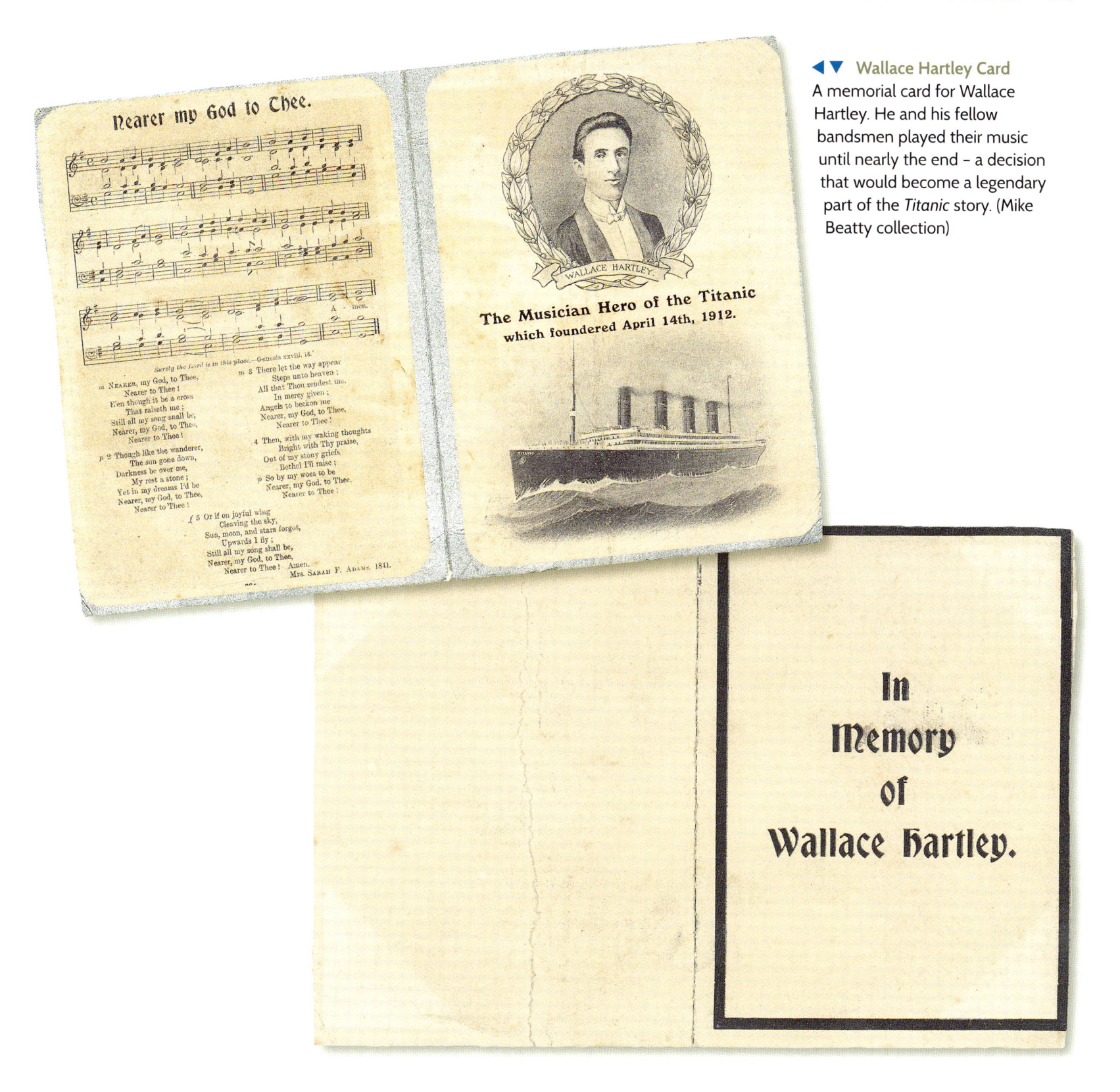

◀▼ **Wallace Hartley Card**
A memorial card for Wallace Hartley. He and his fellow bandsmen played their music until nearly the end – a decision that would become a legendary part of the *Titanic* story. (Mike Beatty collection)

CHARLES HAYS

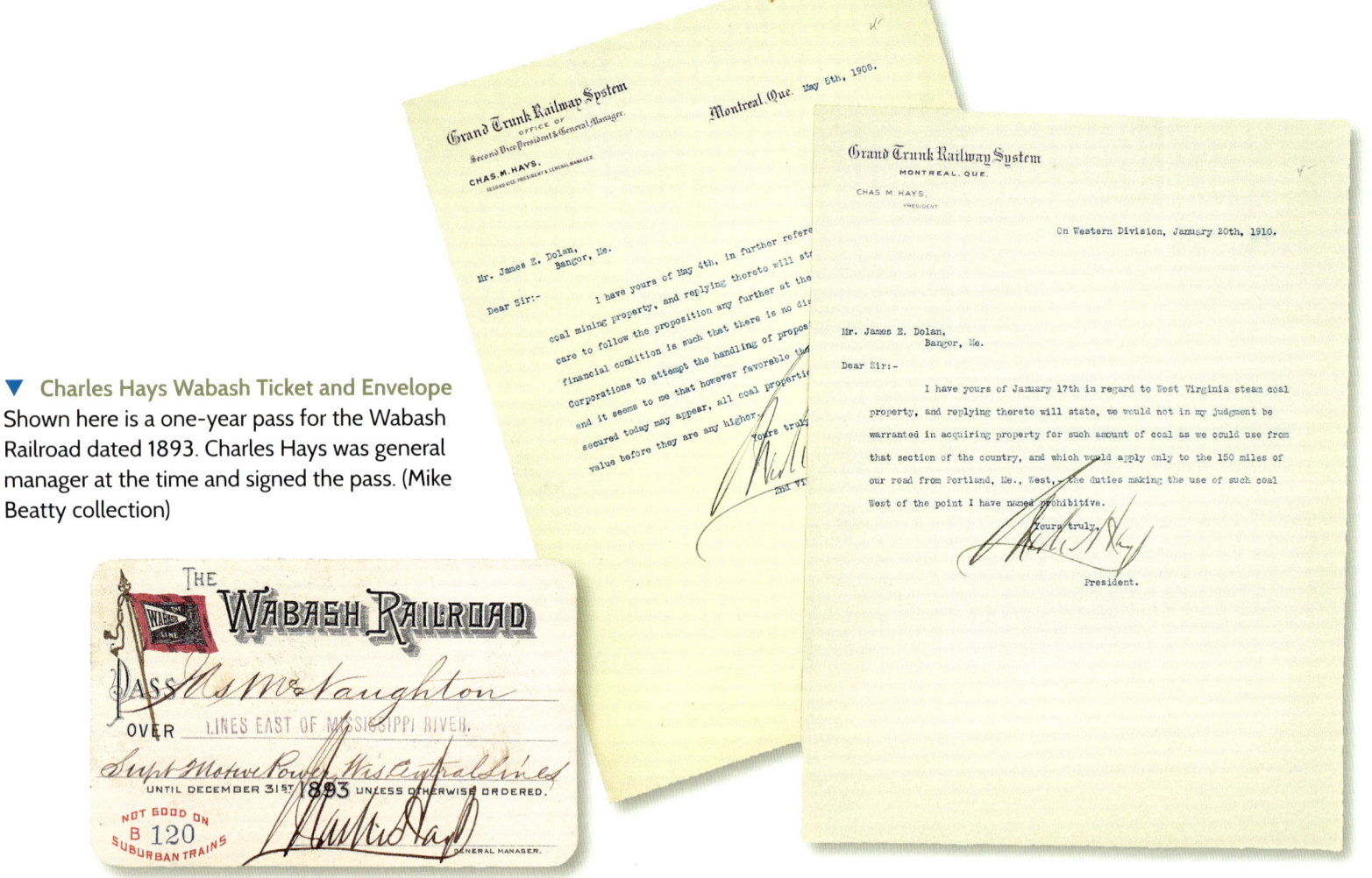

▼ Charles Hays Wabash Ticket and Envelope
Shown here is a one-year pass for the Wabash Railroad dated 1893. Charles Hays was general manager at the time and signed the pass. (Mike Beatty collection)

▲ Charles Hays Business Correspondence
Hays worked his way up through the ranks in the railway industry, first with the Wabash, St Louis and Pacific Railway, and later becoming president of the Grand Trunk Railway. He was returning from business work in London when he boarded the *Titanic* in Southampton. Hays was trying to get back to Canada in time for the grand opening of the Grand Trunk Railway's new hotel Château Laurier in Montreal, but he wouldn't live to see his latest success. (Mike Beatty collection)

▶ Railroad Pass

This pass for the Grand Trunk Railway System was valid until 31 December 1911, and bears Hays' signature as president of the railroad. (John Lamoreau collection)

▼ (left) Memorial Programme

The memorial service for Charles Melville Hays, conducted by Rev Robert Johnston. (Kalman Tanito collection)

▼ (right) Charles Hays Tribute

The July 1912 issue of *THE FRA* paid tribute to Charles Hays. The tribute was written by Elbert Hubbard, who would lose his life three years later in the *Lusitania* sinking. (Mike Beatty collection)

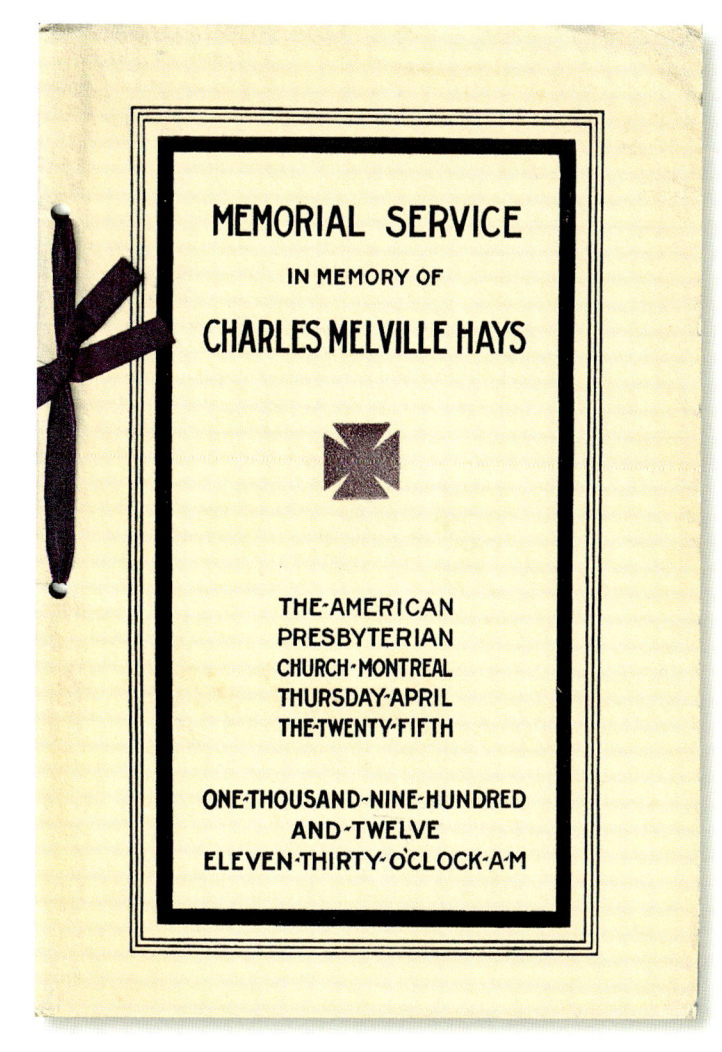

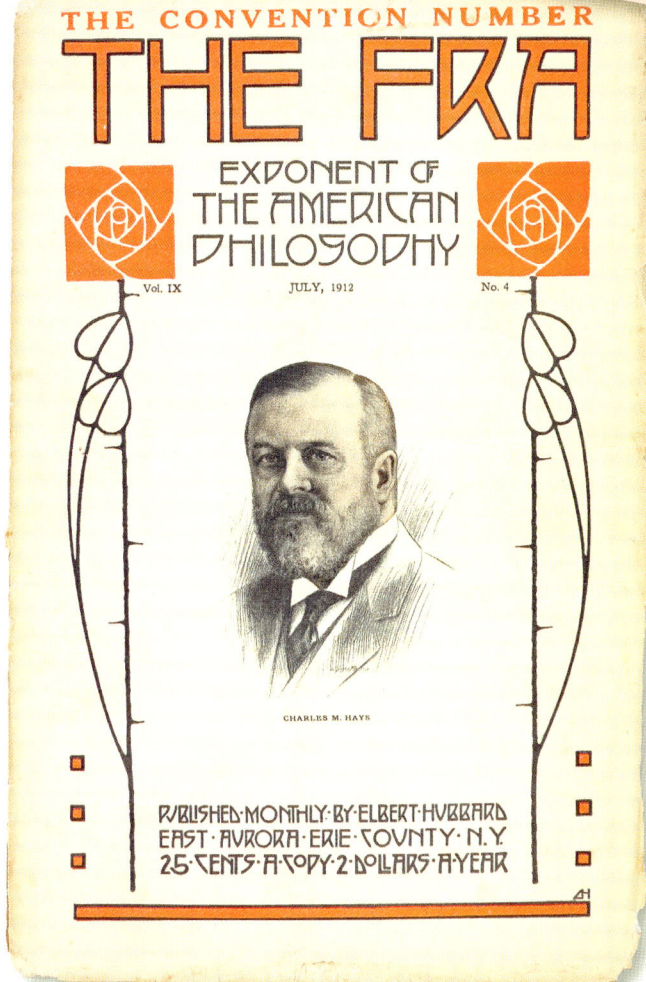

ROBERT HICHENS

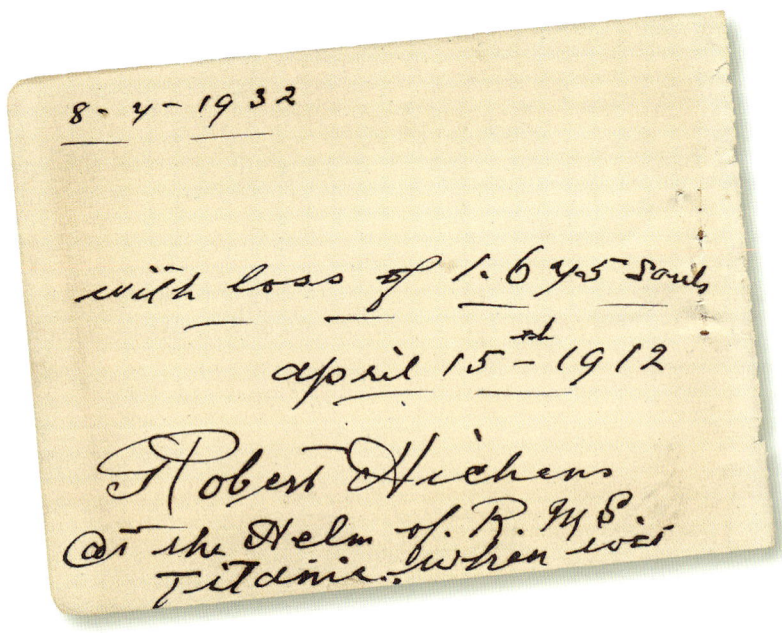

8 - 4 - 1932

with loss of 1.695 souls

april 15th - 1912

Robert Hichens
@ the Helm of R. M S
Titanic. when iced

◀ **Robert Hichens Autograph**

Robert Hichens was on duty at the helm when *Titanic* struck the iceberg at 11:40 p.m. He struggled financially and emotionally for years after the sinking and appears to have signed a few autograph books for money in the 1930s, since several have been discovered over the years. (Mike Beatty collection)

JOSEPH BRUCE ISMAY

▶ **(and opposite)** *Olympic* **Marconigrams**

There was a lot of wireless communication between *Carpathia* and *Olympic* during the day of the rescue. These two messages were received by the *Olympic* and make specific mention of the White Star Line chairman, Bruce Ismay. (Mike Beatty collection)

Form No. 4.—100.—17.8.10.   Deld. Date 15 APR 1912

The Marconi International Marine Communication Co., Ltd.,
WATERGATE HOUSE, YORK BUILDINGS, ADELPHI, LONDON, W.C.

No. OLYMPIC.   OFFICE. 15 APR 1912 ___ 19

CHARGES TO PAY.

Handed in at   CARPATHIA

This message has been transmitted subject to the conditions printed on the back hereof, which have been agreed to by the Sender. If the accuracy of this message be doubted, the Receiver, on paying the necessary charges, may have it repeated whenever possible, from Office to Office over the Company's system, and should any error be shown to exist, all charges for such repetition will be refunded. This Form must accompany any enquiry respecting this Telegram.

Total

To

COMMANDER OLYMPIC.   RECEIVED 3.18 PM N.Y.T.

MR. BRUCE ISMAY IS UNDER AN OPIATE.

ROSTRON.

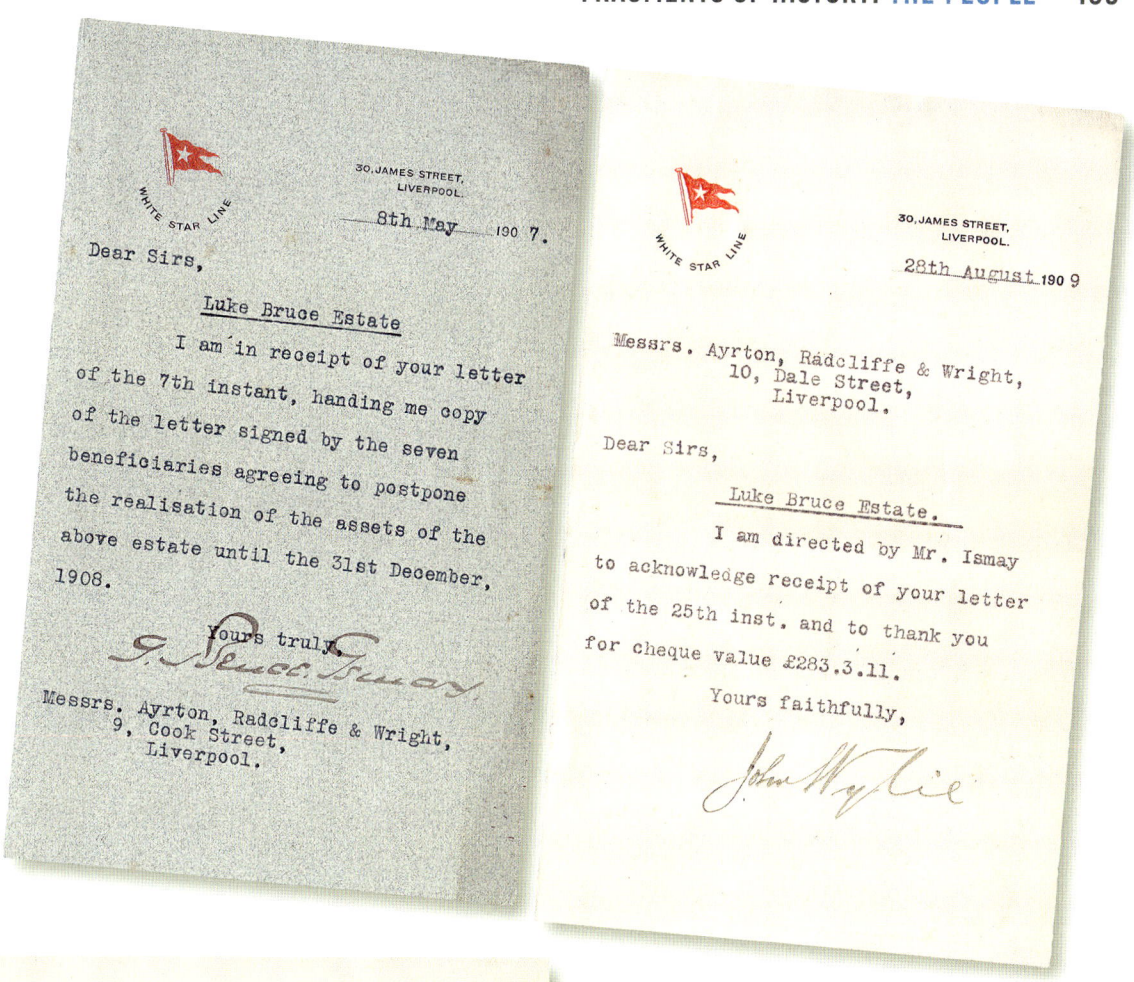

WHITE STAR LINE

30, JAMES STREET,
LIVERPOOL.

8th May 190 7.

Dear Sirs,

Luke Bruce Estate

I am in receipt of your letter of the 7th instant, handing me copy of the letter signed by the seven beneficiaries agreeing to postpone the realisation of the assets of the above estate until the 31st December, 1908.

Yours truly,
J. Bruce Ismay

Messrs. Ayrton, Radcliffe & Wright,
9, Cook Street,
Liverpool.

WHITE STAR LINE

30, JAMES STREET,
LIVERPOOL.

28th August 190 9

Messrs. Ayrton, Radcliffe & Wright,
10, Dale Street,
Liverpool.

Dear Sirs,

Luke Bruce Estate.

I am directed by Mr. Ismay to acknowledge receipt of your letter of the 25th inst. and to thank you for cheque value £283.3.11.

Yours faithfully,
John Wylie

Form No. 4.—100.—17.8.10.

Deld. Date 15 APR 1912

The Marconi International Marine Communication Co., Ltd.,
WATERGATE HOUSE, YORK BUILDINGS, ADELPHI, LONDON, W.C.

No. OLYMPIC.   OFFICE. 15 APR 1912   19

CARPATHIA

Handed in at

CHARGES TO PAY.

This message has been transmitted subject to the conditions printed on the back hereof, which have been agreed to by the Sender. If the accuracy of this message be doubted, the Receiver, on paying the necessary charges, may have it repeated whenever possible, from Office to Office over the Company's system, and should any error be shown to exist, all charges for such repetition will be refunded. This Form must accompany any enquiry respecting this Telegram.

Total

To   COMMANDER OLYMPIC   RECEIVED 3.22 pm NYT

MR. ISMAY ORDERS OLYMPIC NOT TO BE SEEN BY CARPATHIA.

NO TRANSFER TO TAKE PLACE. ROSTRON.

▲ **Bruce Ismay Letters**
Correspondence pertaining to the estate of Bruce Ismay's maternal grandfather, Luke Bruce, on White Star Line stationery. Bruce was one of the trustees of the estate. (Mike Beatty collection)

STEPHEN JENKIN

▶ **Titanic Relief Fund Cheque**
This cheque, dated '1 Jan 1917', is made out to a Mrs K. Jenkins. It is believed it was for the loss of her son Stephen Curnow Jenkin, a 32-year-old victim of the *Titanic* disaster (there is some confusion over the spelling of the last name Jenkin/Jenkins). Stephen Jenkin's mother was named Catherine, but went by 'Kate', and was from the community of Trenwith, near Cornwall. The back of this cheque is signed. 'K. Jenkins, Trenwith'. (John Lamoreau collection)

ALICE JOHNSON

◀ **1920s Johnson, Amundson, Peterson Family**
Survivor Alice Johnson was married three times by the mid-1920s, creating a large blended family. In this previously unpublished family photo are three *Titanic* survivors: Eleanor Johnson (far left); next to her is her mother Alice Johnson; and second from the right is survivor Harold Johnson. (Mike Beatty collection)

▶ **1920s Alice Johnson**
Alice Johnson is shown with her third husband, Carl Peterson, around 1925. (Mike Beatty collection)

▶ **1930s Johnson Family**
Alice Johnson is shown in the middle rear of this photo of her and some of her family. Her son, Harold Johnson (left), was 4 years old when he survived the *Titanic* with his mother. Also shown is Alice's younger daughter, Irene, and Alice's third husband, Carl Peterson. Harold's wife, Harriet, is on the right. This unpublished late 1930s photo is from a family album. (Mike Beatty collection)

HENRY JULIAN

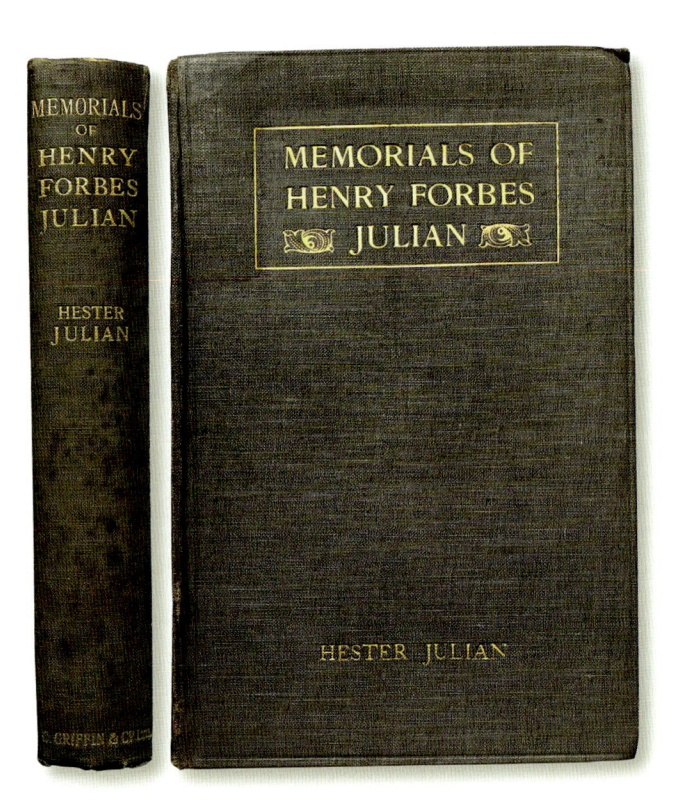

◀ Book

In 1914 Hester Julian, the widow of first-class victim Henry Forbes Julian, published a biography of her late husband. The book included the text of correspondence she'd received from *Titanic* survivor Gladys Cherry. (George Behe collection)

▶ Letter

Two years after the sinking, Hester sent a copy of her late husband's biography to a family friend, along with a black-bordered letter of mourning. The friend tucked the letter inside his copy of the book, and both items eventually found their way into a private collection. (George Behe collection)

Dear Alfred Croft

Many thanks for both your kind letters and enclosure. I am sending the biography as you kindly wish to have it. Remember how <u>very much</u> interested my dear husband was in your Presidential Address at the Devon Assoc. at Teignmouth and in your allusions to my father Mr Pengelly. The Association owes you very much for your keen interest in its work & welfare …

With kind regards,
Very sincerely yours,
Hester Julian

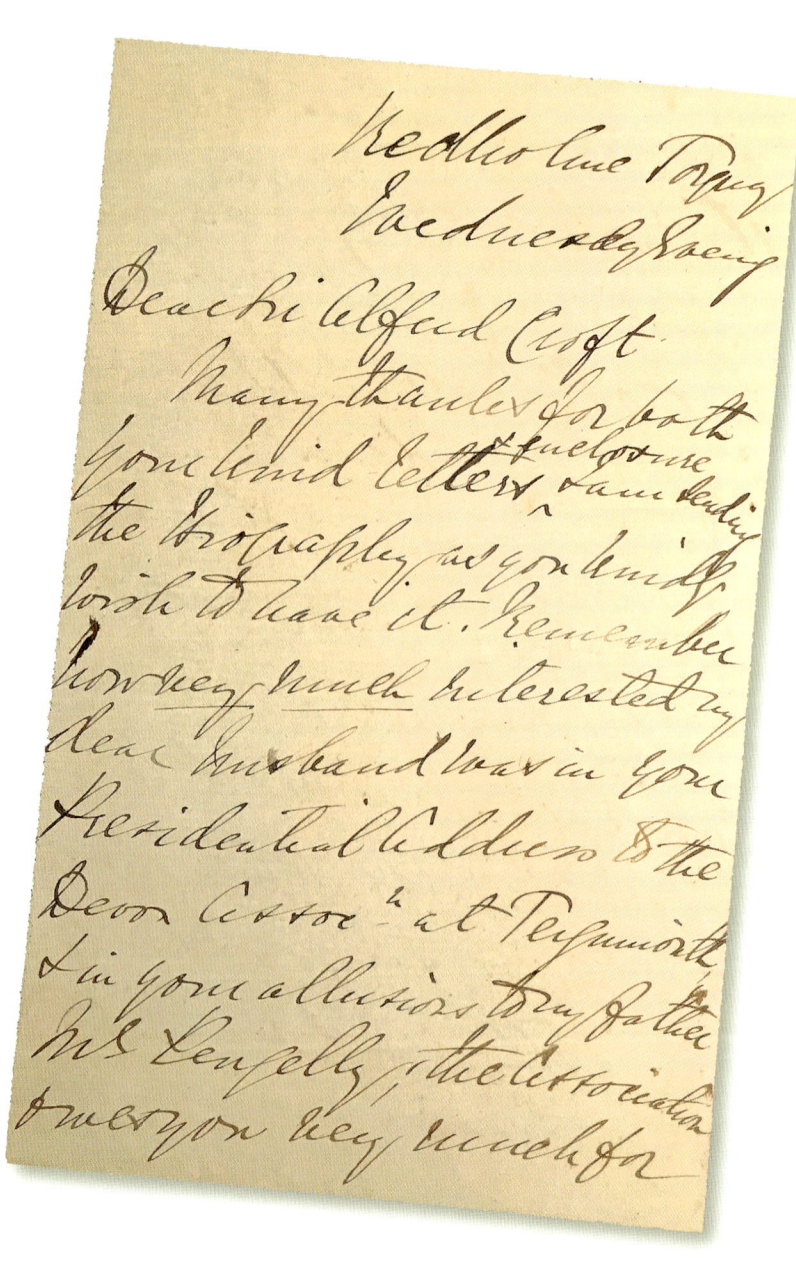

EDWARD KENT

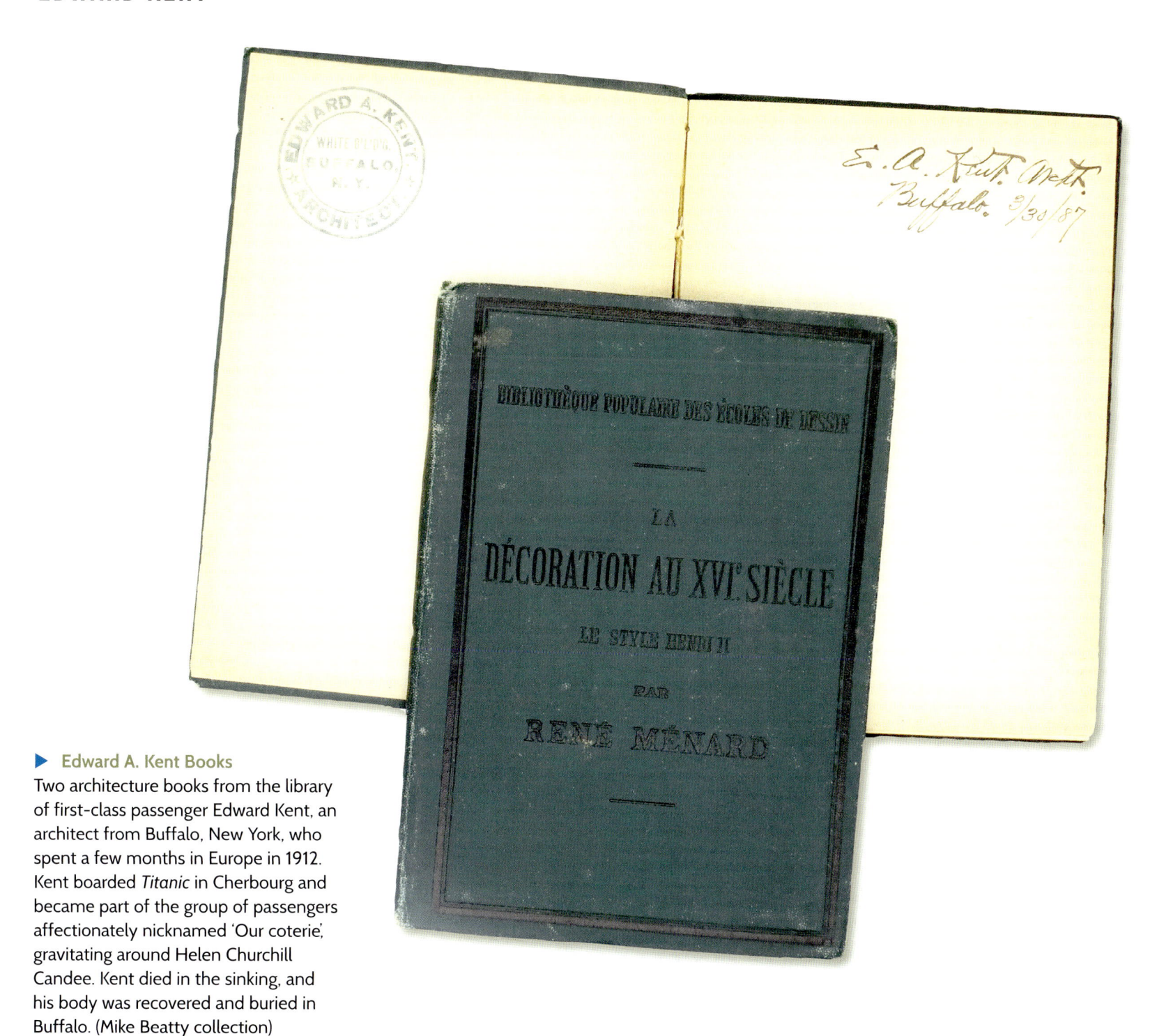

▶ **Edward A. Kent Books**

Two architecture books from the library of first-class passenger Edward Kent, an architect from Buffalo, New York, who spent a few months in Europe in 1912. Kent boarded *Titanic* in Cherbourg and became part of the group of passengers affectionately nicknamed 'Our coterie', gravitating around Helen Churchill Candee. Kent died in the sinking, and his body was recovered and buried in Buffalo. (Mike Beatty collection)

CHARLES KIRKLAND

▼ **Charles Kirkland Family Bible**

The clergy on board *Titanic* hold a special place in the story and probably the least known of them is Rev. Charles Kirkland. The Canadian-born Kirkland was a carpenter who in his early years relocated to Maine. During the 1870s he answered a calling to become an evangelical Baptist minister and travelled around Maine conducting revival meetings. In November 1911 Rev. Kirkland sailed to Scotland to settle the estates of his two uncles. By April 1912, his work was done, and he bought a second-class ticket to board the *Titanic* in Southampton along with his friend, Frank Maybery. Neither man would survive the sinking.

This is Kirkland's personal family Bible and includes entries for his children and some grandchildren. It was first bequeathed to his daughter Myrtle Treadwell before passing through five other family members over the years. (Mike Beatty collection)

THOMAS KNOWLES

▶ **Thomas Knowles Certificate of Discharge**
Thomas Knowles was a *Titanic* crew member who survived the sinking. In 1892 he served aboard the *Mexican*, and in 1900 he survived the foundering of that ship off the coast of South Africa. Knowles lived to be 82. (John Lamoreau collection)

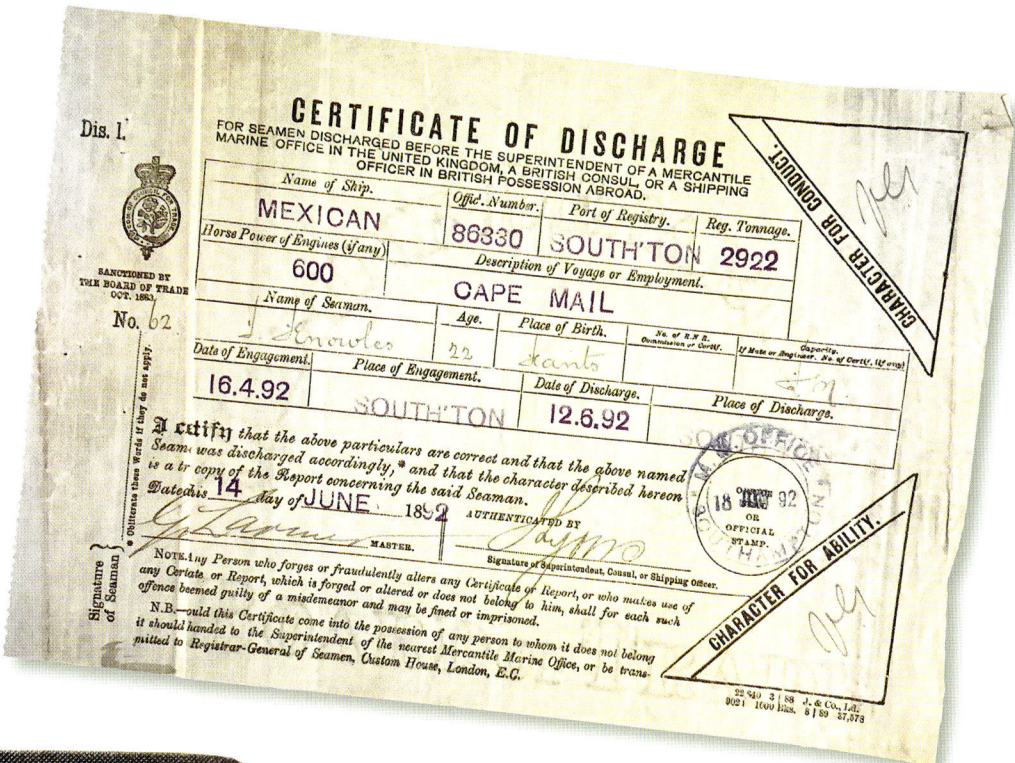

CHARLES LIGHTOLLER

◀ **Book**

A 1935 first edition copy of Commander Charles Lightoller's autobiography, *Titanic and Other Ships*. Lightoller escaped the sinking *Titanic* only after being sucked beneath the ocean's surface by water that was pouring into one of the ship's submerged ventilators. (George Behe collection)

▶ **Lease Agreements**

There is evidence that many ships' officers invested in real estate to supplement their incomes. Here are three lease agreements for properties owned by Charles Lightoller from the late 1920s, and separate letters written by *Titanic*'s chief officer Henry Wilde discuss similar property rentals of his own prior to 1912. (Mike Beatty collection)

▼ *Titanic and Other Ships*

Lightoller's memoir was rereleased in 1938 in a green and brown softcover version. The copy on the right is signed by Lightoller and was given to friends of the family. The copy on the left features the first edition's dust jacket. (Mike Beatty collection)

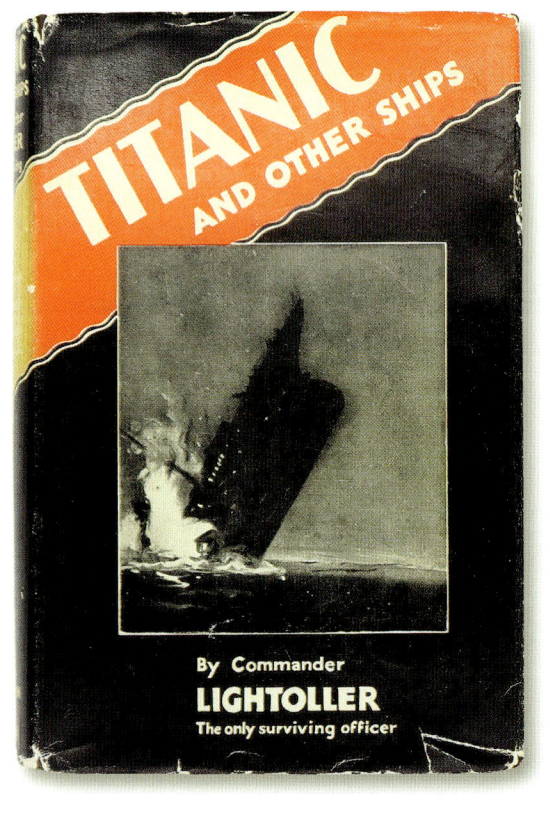

▶ **Lightoller Second World War Photograph**

An unpublished photograph of Lightoller during the war. This is one of a dozen original photographs taken when Lightoller commanded a crew of seven for the British Small Vessels Pool during the war, when he would have been 66 years old. He was positively identified by a grandson as being the man wearing the hat. (John Lamoreau collection)

▶ **Sylvia Lightoller Letter**

Lightoller's wife, Sylvia, sends a letter on memorial stationery after his death in 1952. (Mike Beatty collection)

HAROLD LOWE

▶ **Officer Lowe Code Book**

Sending messages via wireless was an expensive endeavour in the early 1900s. A system of codes was marketed to allow you to send very abbreviated messages that could relay a lot of information. Since the customer paid by the word, this made long messages much cheaper to send. This copy of *The Nautical Telegraph Guide* was published in 1908 and belonged to *Titanic*'s fifth officer Harold Lowe, who made numerous notes inside for coded messages for his father and sister. It's likely Lowe lost the copy he used in the sinking and that this was the one his family used to decipher the messages he sent them, or else he made this copy to replace the one he lost. This copy was obtained directly from Lowe's grandson. (Mike Beatty collection)

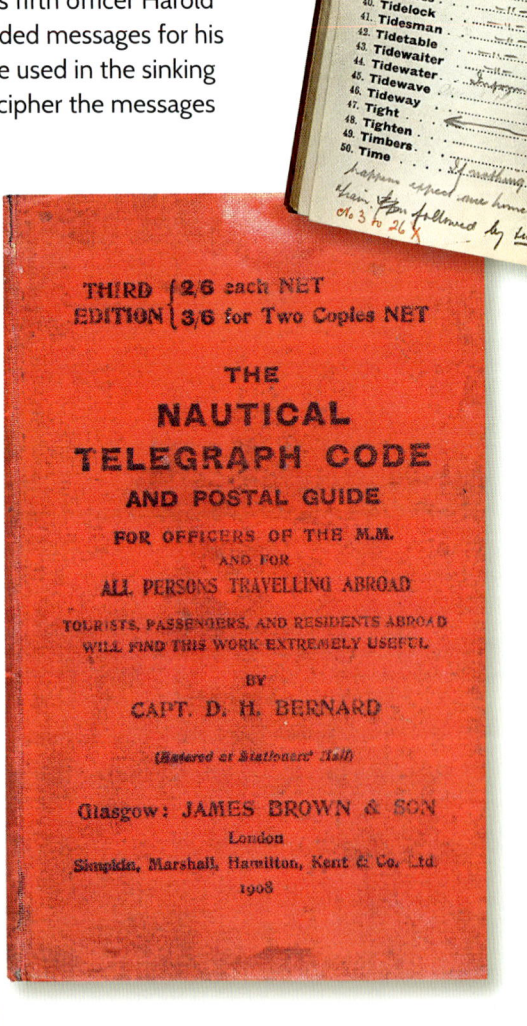

◀ **Filson Young's *Titanic***

One of the very first books published about the disaster was authored by Filson Young and released only thirty-seven days after the sinking. This first edition copy with extremely rare original dust jacket is from the library of Harold Lowe. (Mike Beatty collection)

PAUL MAUGÉ

▶ **Paul Maugé Postcards**

The only survivor of the à la carte kitchen staff was kitchen clerk Paul Maugé. After the sinking he was detained in New York, perhaps to give testimony about the other staff being prevented from going up to the boat deck. While under detention he sent these two postcards home to a possible love interest, Charlotte Antin, and her family, who lived in his home town of Orgeval, France. On 15 May he writes: 'Paul Maugé – Please Madame Antin kindly accept the best wishes of a survivor of the Titanic.' On 8 June he writes to Charlotte's father: 'Paul Maugé Titanic survivor happy to be back on firm land and able to write my name.' She married someone else in 1913, so apparently it never worked out between them. (Mike Beatty collection)

◀ **Paul Maugé Postcards**
Another set of four postcards sent by Paul to Charlotte while in New York City on 19 May 1912. Having a bit of fun, he spells out his name 'P A U L'. (Mike Beatty collection)

HUGH McELROY

▶ **Passenger List**

A first-class passenger list for the 9 October 1903 crossing of the White Star liner *Cedric*. Hugh McElroy, *Titanic*'s future chief purser, was the chief purser on this voyage as well. (Don Lynch collection)

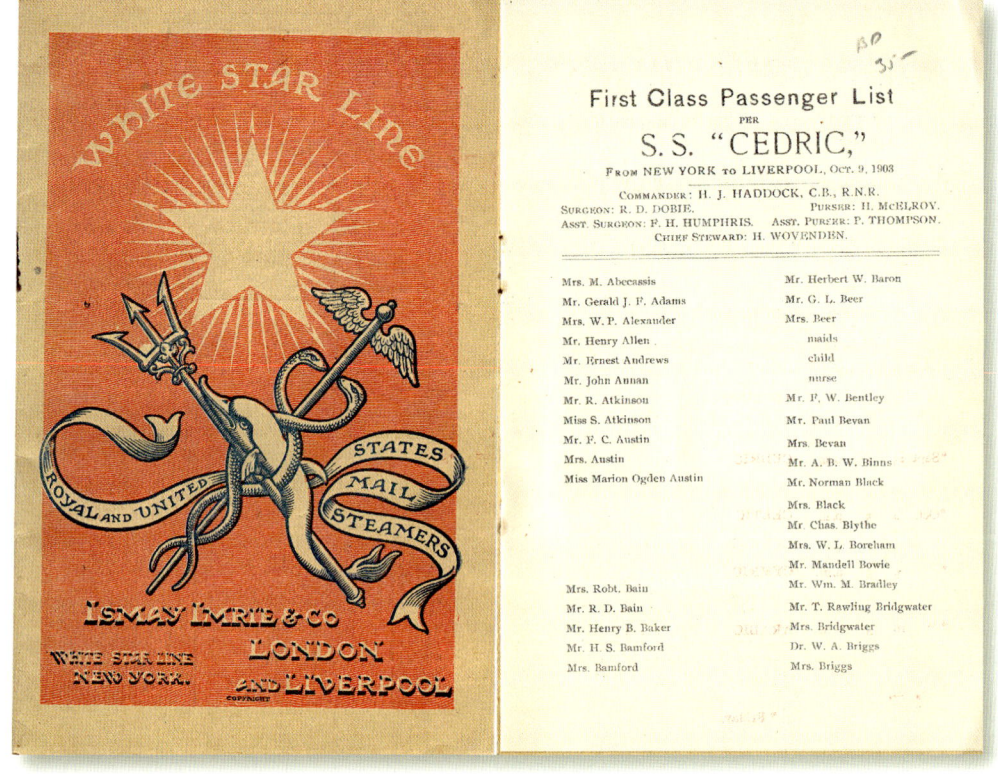

FRANCIS MILLET

◀ **F.D. Millet 1879 Letter**

While in Paris, Francis 'Frank' Millet, a well-known American artist, muralist and author, sent some correspondence related to an order for three statues (Diane de Gabii, Diana the Huntress, and Polyhymnia), to be sent to the Museum of Fine Arts in Boston. (Mike Beatty collection)

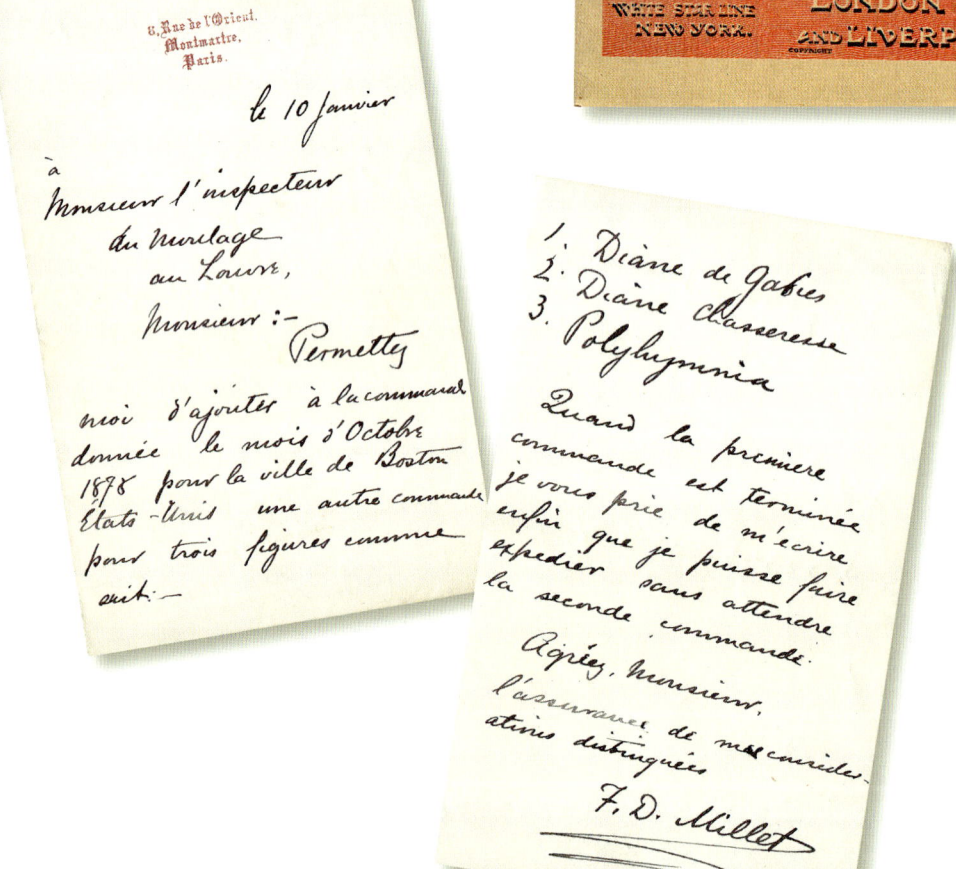

▶ **Frank D. Millet Painting** 'Chloé', featuring a young woman at a spinning wheel, was painted by Millet in his Bridgewater, Connecticut, studio in 1880. It first hung in his studio before being exhibited twice in 1881, and later that year in Boston it sold to a private collector for $350. (Mike Beatty collection)

◄ **Original Art for Millet Article**
In November 1881 Millet had an article published in *Century* magazine, titled 'Costumes in the Greek play at Harvard'. Although Millet was an acclaimed artist, the sketches for the article were drawn by Alfred Laurens Brennan. The original sketch shown here was named 'Jocasta Enters'. A similar sketch used in Millet's article, titled 'Jocasta's Offering', resides at the Library of Congress. (John Lamoreau collection)

▶ **Signed Framed Millet Print**
Millet's 'A Portrait of Mrs. Millet' (1883). This hand-signed print is unusual in two ways: it's almost the same size as the original oil painting, and the antique frame moulding matches the design of the couch Mrs Millet is sitting on. The original oil was last sold in 2007 for $79,000 plus commission. (John Lamoreau collection)

▲ **Bookplate**
This book from Millet's personal library features a bookplate designed by the artist himself. (Mike Beatty collection)

◀ *A Capillary Crime etc.*
Frank Millet was not only a well-known artist but an established author as well. In 1892 he published *A Capillary Crime etc.*, and wrote a dedication in this first edition copy. (Mike Beatty collection)

◀ Book

Frank Millet's 1899 book *The Expedition to the Philippines*, which describes his exploits as a correspondent in that country during the Spanish–American War. (George Behe collection)

▲ Book

An 1893 first edition book, *The Danube: From the Black Forest to the Black Sea*, by Francis Davis Millet. Millet was multi-talented, even though he became better known as an artist. (John Lamoreau collection)

▶ Medals

Millet was not only an author and artist; he also designed medals for military service for the United States government. Pictured here are two of the many he created. The first is an original medal for the Army Civil War Campaign, established by the US War Department on 21 January 1907, and the second is an original medal for the 'Indian Wars', or US Army Indian Campaign Medal, congressionally approved on 11 January 1905. (John Lamoreau collection)

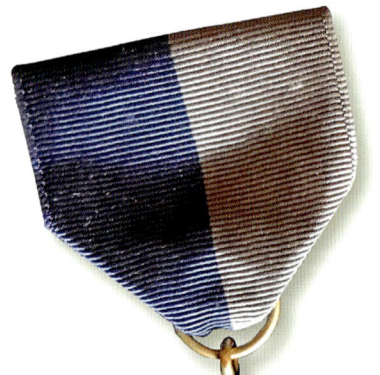

▼ **Cleveland Trust Company Murals**

Millet was commissioned by The Cleveland Trust Company to paint a series of thirteen murals for its new building. The series, completed in 1910, was called 'The Development of Civilization in America' and was installed in the building's rotunda. This booklet was published for the unveiling of the murals. (Mike Beatty collection)

Copyright 1909 by F. D. Millet

SURVEYING THE SITE OF CLEVELAND

IN this picture Moses Cleaveland is seen surveying the site of the city which now bears his name. He has set up his transit, by means of which fixed lines are established, on an elevated bit of land from whence long vistas are obtainable. His young assistant is using a stump as a table and making notations on the map as the surveyor directs. This is invariably the initial step in laying out a town or city. It was as a surveyor, it will be remembered, that Washington began his career.

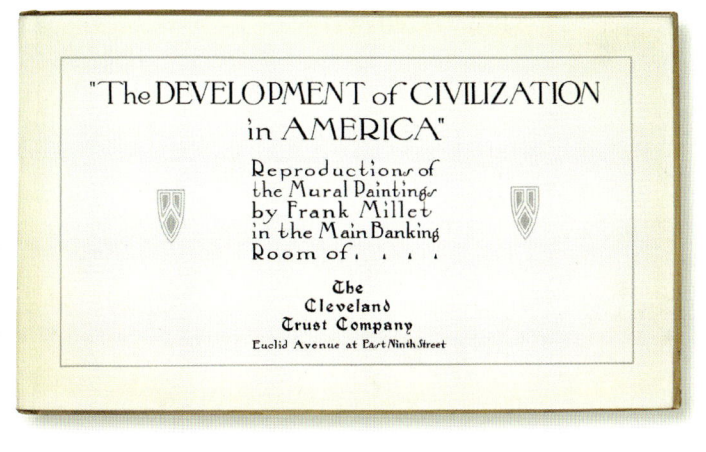

F. D. MILLET
1256 WISCONSIN AVENUE N. W.
WASHINGTON, D. C.

Feb 6 1912

My dear Mr Pease ~ I was delighted to get your excellent and most interesting letter, yesterday and the photograph which came a good deal damaged but can be repaired somewhat and will serve me perfectly well. It is the best photograph of a whaler I ever saw and I am very glad indeed to get it. Also the No 8 of the old Dartmouth Historical Sketches, full of meat, came to hand and I have read the marked page and a good many of the others already, while waiting for this large room to get room enough to work in. It is greatly encouraging to hear that they will permit me to ignore those electroliers and I am sure they will never regret it. Thank you very much for the photograph and the pamphlet and for your kind offices in relation to the electric fixtures. I hope to get at the work early in May. I have to run over to Rome first but I shall be always studying the subjects and hope to get a series which will be a record of the history at once instructive and decorative. Of course whaling will bear a prominent part but I think I can also work in all sorts of incidents and events which will enrich the series and add to the interest. As one studies a problem like this the ideas develope very fast and the trouble usually is to keep them down to reasonable limits. I can already see scores more pictures than I can put on the walls.

I shall have to come down to make accurate measurements and templates as soon as I get back from Rome and then I hope I shall not be so much rushed as I was on my

◀ F.D. Millet 1912 Letter
A letter written by Millet to his close friend Zephaniah Pease, editor of the *New Bedford Mercury* newspaper. The letter is dated 6 February 1912, shortly before Millet sailed to Europe with his friend Major Archibald Butt. In the letter Millet discusses his plans for painting whaling murals for the New Bedford Public Library in Massachusetts, which was then in the process of being remodelled, and he mentions he'll be working on the design of the murals while in Rome. It's believed that Millet's mural sketches were lost with him in the *Titanic* disaster. (John Lamoreau collection)

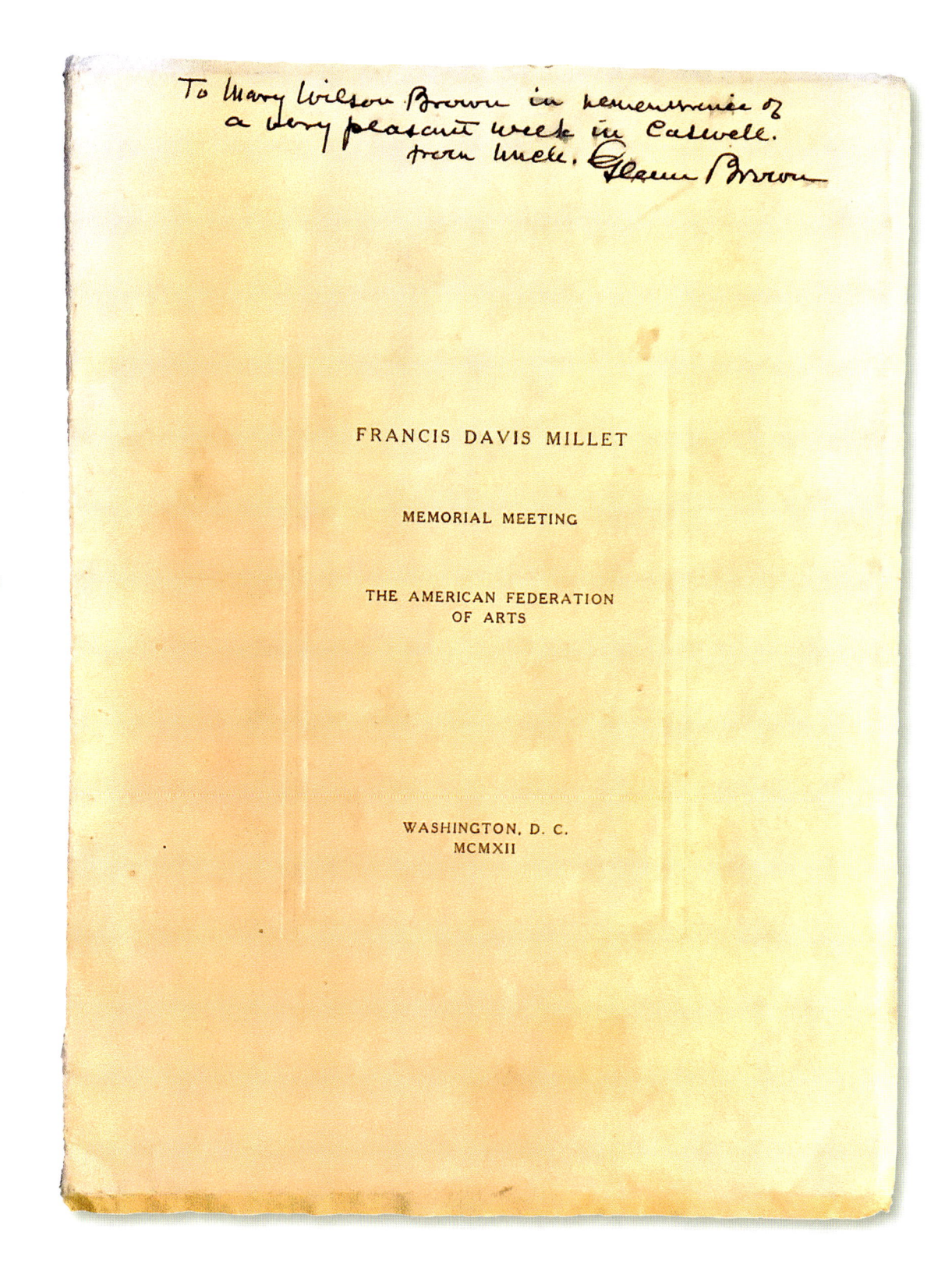

▶ **F.D. Millet Memorial Book**
This book is from the Francis Davis Millet Memorial Meeting of the American Federation of Arts, held in The National Museum, Washington, DC, in 1912. While not well known today, Millet was one of the most famous and beloved passengers on the *Titanic*. The minutes from the memorial meeting state, 'We have come not to do injustice to Francis Millet's example by mourning and lamentation, but to celebrate the achievement of his long and useful and joyous life. He possessed in a very high degree many of the qualities which men at their best, in their noblest moods, most delight to honour and most sincerely believe to be a part of the saving grace of the world.' (John Lamoreau collection)

LEDGWOOD TERRACE
MALDEN

April 28, 1912 –
Editor of New Bedford
Mercury: —
Dear Sir,
As you have
been so kindly inter-
ested in publishing
So much about my
brother, Frank D. Millet
I am going to make

▲ **Lucia Millet Letter**
A four-page letter written by Millet's sister, Lucia Millet Baxter, to Zephaniah Pease. The letter reads in part: 'The body has been found and met at Halifax by Laurence Millet, the oldest son, on arriving in Boston it will be cremated by cable request from his widow in England.' (John Lamoreau collection)

▶ **Bust**
A bust of F.D. Millet, executed by Albin Polasek in Rome, Italy, in 1912. According to the Albin Polasek Museum, ten of them were cast and given to the Pennsylvania Academy of the Fine Arts, Harvard University, the American Academy in Rome, and New York University. This is one of them, found in England. (Kalman Tanito collection)

▲ **Millet-Butt Memorial Press Photograph**
This original press photograph is dated 8 February 1913. Major Archibald Butt and Francis D. Millet sailed on the *Titanic* together, and the press release on the back of the photograph reads in part: 'TRIBUTE TO TWO OF *TITANIC*'S HEROIC DEAD … this design for the memorial to Major Butt and Frank D. Millet, two famous Washingtonians who went down in the *Titanic* disaster, has been approved by President Taft and the work on the memorial to be commenced at once. The knight in armour represents Major Butt and the bas relief of the fine arts represents the artist Millet. The reliefs are to be on each side of the fountain to be erected in the park just south of the White House.' The memorial fountain still stands in that same location. (John Lamoreau collection)

JACOB MILLING

▲ ▶ Jacob Milling Postcard

Danish engineer Jacob Milling was planning to travel to the US to study railway machinery for two months. On 9 April 1912, the day before sailing, he sent this postcard to his wife Augusta while staying in Southampton: 'Dear Augusta! This is the last thing you will hear from me from this side of the Atlantic. I am staying at Banen's Hotel, it's not cheap but comfortable. From my window, I can see the ship in the dock'. This was the last letter Milling would ever write to his wife, because he did not survive the sinking of the *Titanic*. His remains were later recovered from the sea and were returned to his widow. (Trevor Powell collection)

CLARENCE MOORE

◀ **Clarence Moore Portrait**
Clarence Moore, a Washington DC banker and businessman, gave out this signed portrait for Christmas 1908. In April 1912 he and his friend Archie Butt both lost their lives when the *Titanic* went down. (Mike Beatty collection)

▼▶ **Clarence Moore Photo Album**
This album from around 1905–10 features photos of Clarence Moore and his wife Mabelle on vacation. Inside also features Mabelle's bookplate. (Mike Beatty collection)

HELEN NEWSOM

◄◄ ▲ Newsom Trophy
The Pretty Brook Tennis Club mixed doubles prize (1933) for Mrs Karl Behr (Helen Newsom), *Titanic* survivor. (Kalman Tanito collection)

WILLIAM O'LOUGHLIN

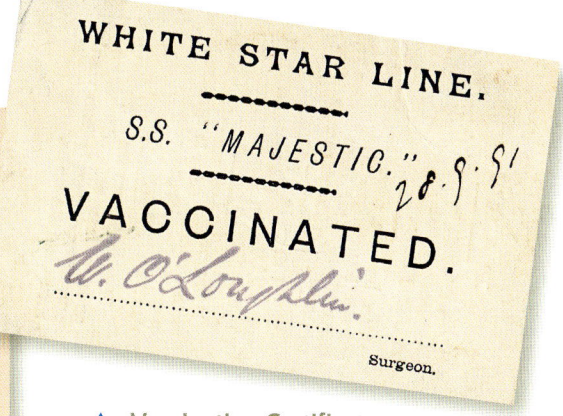

▲ Vaccination Certificate

Dr William O'Loughlin was the beloved elderly surgeon on the *Titanic*. In 1891 he was serving on the *Majestic* and stamped this vaccination certificate for an immigrant. He died in the disaster, and his body is not known to have been recovered. (Kalman Tanito collection)

▲ Passenger List

An *Oceanic* passenger list for 5 June 1901, with Dr William O'Loughlin acting as the chief surgeon. Also named on this passenger list are Mrs J. Pierpont Morgan, Miss Morgan and W. Forbes Morgan. (Don Lynch collection)

▶ Bronze Plaque

On 22 April 1912 the *New York Times* reported on Dr O'Loughlin's bravery: 'Survivors say they saw Dr. O'Loughlin on deck going from one to another of the frightened passengers, soothing them and aiding them in getting into the lifeboats.' Known for his generosity and for volunteering at St Vincent's Hospital in New York City, money was raised from around the world to build a seventeen-bed emergency room ward at St Vincent's in his name. The ward was dedicated in 1914, and a bronze 'tablet' was hung in the good doctor's honour. The memorial plaque measures 52 inches by 38 inches. (John Lamoreau collection)

HELEN ØSTBY

▶ **Østby Sheet Music**
Helen Ragnhild Østby was a first-class passenger on the *Titanic* and was returning to America with her widowed father, Engelhart Cornelius Østby, after a tour of Europe and North Africa. Mr Østby often took Helen on business trips to Europe, and on one such trip in September 1907 they visited Berlin, where this sheet music was obtained. Helen survived the sinking of the *Titanic*, but her father did not. (John Lamoreau collection)

◀ **Østby Necklace**
An antique sterling silver filigree citrine drop necklace made by the Østby & Barton Company, a jewellery manufacturing firm co-founded in 1879 by Engelhart Cornelius Østby. (John Lamoreau collection)

OCEAN LINER TITANIC—LARGEST STEAMER IN THE WORLD.
Sunk by iceberg on maiden trip off Halifax, April 15, 1912; 1,500 people drowned. Length, 882 feet; breadth, 92 feet; number of steel decks, 11; watertight bulkheads, 15; passengers accommodated, 2,500; crew, 860; tonnage registered, 45,000; tonnage displacement, 66,000; cost, $7,500,000.

▲ ◀ **Østby-related Postcard**

This memorial postcard was mailed by *Carpathia* passenger Hope Chapin's father D. Russell Brown. Brown, a former governor of Rhode Island, travelled to New York City after the sinking to meet the *Carpathia*. Newlyweds Hope and Howard Chapin, who had embarked on the *Carpathia* on their honeymoon, were reunited with their longtime acquaintance Helen Østby after the rescue and offered their cabin to the survivor. Postmarked 20 April 1912 and addressed to his son-in-law's family, Brown writes: 'We are so sorry to not find Mr [Engelhart] Østby. Hope says Miss Østby was very brave and assisted greatly in the care of survivors who were injured.' (Trevor Powell collection)

RICHARD PARSONS

▲ ▶   Richard Parsons Postcards
Second-class saloon steward Richard Parsons sent home three postcards during the month of September 1911. He worked on *Olympic* during the summer of 1911 but briefly transferred to *Majestic* before returning to *Olympic* in late September and subsequently being reassigned to *Titanic* on 4 April 1912. He did not survive the sinking. (Mike Beatty collection)

AUSTIN PARTNER

Manitoba Club,
Winnipeg.

Aug 6. 1910

My dear Father

I am still held
up here but hoping
now to leave in a day
or two to sail about
the 18th for home.

This will mean that
I cannot see you by
your birthday & I
am writing to wish
you very many happy

June 11. 1910.

My dear Father

I want to write you
just a line while I have
time to say how sorry I
... a you were
... getting your
... letters. I was so
... to have such
... the next. but
... "pride goeth
... all" & your
... health perhaps
... you to take
... otherwise

...derful ride
... be very glad
... to inspect
... coal forests
... mines + what
... of my
... probably
... S. Francisco.

Much love to you all

Your affec Son

Austin

◀ **Austin Partner 1909–10 Letters**

Austin Partner was a stockbroker from England who spent much time in the United States and Canada for business. Here he wrote several letters home to his father, Rev. Richard Partner, in which he updated his family on his travels. For the most part he was enjoying his time and the hospitality he was receiving, although occasionally he tired of it. On 11 June 1910 he wrote: 'I've had enough of hotel and club life and I am just a bit bored of talking high finance all day and half the night sometimes. Still I might be doing worse and I only ought to be thankful that I have got the work to do.' (Mike Beatty collection)

▲ **Austin Partner 1910 Letter**
Partner wrote this lengthy letter to his father on 21 May 1910. In it he described his 3,400-mile train ride from New York to Mexico City, where he saw the Aztec ruins and many other sites in Mexico. (Mike Beatty collection)

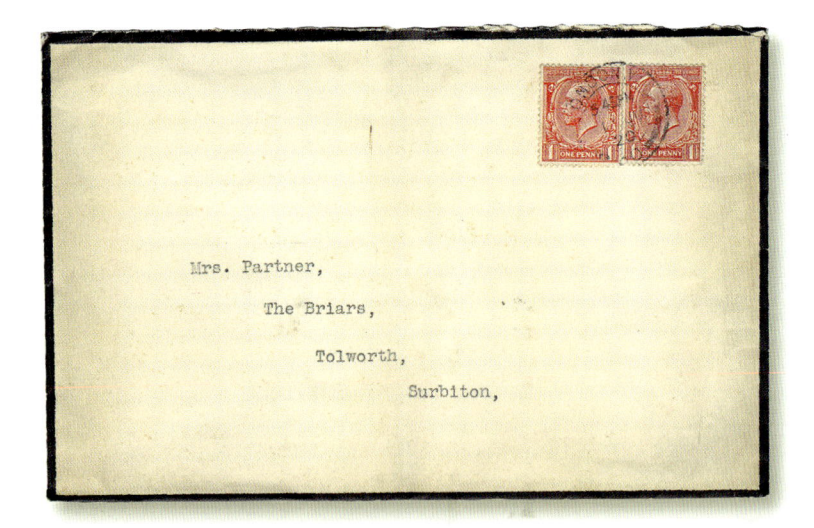

Mrs. Partner,

The Briars,

Tolworth,

Surbiton,

Mʳˢ Austin Partner

desires to express

her gratitude for

kindness & sympathy

shewn her in

her great sorrow.

The Briars,
Ewell Road,
Surbiton.

Reprinted from the " Surbiton Times "
of Friday, May 24th, 1912.

———

IN MEMORIAM.

MR. AUSTIN PARTNER

(A VICE-PRESIDENT OF THE TOLWORTH DEBATING
SOCIETY WHO PERISHED IN THE WRECK OF
THE "TITANIC," 14TH APRIL, 1912.)

Adieu! for safe within His ruling hands,
    Thy manly noble spirit now we leave;
Assured that Captain, who all-wise commands,
    Hath some dear holy purpose to achieve.
Too true, 'tis hard to think thee dead, who late
    With cheery voice addressed our thoughtful
        throng,
Contending in the lists of keen debate,
    For thy convictions 'twixt the right and
        wrong.
And wrongs there are, the curse of greed, and
        pride
    And laws which Time and Science make
        effete,
While man, vain man! sleeps on till woe betide
    And ruin, ruthless ruin, is complete:—
To face such foes, in life's last hour, thy man-
        hood proved above,
And joined a League of Mercy and a Brother-
        hood of Love.

Ah! what thy thoughts on that huge sinking
        ship,
    When horrors midnight orgy on it burst!
The crowd of frailty in the wreck's fell grip;
    The startling cry "Women and children
        first";
The grief-wild fond farewells, as lifeboats tore
    The dearest kin apart,—for ever lost;
And left thee ranked with noble hundreds
        more,
    One of that brave and self-denying host.
Here to sweet rural calm thy form we bear
    (Snatched from the grasping unconquerable
        sea)
Whilst on thy silent lips still dwells thy prayer,
    "Nearer, my God, to Thee, nearer to Thee."
Comes there not now a "still small voice," as
        o'er yon icy spray,
    "The Father of the fatherless, will wipe all
        tears away?"
    Tolworth, Surbiton.   J. R.

◄▲ **Austin Partner Mourning Stationery**
A piece of mourning stationery and accompanying envelope for Partner, and a memorial poem dedicated to his memory. (Mike Beatty collection)

JOHN PHILLIPS

▲ **Jack Phillips Postcard**
A postcard from *Titanic* Marconi operator John 'Jack' Phillips to his sister, dated February 1907, and signed 'Love Jack'. (John Lamoreau collection)

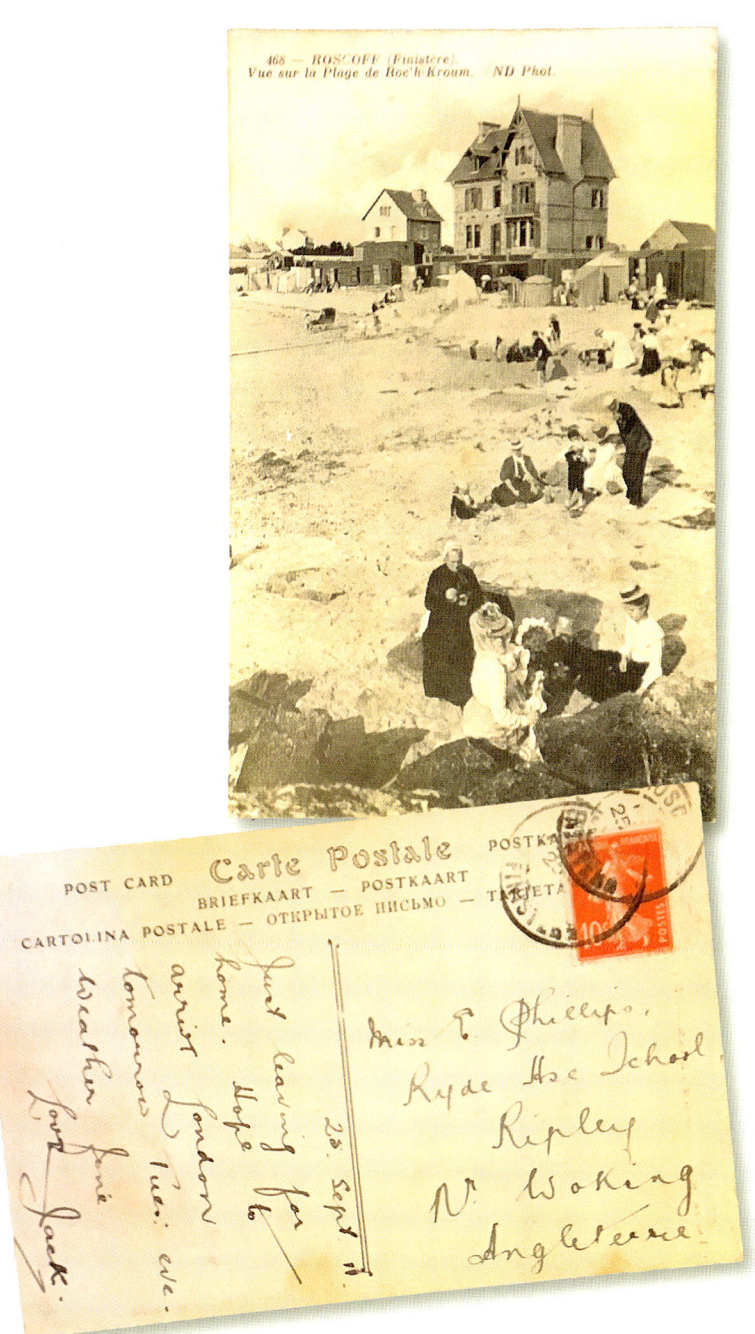

▲ **Jack Phillips Postcard**
Another postcard from Phillips to his sister, dated September 1911. The postcard was mailed from France and was sent to his sister's address in *Angleterre*. (John Lamoreau collection)

▲ **Jack Phillips Postcard**

In November 1911 Jack Phillips was working on the *Oceanic*. During a layover in Southampton he wrote a postcard to his sister about his plans for the upcoming holidays. (Mike Beatty collection)

WILLIAM PIRRIE

◀ **Lord Pirrie Letter**

This White Star Line letter signed by Lord William Pirrie is dated 18 December 1909. Pirrie was chairman of Harland & Wolff, builders of the *Titanic*, for almost thirty years. (John Lamoreau collection)

◀ ▼ **Mrs Pirrie Letter to Mrs Dewey**
Margaret Pirrie, wife of Lord Pirrie, sent a letter of
acknowledgement to United States Navy Admiral George
Dewey's wife, Mildred Dewey, who had sent a thoughtful letter of
sympathy over the *Titanic* disaster. (Mike Beatty collection)

HERBERT PITMAN

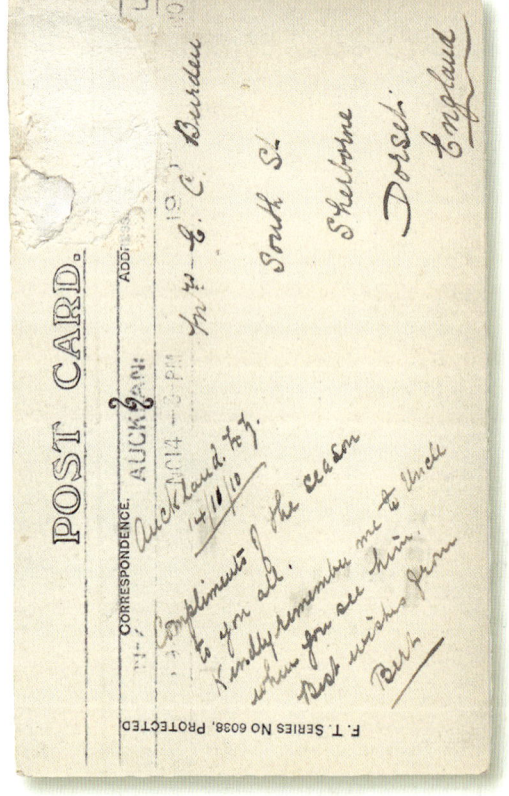

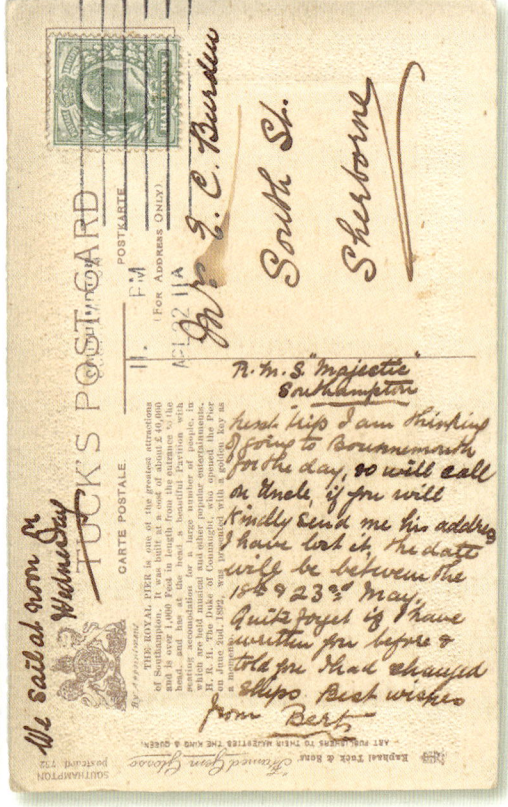

◀▲ **Herbert Pitman Postcards**
Titanic's third officer, Herbert Pitman, sent messages home in 1910 and 1911 while working on board the *Majestic*. (Mike Beatty collection)

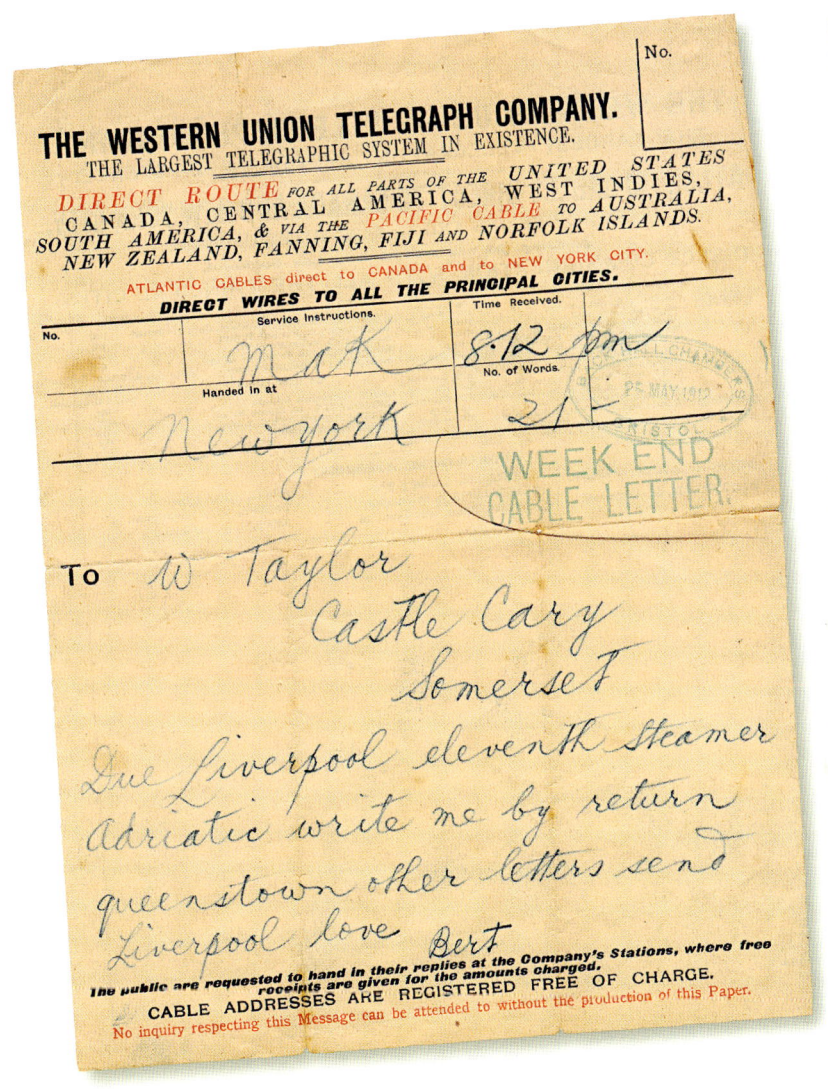

▲ **Telegram**

Third Officer Pitman was detained for the United States Senate Inquiry when he arrived in New York on the *Carpathia*. When he was released after giving his testimony, he returned from Washington to New York and boarded the *Adriatic* for England, where he would have to testify at the British Inquiry. Just before boarding, he sent this telegram to his sister. (Mike Beatty collection)

▶ **Passenger List**

An *Olympic* passenger list for 14 September 1921. By this late date Pitman had assumed the duties of an assistant purser due to his failing eyesight. (Don Lynch collection)

WALTER PORTER

▶ **S. Porter & Company Advertising**

Walter Chamberlain Porter was a first-class passenger who died on the *Titanic*. In 1903 he became a co-owner of the Samuel Porter Last Manufacturing Company, a business his father had started. This metal display item, stamped S. PORTER & CO, was used for advertising purposes. (John Lamoreau collection)

JANE QUICK

▼ **Photo**

Second-class passenger Jane Quick and her daughters, Winnifred and Phyllis, left the *Titanic* in lifeboat 11 and survived the disaster. Here Jane is seen in a photograph taken around the time of the disaster. (George Behe collection)

◀ **Photo**

Here we see Jane Quick seated between her two little girls – Winnifred (left) and Phyllis (right). Jane's husband, Fred (standing), was awaiting their arrival in Detroit when he learned that the *Titanic* had gone down. After he hurried to New York to meet his family on the *Carpathia*, Jane's first words to her husband were, 'Oh Fred, what a funny hat you're wearing!' (George Behe collection)

▶ Souvenir Flag

While on the train taking them to their new home in Detroit, little Phyllis Quick discovered something secreted in her mother's coat pocket – a small souvenir flag that Mrs Quick had purchased while on the *Titanic*. 'Mine!' Phyllis exclaimed to her father when he attempted to examine the flag more closely. (George Behe collection)

◀ Saved Items

In addition to the little flag, Jane Quick saved several other items from being lost on the *Titanic* – a small tin box with bicyclists engraved on its cover, and four small-denomination British coins. (George Behe collection)

LUCY RIDSDALE

▶ **Lucy Ridsdale** *Carpathia* **Message**
Second-class survivor Lucy Ridsdale sent this message from the
rescue ship *Carpathia* stating that she was saved. Due to the great
volume of messages it was never transmitted, and her family had to
wait until she arrived in New York to find out she had been rescued.
(Mike Beatty collection)

ELISABETH ROBERT

▼ **Elisabeth Robert Letter, 1938**
Elisabeth Robert travelled first class on the *Titanic* with her niece,
Elisabeth Walton Allen, and her daughter, Georgette Madill, all
three of whom survived the sinking. This letter is accompanied
by the original mailing envelope addressed in Robert's hand. (John
Lamoreau collection)

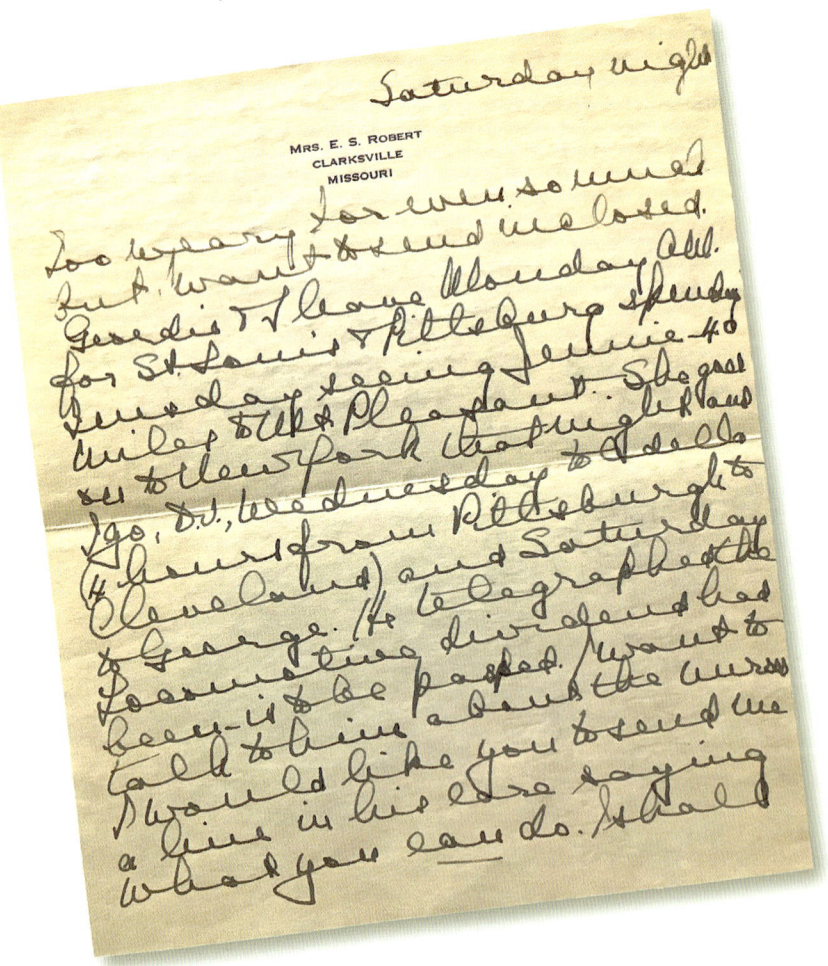

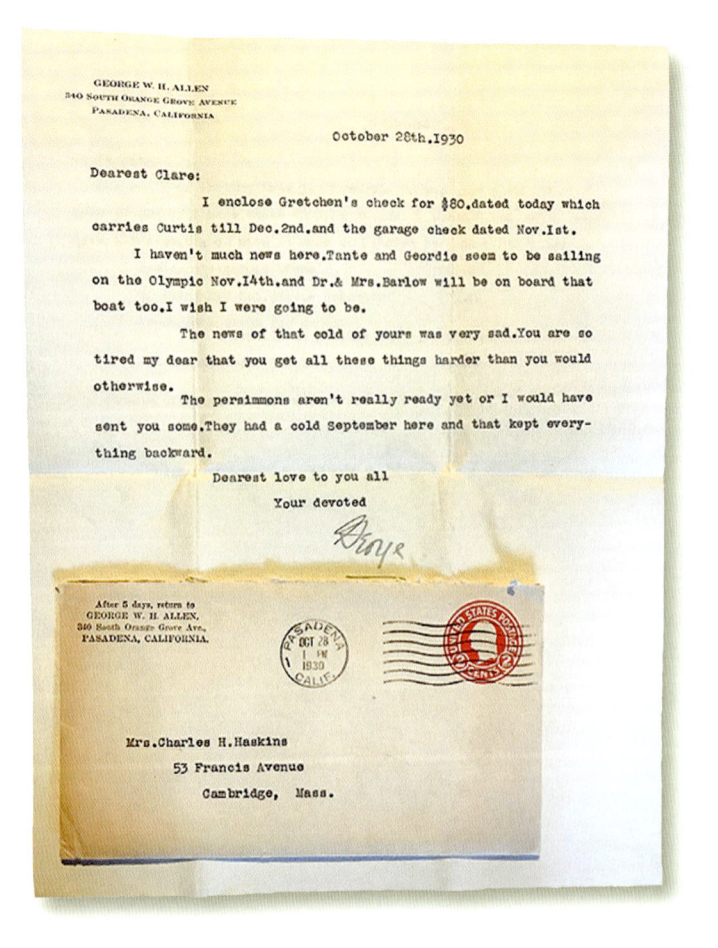

EDITH ROSENBAUM

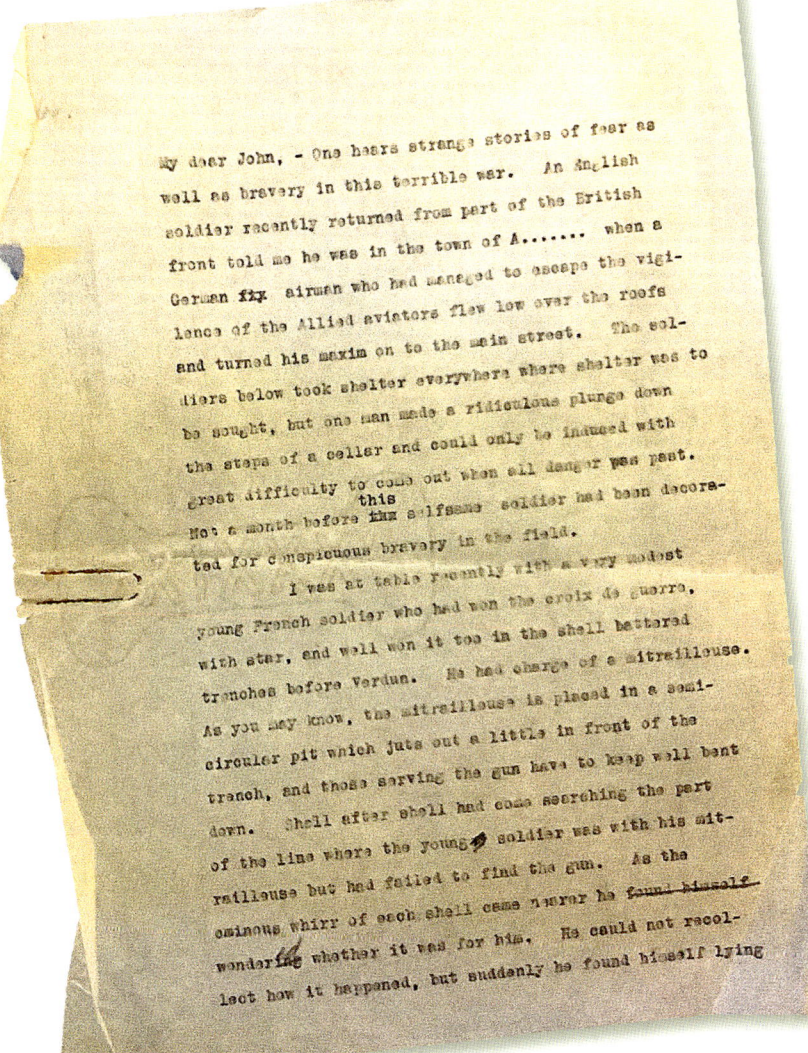

◀ **First World War Edith Rosenbaum Letter**
A letter from a group of six such letters written by *Titanic* survivor Edith Rosenbaum. Edith was living in France as a fashion correspondent when the Great War broke out, and she became one of the world's first female, on-the-scene, war correspondents. Her letters are rich in historical detail, with vivid descriptions of the horrors she saw. (John Lamoreau collection)

▼ **Business Card for Edith Russell**
This card from the former Edith Rosenbaum was sent to Robert Forrest (collector/researcher) by Walter Lord, who wrote a note on the back. (Mike Beatty collection)

◀◀ **Letter**
This letter is from George Walton Holker Allen (1889–1973) and is written to his sister, Clare Haskins; they were the siblings of Elisabeth Walton Allen, who survived the sinking alongside their aunt, Elisabeth Walton Robert, and cousin, Georgette Alexandra Madill. This letter, dated 28 October 1930, reads: 'Tante and Geordie seem to be sailing on the *Olympic* Nov. 14 …' Tante is German for 'aunt' and refers to Mrs Robert, while 'Geordie' was Georgette Madill's nickname. One can only wonder how the *Titanic* survivors felt when they stepped on board the *Titanic*'s older sister. (John Lamoreau collection)

GEORGE ROSENSHINE

▶ Rosenshine Stationery

George Rosenshine, along with his brothers Albert and Max, ran Rosenshine Brothers, which specialised in importing feathers, flowers and other millinery items. This letter was from their business. Along with his mistress Gertrude Thorne, George boarded the *Titanic* in Cherbourg under the alias 'George Thorne' after enjoying a few months of business and pleasure in Europe. Gertrude survived the sinking, but George was one of the first-class passengers who lost his life. His body was recovered and buried in New York. (Mike Beatty collection)

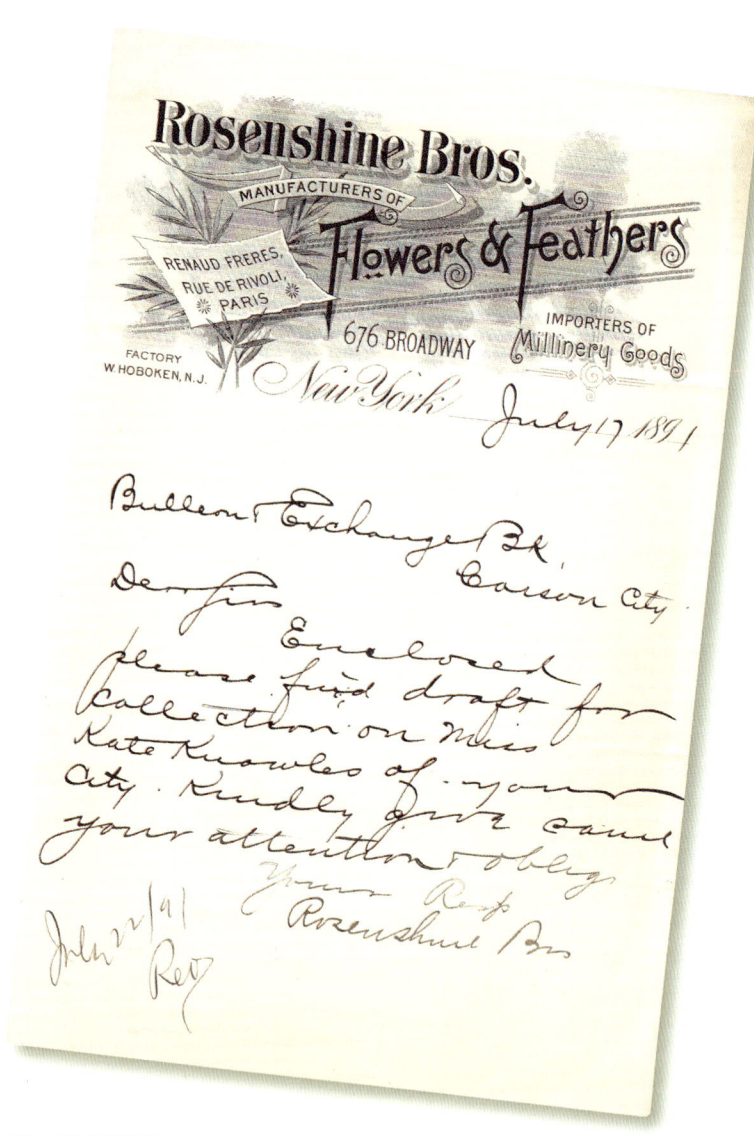

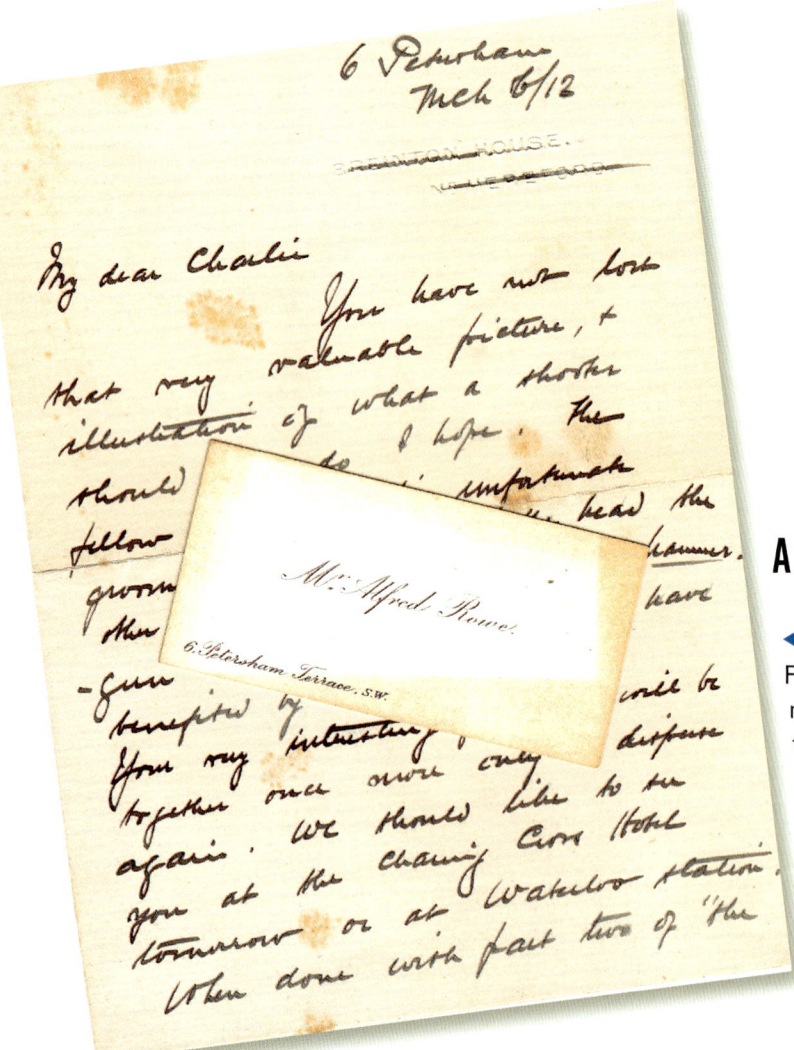

ALFRED ROWE

◀ Alfred Rowe Calling Card

First-class passenger Alfred Rowe owned a ranch in Texas and regularly made trips from England to America to oversee it. It was on one of these trips that Rowe booked a first-class passage on *Titanic*. He regularly wrote to his brother Charlie, including this letter, which was written a month before he lost his life on the *Titanic*. A few weeks after the sinking his body was recovered and forwarded to his brother in England along with the effects found on his body. One such item was a wallet with a few personalised calling cards inside, and the staining on this card showing where another card laid on top of it is still evident. (Mike Beatty collection)

EMILY RYERSON

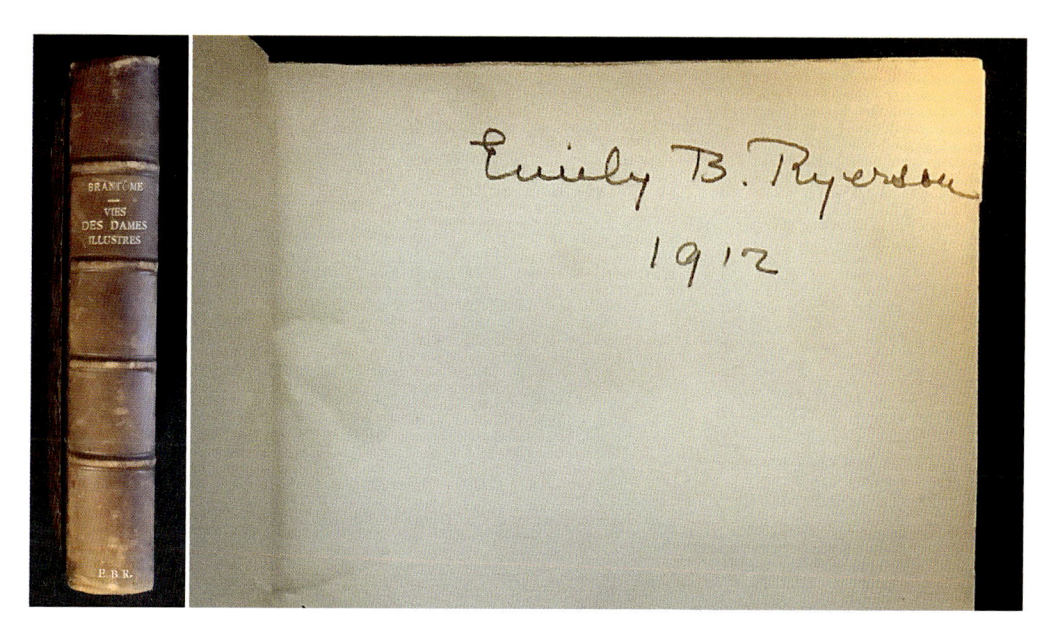

◀ **Ryerson Book**

A book from the estate of Miss Emily Borie Ryerson signed and dated '1912' by Miss Ryerson, who was 18 years old at the time of the sinking. Her initials 'E.B.R.' are stamped in gilt on the spine. The book, *Vies des dames illustres* (*Lives of Illustrious Ladies*), is by Pierre de Brantôme and measures 7¼ inches by 4½ inches. (John Lamoreau collection)

▶ **Ryerson Marconigram**

In the days following the disaster, first-class survivor Emily Ryerson attempted to send this Marconigram to her brother-in-law in Philadelphia. It reads: 'Arthur missing – rest safe – Ryerson. Arriving [in] New York Thursday. Carpathia.' (Trevor Powell collection)

ADOLPHE SAALFELD

◀ **Adolphe Saalfeld Bottles**
German-born chemist Adolphe Saalfeld was travelling on board *Titanic* to the United States to expand his fragrance company based in Manchester, England. He brought with him samples of floral perfumes that were lost in the sinking, but Saalfeld himself was fortunate enough to survive. These two bottles from his company still smell of pineapple and strawberries. (Mike Beatty collection)

WILLIAM SLOPER

▶ ▼ Sloper Biography

In 1949 survivor William Sloper published a biography of his father titled *The Life and Times of Andrew Jackson Sloper 1849-1933*, in which he included a special chapter describing his own experiences during the *Titanic*'s maiden voyage. This copy with the original dust jacket belonged to his personal secretary, Lillian Braunstein, inside which she kept some 1940s portraits of Sloper and news clippings about the book's release. (Mike Beatty collection)

EDWARD J. SMITH

THE LATE
CAPTAIN E. J. SMITH, R.N.R.
OF THE ILLFATED LINER "TITANIC".
"GREATER LOVE HATH NO MAN THAN THIS,
THAT A MAN LAY DOWN HIS LIFE FOR HIS FRIENDS."

Published by Tom Harvey, Redruth.

▲ **Postcard**
A post-disaster postcard honouring the late Captain Edward J. Smith by utilising the lyrics and music of 'Nearer My God, to Thee'. (George Behe collection)

◄ **Postcard**
This card's photograph of Captain Smith was taken on 10 April 1912, outside the *Titanic*'s first and second officers' cabins while the vessel was preparing to leave Southampton on her maiden voyage. The debris around Smith's feet might be fragments of decorative plants that were delivered to the ship the previous evening. (George Behe collection)

▶ **E.J. Smith Signature**

This signature came from a 'children's birthday book' that was gifted to a Bertha Chaplin on 6 March 1883, as a gift from her grandmother. She must have moved in affluent circles, because the book is filled with signatures of viscounts, members of Parliament, musicians, actors and other peers. Each individual signed under the date of their own birthday, and Captain Smith signed under his, 27 January. (John Lamoreau collection)

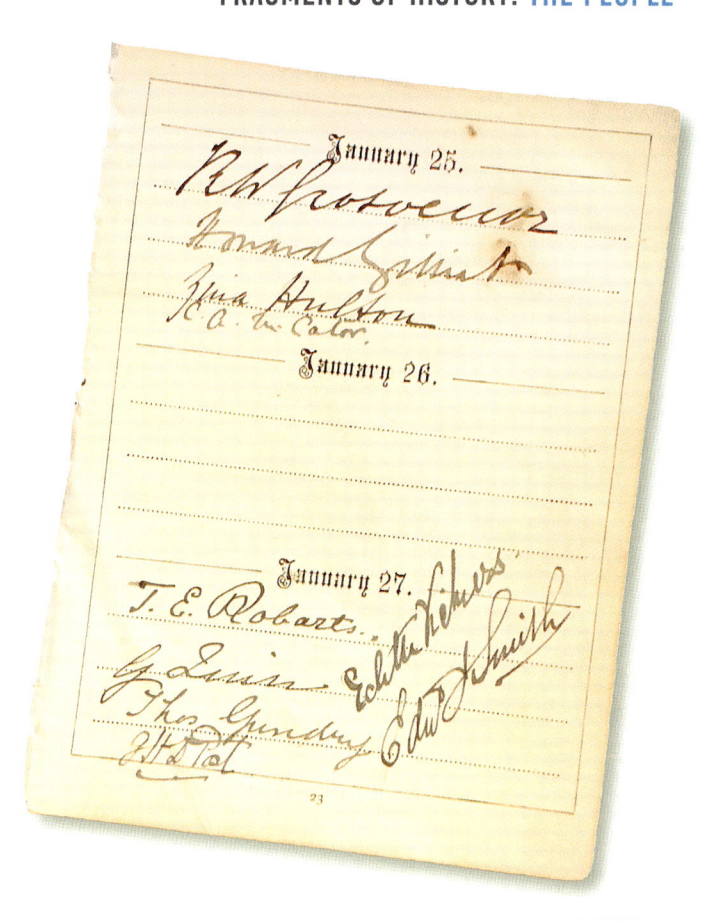

▼ **Discharge Book and Certificate**

The certificate book of Able Seaman John Callaghan, who served on several occasions under Captain Smith. This certificate for his service on the *Majestic* in October 1895 has been hand-signed by the captain. (Kalman Tanito collection)

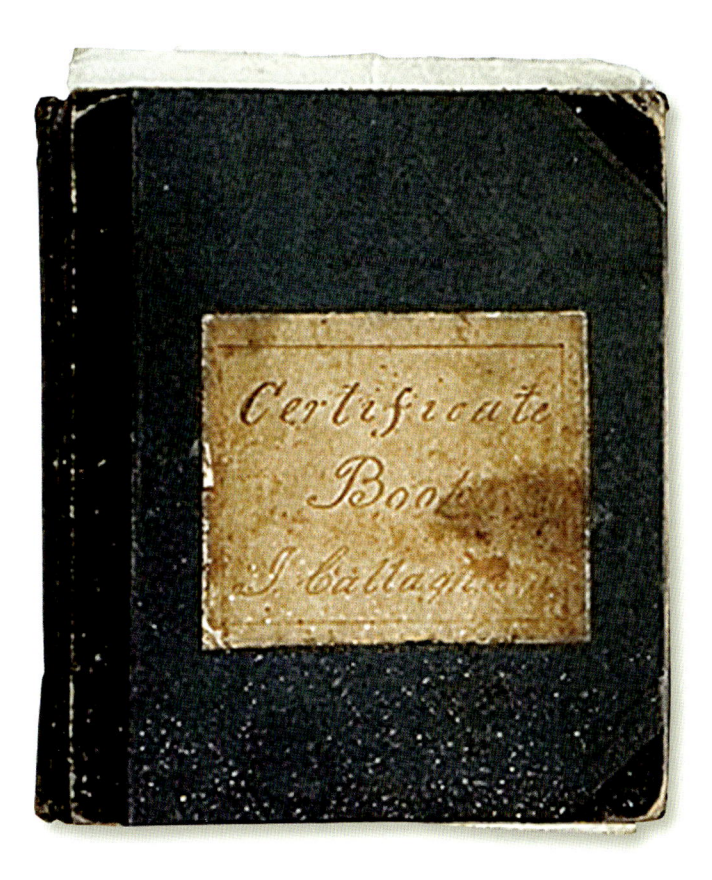

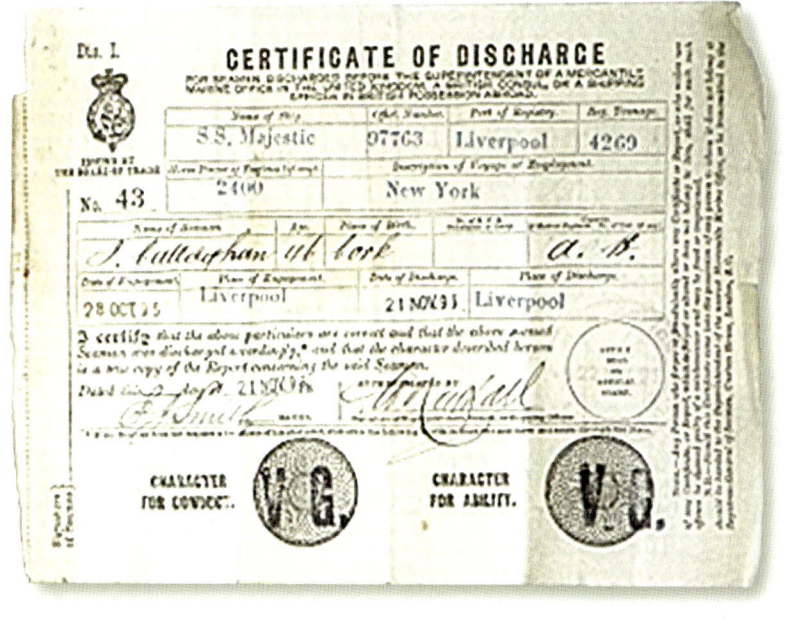

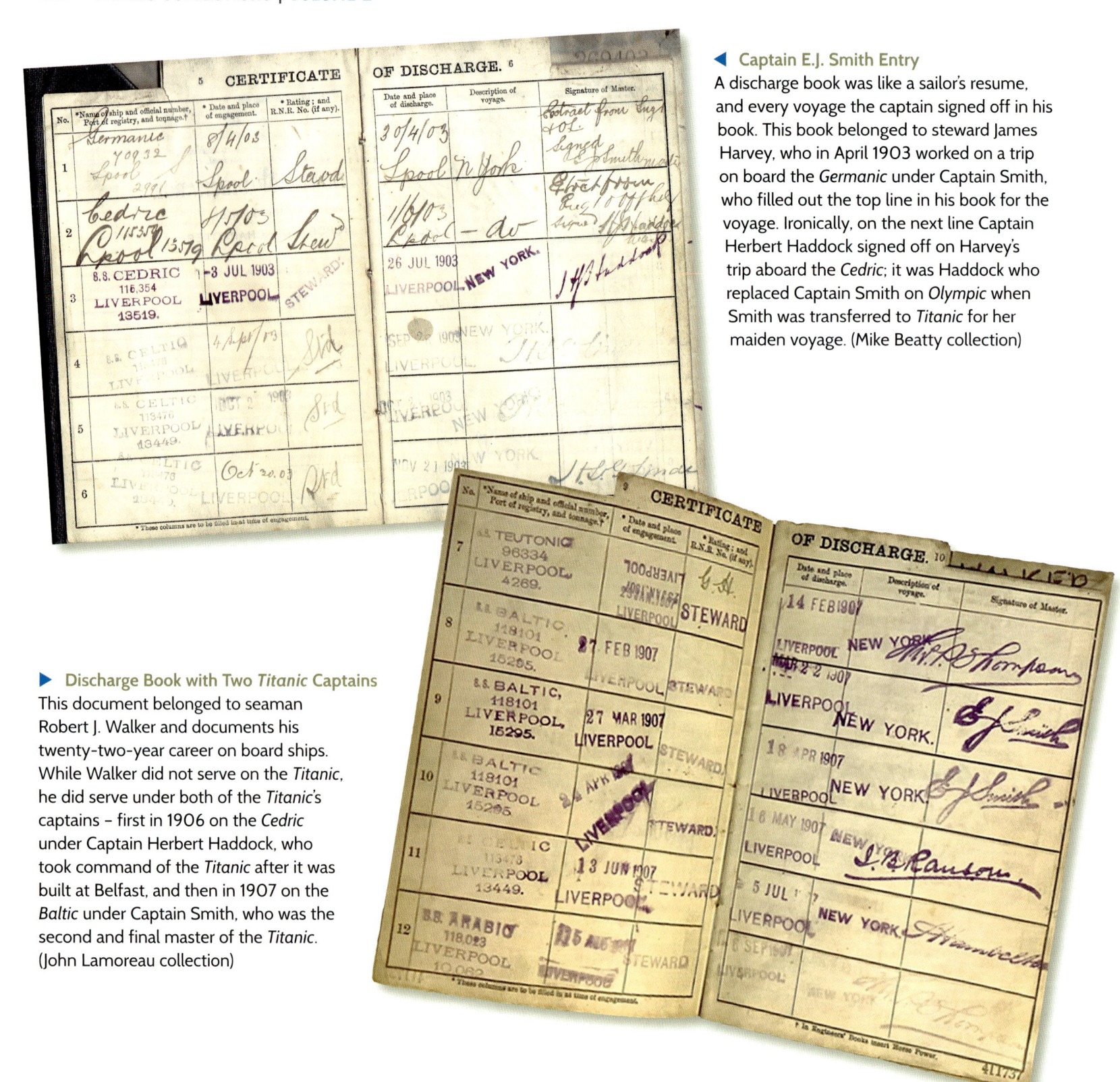

◀ **Captain E.J. Smith Entry**
A discharge book was like a sailor's resume, and every voyage the captain signed off in his book. This book belonged to steward James Harvey, who in April 1903 worked on a trip on board the *Germanic* under Captain Smith, who filled out the top line in his book for the voyage. Ironically, on the next line Captain Herbert Haddock signed off on Harvey's trip aboard the *Cedric*; it was Haddock who replaced Captain Smith on *Olympic* when Smith was transferred to *Titanic* for her maiden voyage. (Mike Beatty collection)

▶ **Discharge Book with Two *Titanic* Captains**
This document belonged to seaman Robert J. Walker and documents his twenty-two-year career on board ships. While Walker did not serve on the *Titanic*, he did serve under both of the *Titanic*'s captains – first in 1906 on the *Cedric* under Captain Herbert Haddock, who took command of the *Titanic* after it was built at Belfast, and then in 1907 on the *Baltic* under Captain Smith, who was the second and final master of the *Titanic*. (John Lamoreau collection)

Clockwise from left:

Photograph Captain Smith conducting a bridge inspection on the *Baltic*'s maiden voyage in 1904. (Kalman Tanito collection); **Rendering** An artist's rendering of the White Star liner *Majestic* was printed on this large card, and signed by Smith, then her captain. (Don Lynch collection); **Memorial Tablet** In 1913 Swiss-born sculptor Frank Lutiger created this bas-relief bronze memorial tablet commemorating Captain Smith. (Trevor Powell collection)

JOHN SMITH

▶ **Relief Fund Cheque**

John Richard Smith was one of the postal clerks on board *Titanic*. When the great vessel struck the iceberg, the postal workers worked heroically to carry sacks of mail to a higher deck, but their efforts were in vain. All five postal clerks died in the sinking, and this relief cheque is made out to John's possible wife, M.A. Smith. (Mike Beatty collection)

LUCIAN SMITH

◀ **Lucian Smith Reference Postcard**

This postcard is dated 23 April 1912, and the female writer looks to have known first-class passenger Lucian P. Smith, who perished in the sinking. She writes: 'I suppose you have read of the disastrous wreck of the Titanic in which Lucian P. Smith lost his life.' Lucian was able to get his pregnant wife, Mary Eloise Smith, safely into a lifeboat, and on 12 November 1912 she gave birth to Lucian Philip Smith II. (John Lamoreau collection)

JULIA SMYTH

▲ Letter

This letter was written by third-class survivor Julia Smyth to her mother back in Ireland a few weeks after arriving in New York on the *Carpathia*. Julia was emigrating from Pottlebawn, Ireland, to New York City, where her brother Henry already lived. She became sick while on the *Carpathia*, eventually coming down with scarlet fever, and it was only after her recovery that she finally was able to write this letter home. The letter was stashed up in the rafters of her mother's home and forgotten about until 1950, when her son-in-law was replacing the roof and rediscovered it. (Mike Beatty collection)

MARGARETTA SPEDDEN

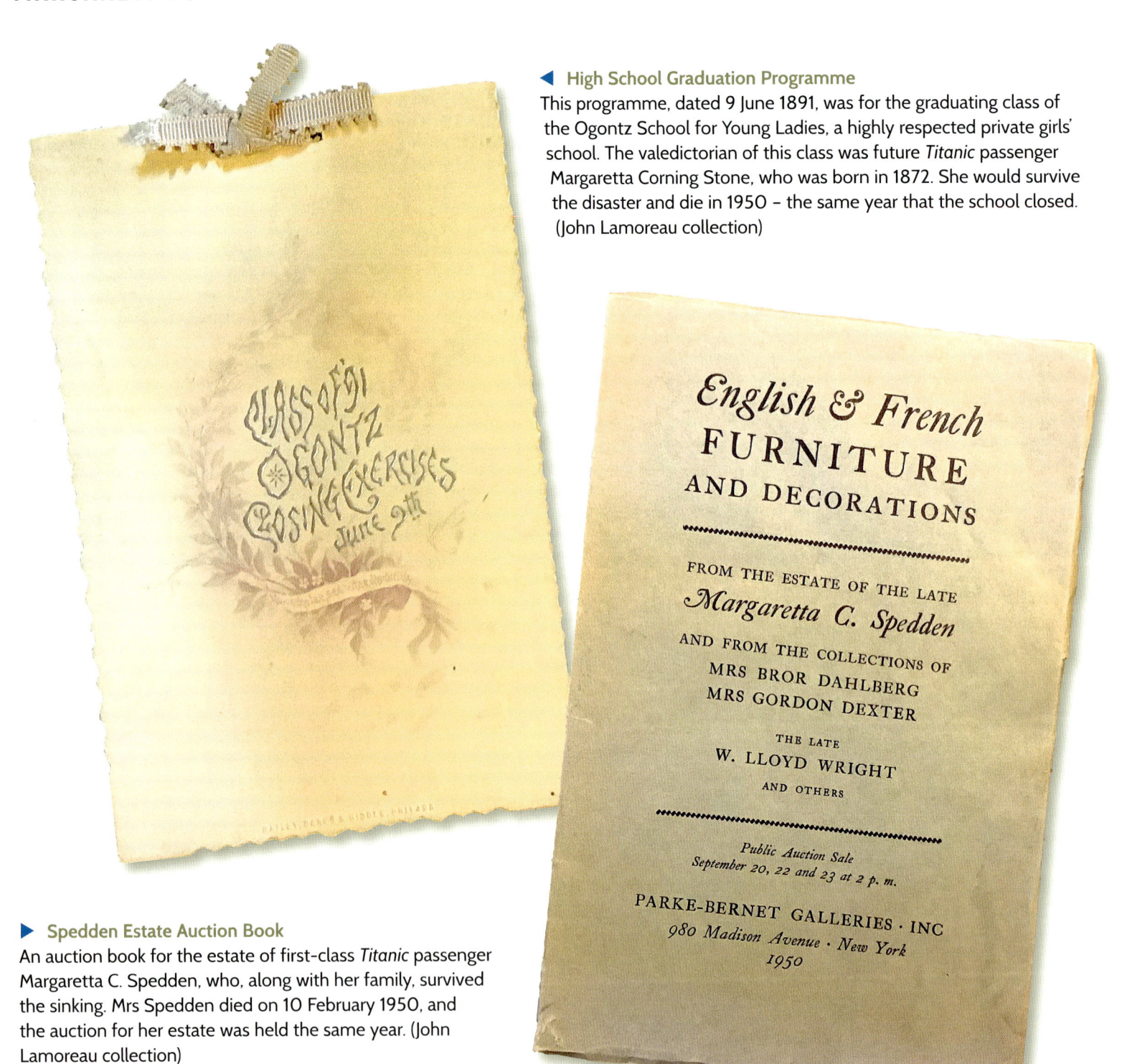

High School Graduation Programme

This programme, dated 9 June 1891, was for the graduating class of the Ogontz School for Young Ladies, a highly respected private girls' school. The valedictorian of this class was future *Titanic* passenger Margaretta Corning Stone, who was born in 1872. She would survive the disaster and die in 1950 – the same year that the school closed. (John Lamoreau collection)

Spedden Estate Auction Book

An auction book for the estate of first-class *Titanic* passenger Margaretta C. Spedden, who, along with her family, survived the sinking. Mrs Spedden died on 10 February 1950, and the auction for her estate was held the same year. (John Lamoreau collection)

SAMUEL STANTON

▲ ▶ **Bookplates**
Bookplates of Samuel Ward Stanton, a famous painter
and second-class passenger who lost his life on the *Titanic*.
(Kalman Tanito collection)

WILLIAM T. STEAD

▶ **William T. Stead Portrait**
Cabinet card portrait with autopen signature of William T. Stead from the early 1890s. Mr Stead was a British newspaper editor and investigative journalist, and was one of the more famous *Titanic* passengers. (Mike Beatty collection)

◀ **William T. Stead Story**
In 1892 Stead published this story to coincide with the Chicago Exhibition. In one part of the story, the White Star liner *Majestic* rescues passengers from another ship after it struck an iceberg. Twenty years later Stead would lose his life in an eerily similar situation. (Mike Beatty collection)

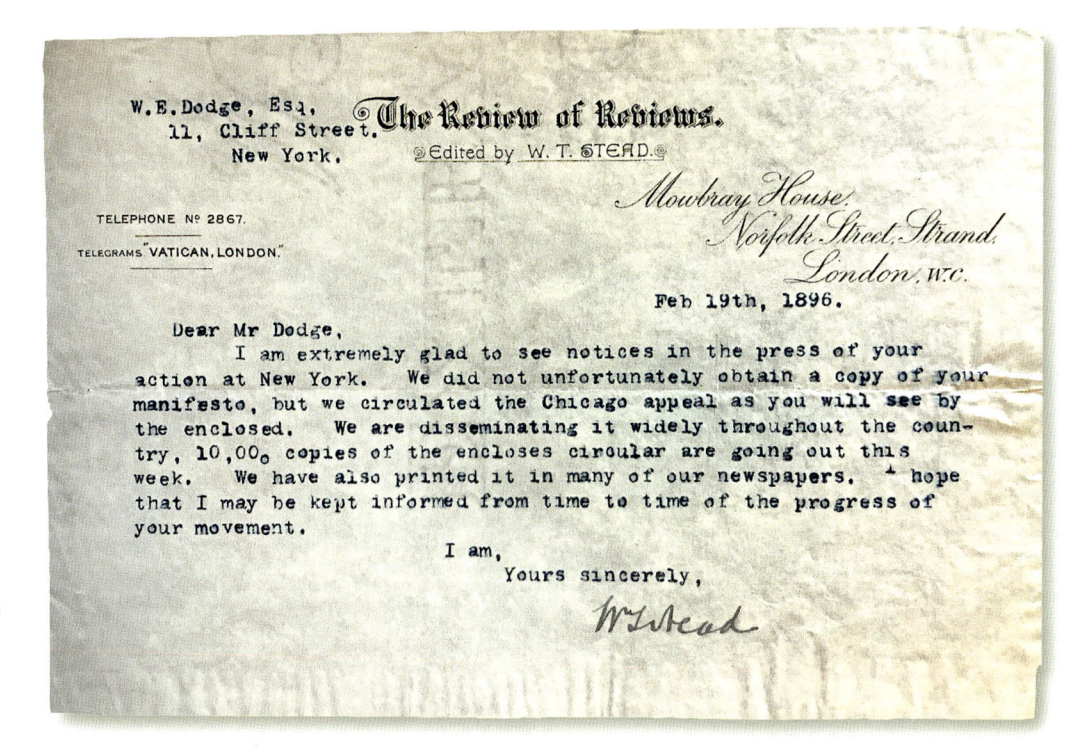

▶ William T. Stead Letter
This letter from Stead to William Earl Dodge Jr is dated 19 February 1896. Remembered as a social reformer and pacifist, Stead was travelling to New York on the *Titanic* to give a speech on world peace at Carnegie Hall. (John Lamoreau collection)

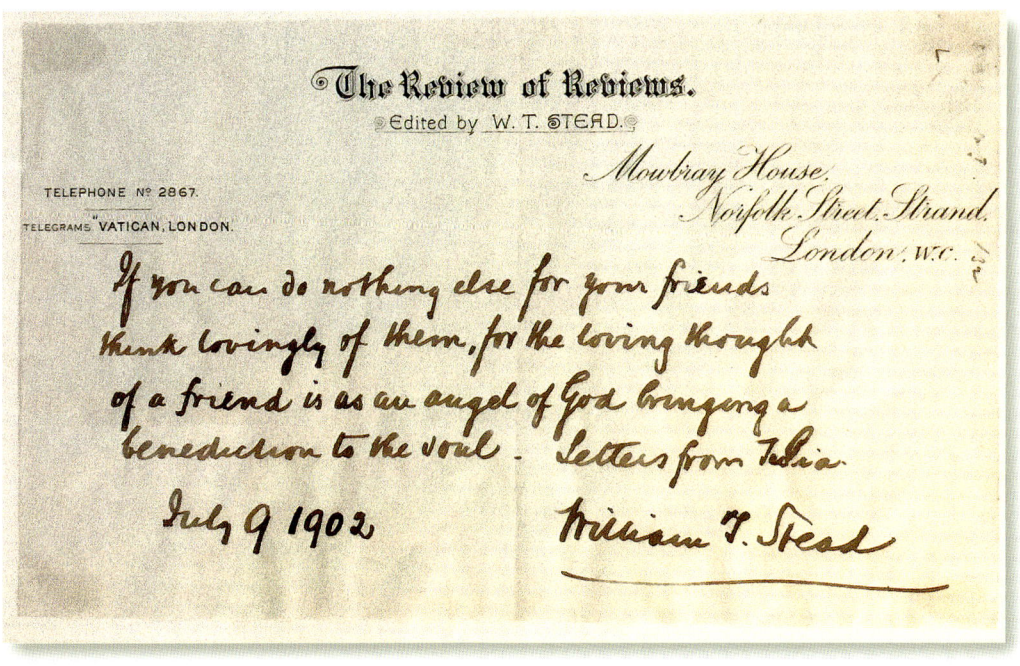

▶ William T. Stead Letter
A 1902 note from Stead quoting 'Julia' from his book *After Death: Letters from Julia.* Stead believed he could communicate with the dead through 'automatic writing' and was certain that a deceased woman by the name of Julia Ames could communicate through him. Stead may have discovered the truth or falsehood of his beliefs after he lost his life when the *Titanic* went down. (John Lamoreau collection)

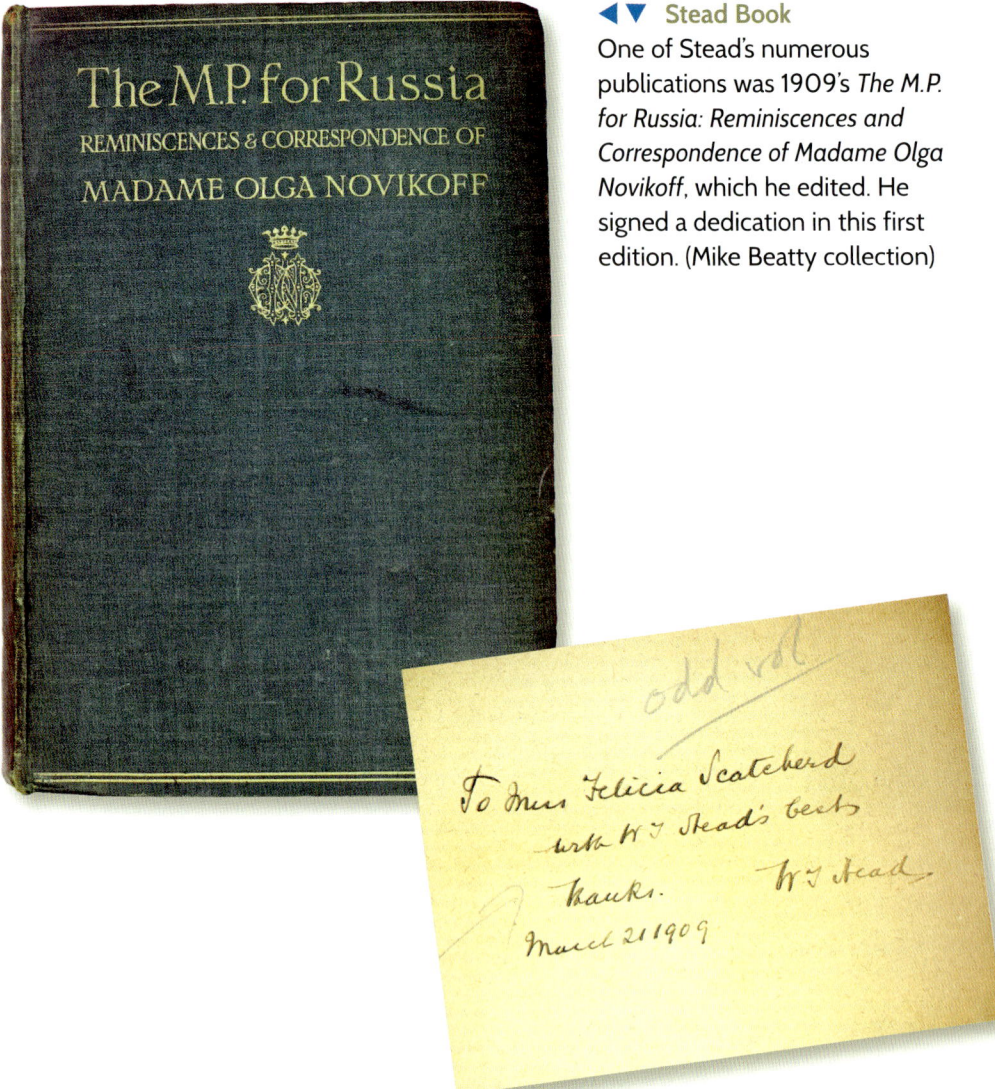

◀▼ Stead Book
One of Stead's numerous publications was 1909's *The M.P. for Russia: Reminiscences and Correspondence of Madame Olga Novikoff*, which he edited. He signed a dedication in this first edition. (Mike Beatty collection)

▶ *How I Know that the Dead Return* **(1909) and** *After Death: New and Enlarged Edition of Letters from Julia* **(Published Posthumously in 1914), by William T. Stead**
Mr Stead was intrigued by the paranormal and formed a small spiritualist group called 'Julia's Bureau' after his friend, journalist Julia Ames, passed away in Boston in 1891 and subsequently became one of Stead's personal 'spirit guides'. Stead's books about the paranormal describe anecdotal accounts of alleged spirit communication between the living and the dead, and after Stead's own death on the *Titanic* fellow spiritualist James Coates expressed his own opinion on this same subject when he published a 1913 book titled *Has W.T. Stead Returned?* (John Lamoreau collection)

CHARLES STENGEL

▲ ▶ Charles Henry Stengel
Carpathia Messages

New Jersey native Charles Stengel boarded the *Titanic* at Cherbourg with his wife Annie May. They were rescued in lifeboat 1, which controversially became nicknamed 'the money boat' because of its small number of occupants – all of whom were from first class. After boarding the *Carpathia*, Mr Stengel sent these two messages notifying acquaintances that he was rescued. (Mike Beatty collection)

IDA AND ISADOR STRAUS

▶ **Isidor Straus Letter**

A 14 December 1899 letter from the hand of *Titanic* victim Isidor Straus demonstrates the man's character and compassion. The letter was addressed to 'Prof. D.G. Lyon, Harvard University'. (David Gordon Lyon occupied the Hollis Chair of Divinity at Harvard's Divinity School.) Included with Straus' letter was a cheque for $50, to be used for the 'nourishment' of a student. Adjusted for inflation, the financial gift was equivalent to over $1,850 in 2023. (John Lamoreau collection)

▼ **(left) Straus Glass Name Card Holders**

Three of eight holders are pictured. These glass card holders were owned and used by Isidor and Ida Straus and were made in France in 1875, with a hunt scene of a wolfhound holding a goose. Straus' descendants report there was always concern when grandchildren played with them after dinner. (John Lamoreau collection)

▼ **(right) Straus Crystal Stemware**

From the estate of *Titanic* passengers Isidor and Rosalie Ida Straus came a partial set of crystal glasses with an early 1900s design. The full set was divided and gifted to Straus family members; the partial set shown here includes four champagne flutes, five cordials and four smaller liquor glasses, all having the floral swag tied with a bow design. (John Lamoreau collection)

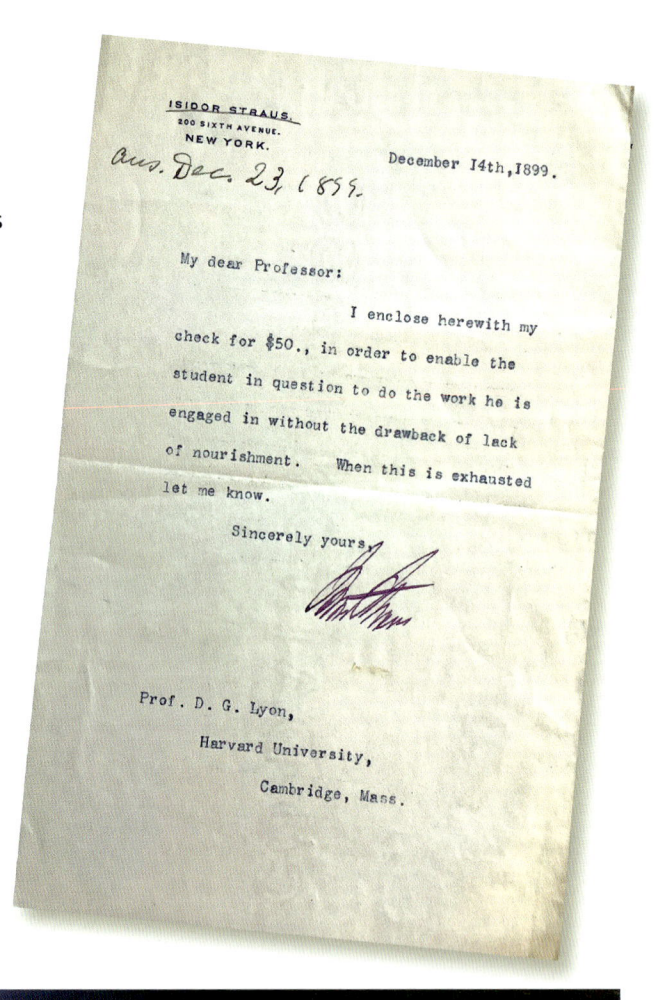

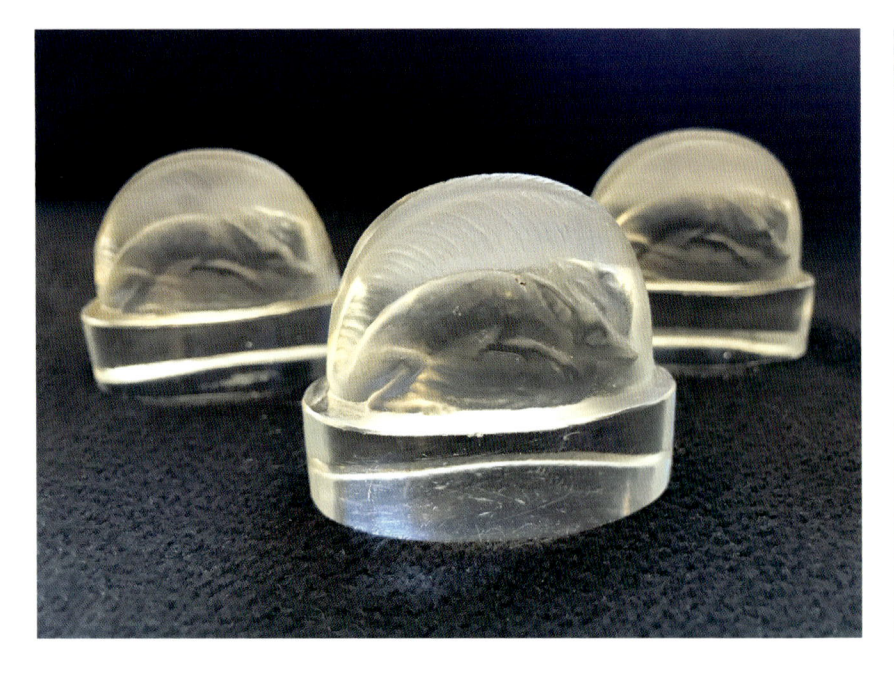

◀ **Souvenir Pin**

After placing her maid Ellen Bird in a lifeboat, Ida Straus and her husband Isidor remained standing on the *Titanic*'s boat deck only to lose their lives when the great ship went down. In the aftermath of the disaster, employees at Macy's Department Store in New York City wore celluloid pins like this one to mourn the loss of Isidor, who was a co-owner of the retailer. (Trevor Powell collection)

ELMER TAYLOR

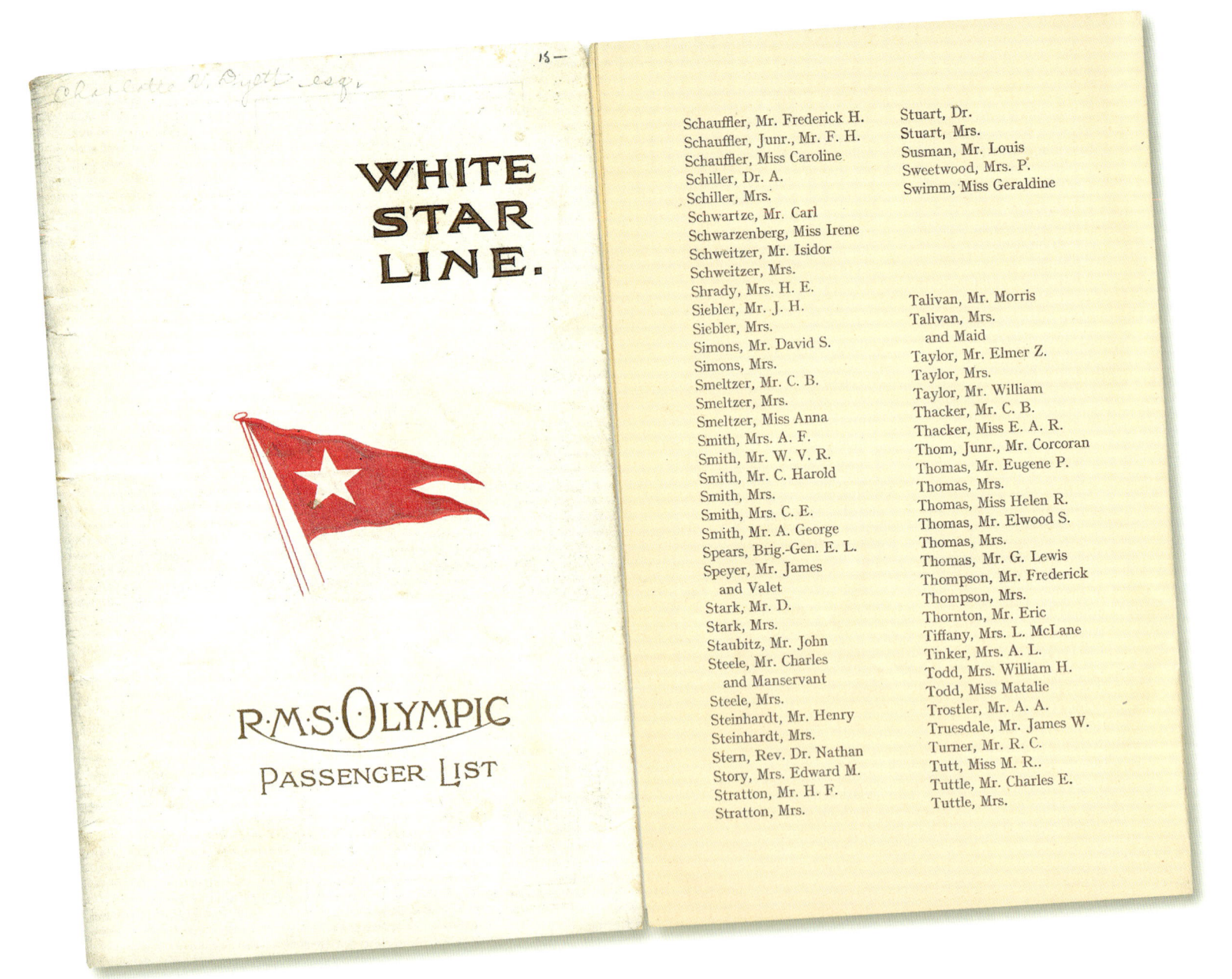

Schauffler, Mr. Frederick H.
Schauffler, Junr., Mr. F. H.
Schauffler, Miss Caroline
Schiller, Dr. A.
Schiller, Mrs.
Schwartze, Mr. Carl
Schwarzenberg, Miss Irene
Schweitzer, Mr. Isidor
Schweitzer, Mrs.
Shrady, Mrs. H. E.
Siebler, Mr. J. H.
Siebler, Mrs.
Simons, Mr. David S.
Simons, Mrs.
Smeltzer, Mr. C. B.
Smeltzer, Mrs.
Smeltzer, Miss Anna
Smith, Mrs. A. F.
Smith, Mr. W. V. R.
Smith, Mr. C. Harold
Smith, Mrs.
Smith, Mrs. C. E.
Smith, Mr. A. George
Spears, Brig.-Gen. E. L.
Speyer, Mr. James
and Valet
Stark, Mr. D.
Stark, Mrs.
Staubitz, Mr. John
Steele, Mr. Charles
and Manservant
Steele, Mrs.
Steinhardt, Mr. Henry
Steinhardt, Mrs.
Stern, Rev. Dr. Nathan
Story, Mrs. Edward M.
Stratton, Mr. H. F.
Stratton, Mrs.

Stuart, Dr.
Stuart, Mrs.
Susman, Mr. Louis
Sweetwood, Mrs. P.
Swimm, Miss Geraldine

Talivan, Mr. Morris
Talivan, Mrs.
and Maid
Taylor, Mr. Elmer Z.
Taylor, Mrs.
Taylor, Mr. William
Thacker, Mr. C. B.
Thacker, Miss E. A. R.
Thom, Junr., Mr. Corcoran
Thomas, Mr. Eugene P.
Thomas, Mrs.
Thomas, Miss Helen R.
Thomas, Mr. Elwood S.
Thomas, Mrs.
Thomas, Mr. G. Lewis
Thompson, Mr. Frederick
Thompson, Mrs.
Thornton, Mr. Eric
Tiffany, Mrs. L. McLane
Tinker, Mrs. A. L.
Todd, Mrs. William H.
Todd, Miss Matalie
Trostler, Mr. A. A.
Truesdale, Mr. James W.
Turner, Mr. R. C.
Tutt, Miss M. R..
Tuttle, Mr. Charles E.
Tuttle, Mrs.

▲ **Passenger List**
An *Olympic* passenger list for her 3 September 1924 crossing.
Titanic survivor Elmer Taylor was a passenger on this voyage.
(Don Lynch collection)

JOHN B. THAYER

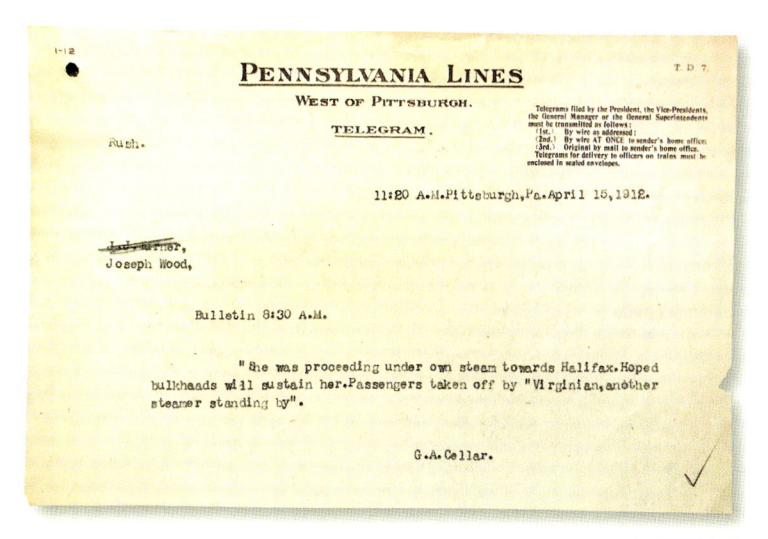

▶ **Press Bulletin**

On the morning of 15 April 1912 news of *Titanic*'s collision with the iceberg was beginning to trickle into newspaper offices around the world. The optimistic bulletin shown here was telegraphed to the Pennsylvania Railroad, whose second vice president, John B. Thayer, was a passenger on the great ship. (George Behe collection)

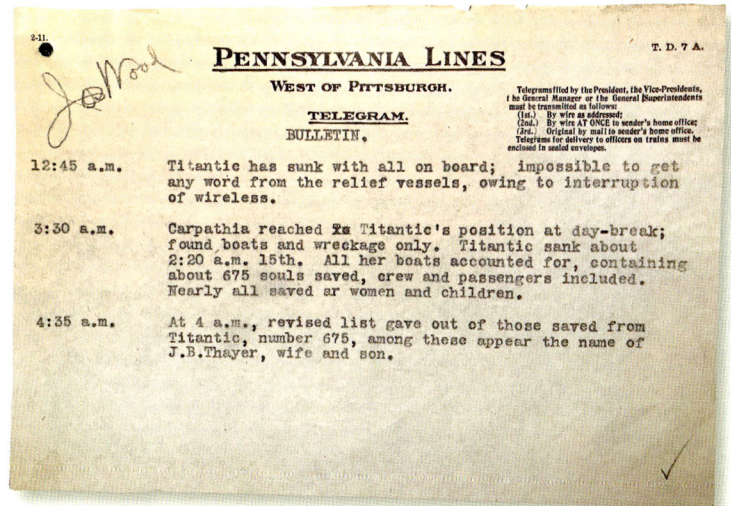

▶ **Press Bulletin**

During the wee hours of 16 April the true horror of the *Titanic* disaster was becoming known around the world. This bulletin was telegraphed to the Pennsylvania Railroad bearing the optimistic news that John B. Thayer and his family had apparently all survived the disaster. (George Behe collection)

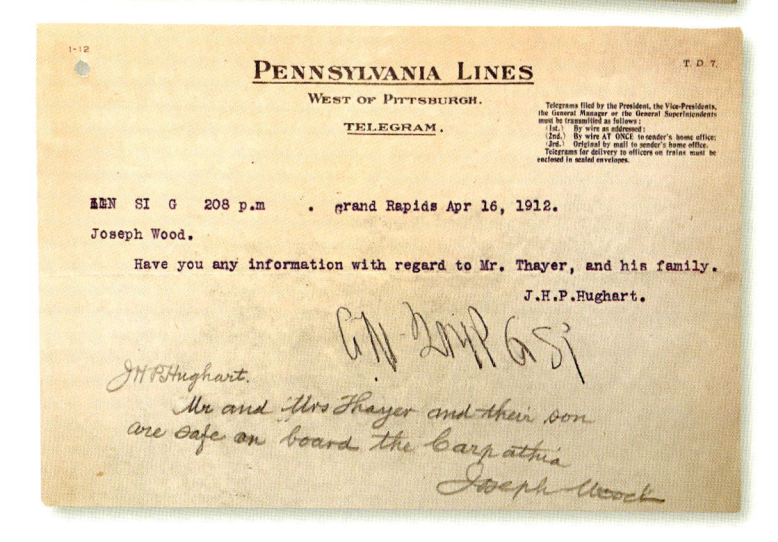

▶ **Press Bulletin**

On the afternoon of 16 April it was still believed that John B. Thayer and his family were all safe on board the rescue ship *Carpathia*. (George Behe collection)

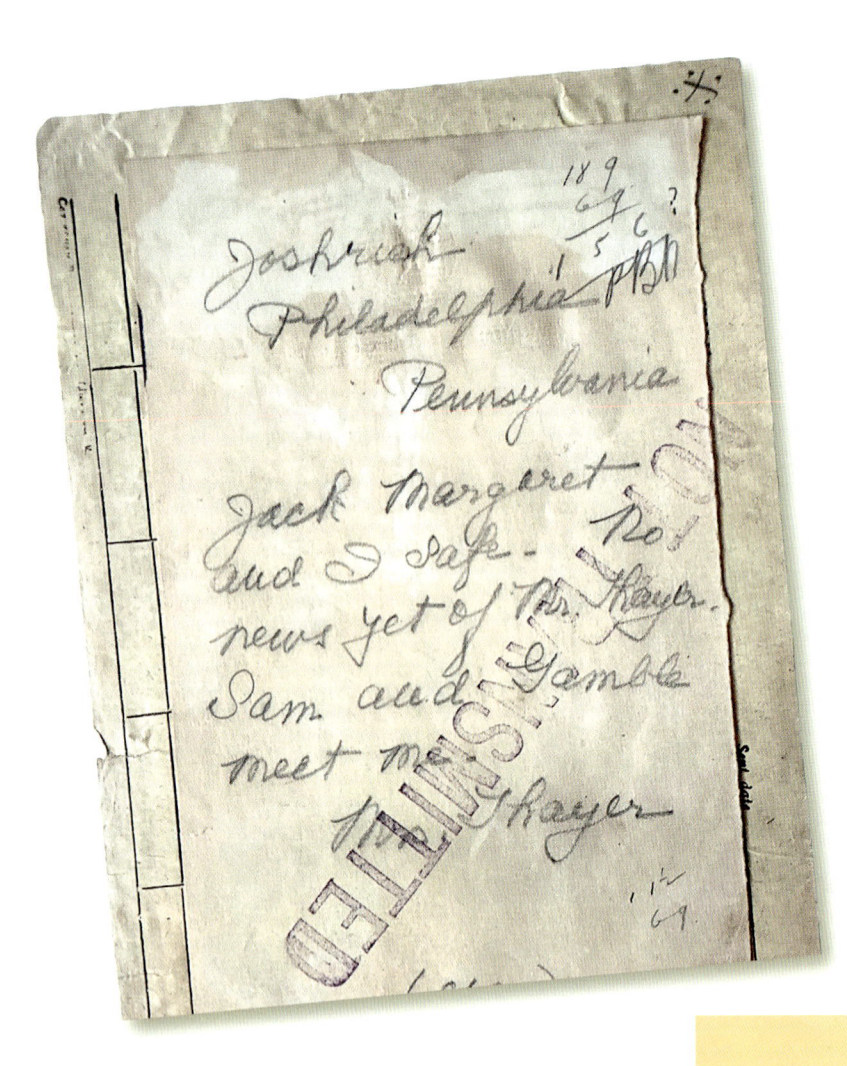

◀ Thayer Marconigram
Shortly after being rescued, first-class survivor Marian Thayer hastily scribbled this message on the back of some *Carpathia* stationery. Addressed to her husband's business partner in Philadelphia, it reads: 'Jack, Margaret and I safe. No news yet of Mr. Thayer. Sam and Gamble meet me. Mrs. Thayer.' (Trevor Powell collection)

▶ Telephone Bulletin
After *Carpathia* arrived in New York on the evening of 18 April, the following morning Joseph Wood, second vice president of the Pennsylvania Railroad, sent a telegram to the Thayer family expressing his heartbreak over the fact that his friend John B. Thayer had gone down with the *Titanic*. (George Behe collection)

THE   PENNSYLVANIA   LINES

5M. 9-11. B2.

WEST OF PITTSBURGH.

OFFICE OF THE FIRST VICE-PRESIDENT.

ROOM 909, UNION STATION,

PITTSBURGH, PA. April 19th, 1912.

BY TELEPHONE TO PHILADELPHIA. 10:50 am

Walter Thayer,
        Philadelphia, Pa.

        After hoping against hope since Tuesday we are simply heartbroken to know that poor John is gone.   Able, indefatigable, heroic, beloved of all, words cannot express how deeply we mourn his tragic fate.   To his wife, children and relatives we tender our deepest sympathy.

                            Joseph Wood.

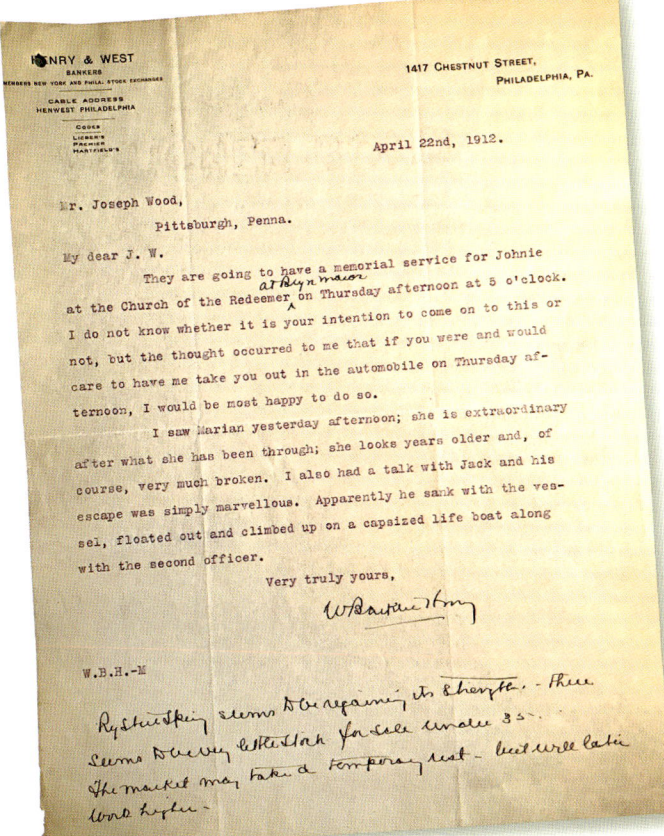

◀ **Letter**

After the collision, John Thayer helped his wife Marian into lifeboat 4 and then lost his own life when the *Titanic* went down. On 22 April 1912 a fellow employee of the Pennsylvania Railroad wrote a letter to first vice president Joseph Wood describing the upcoming memorial service for John and detailing his own impressions of John's stricken wife and son, both of whom survived the disaster. (George Behe collection)

JOHN B. 'JACK' THAYER

▶ **Thayer Account**

In 1940 Jack Thayer privately published 500 copies of his *Titanic* account for friends and family. This copy is No. 13 and was given to his nephew Harry Thayer. (Mike Beatty collection)

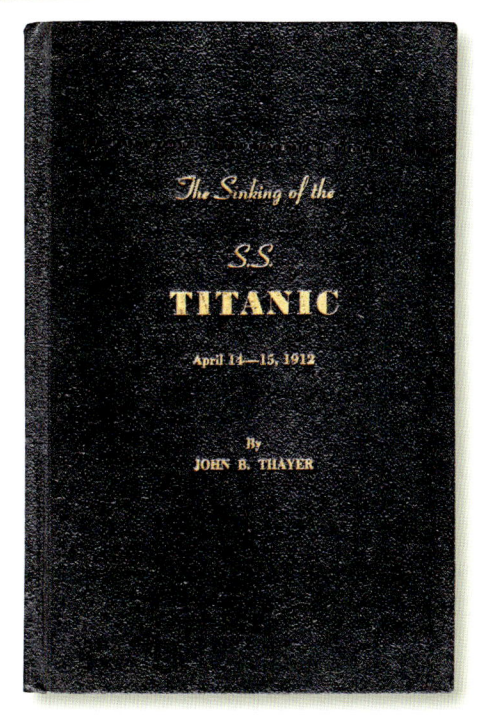

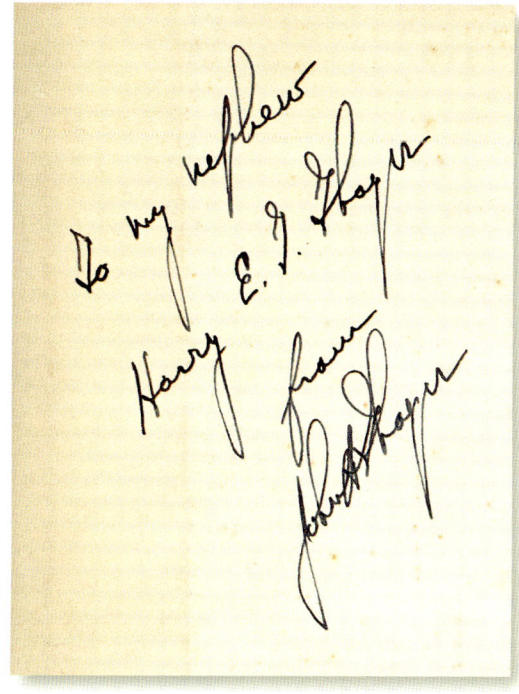

GERTRUDE THORNE

▶ **Gertrude Thorne Marconigram**
Gertrude Maybelle Thorne boarded *Titanic* at Cherbourg with her married lover George Rosenshine. To hide their romantic relationship, George took her last name of Thorne when he booked passage. Only Gertrude survived the sinking, and she sent this Marconigram from the *Carpathia* in the hope that George was safe on board another rescue ship. (Mike Beatty collection)

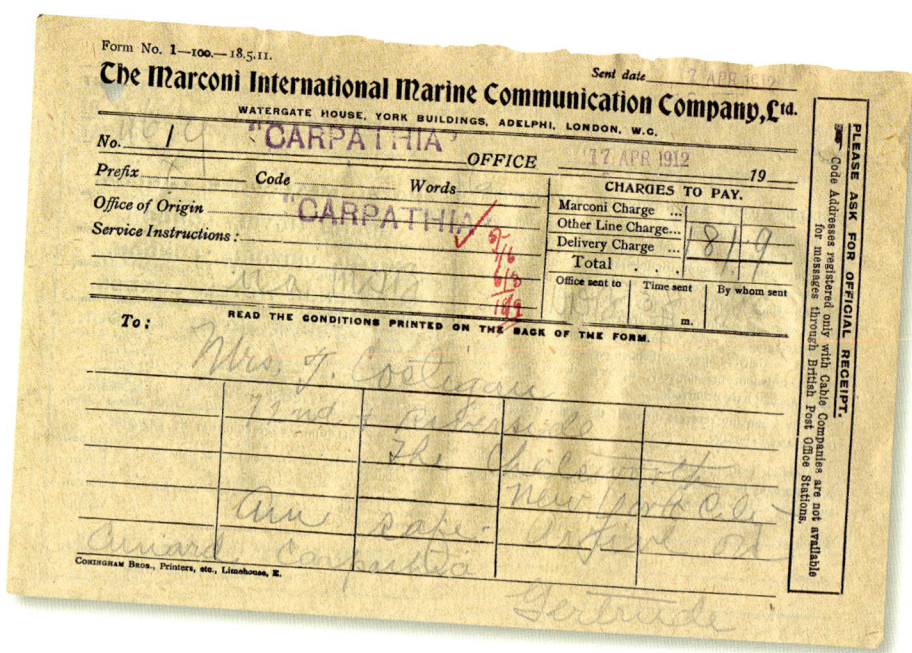

EDWINA TROUTT

◀ **Edwina Troutt**
Miss Edwina Troutt, of Bath, England, was travelling alone in second class to take up permanent residence in the United States. Five years later she had settled in southern California, where she had this studio portrait taken. (Don Lynch collection)

Sace Blue Straw Hat
Black Crinoline Hat.
Black Fur Hat
Black Felt Hat.
1 Sailor made suit Blue
1 Black serge suit
1 Brown Broad cloth suit
3 pairs Boots   1 Pair Shoes
1 silk petticoat
3 best sets lingerie
3 everday sets lingerie
1 Lace Dress
2 Black Taffeta Dresses
1 Sea green evening Dress
1 Long coat Black serge
1 Ink stand
2 Trays
2 Hoggarths Pictures
Money $112·00.
3 summer dresses.
6 Night gowns

(margin, vertical): Titanic losses in one trunk.   Wins

3 all wool underwear.
2 Elastic stockings
1 Matinee coat.
Stockings
Gloves
Hand Kerchiefs
Linen
Trunk $14·00.
2 suit cases
1 set Furs.
8 Blouses.
1 Muslin Dress
1 Woolen sweater coat
1 Large Fancy Table cloth.
Toilet articles
2 linen & lace petticoats
1 gold watch. 3 gold rings
12 yards Blue serge
1 Sterling marmalade slicer

▲ List of Losses

Many survivors submitted claims for their losses as part of a class action lawsuit against the White Star Line. Here, on two sides of a scrap of paper, Troutt has listed her lost belongings. Across the margin is written: 'Titanic losses in one trunk. Wins.' The list is a fascinating description of the complete wardrobe of a single, middle-class, young Englishwoman. (Don Lynch collection) belts on & leave every thing, & go up on Boat deck. The officers assured us it was only a precaution & many a joke was being passed & in my eyes I saw no panic whatever. I remained on the deck seeing the life boats launched still not realizing the peril we were in. I could hear the men shout. Stand back & make room for the ladies be English. Screams were then raised through the parting of men & wives & the continual cry was Harry John or so & so I dont want to go. one man was shouting wholl take my baby then seeing I could be of use I cried I will so was thrown into the boat & the baby given over to me. the child was about 3 months old & was crying with hunger. blankets was thrown in after & were able to keep the child warm its Mother had gone with two other children ahead of us. & the child was delived to here on Board the Carpathia at 7 oclock

The distress signal was repeatedly going off while we were on boat deck. & when we reached the water twas then only we could believe that the Titanic was sinking. In sight of all of us She sunk within a half hour of departure. The men acted magnificently. Our seamen were singing Pull for the Shore sailors. & rowing for their life. we had a lamp, no oil in it. but managed to catch another life boat with a light. The men tied them together & let them drift until we could see the lights of the Carpathia. Then they turned around & made for her which was in readiness. Blankets hot drinks, & nothing spared us. *reached her 6.30.* The passengers of the Carpathia helped to clothe us, but the cries of the women for their husbands & lost sons was terrible. boats were being emptied on both sides of the ship. Special prayers were read & all pleasures were stopped.

▲ **Disaster Account**

On a tablet of paper Troutt wrote a hurried account of the disaster, some pages of which appear to be missing. In it she describes the men yelling for people to stand back and 'Be English' as the boats were loaded, distress rockets being sent up, her taking charge of a baby, and of their lifeboat tying up to another as they waited for rescue. (Don Lynch collection)

▶ **Diary**

After writing her initial description of the sinking, Troutt used the tablet of paper to begin a diary that begins when the *Carpathia* docks. She describes the screams of those waiting on the pier, of her cousins meeting her and bringing a change of clothes with them, and the difficulty her cousin Jim had navigating his automobile through the crowds of people. In subsequent days she described giving a telephone interview, being gifted clothes by Macy's Department Store, contacting the Red Cross for relief funds, and even attending a memorial service for one of the first-class passengers. (Don Lynch collection)

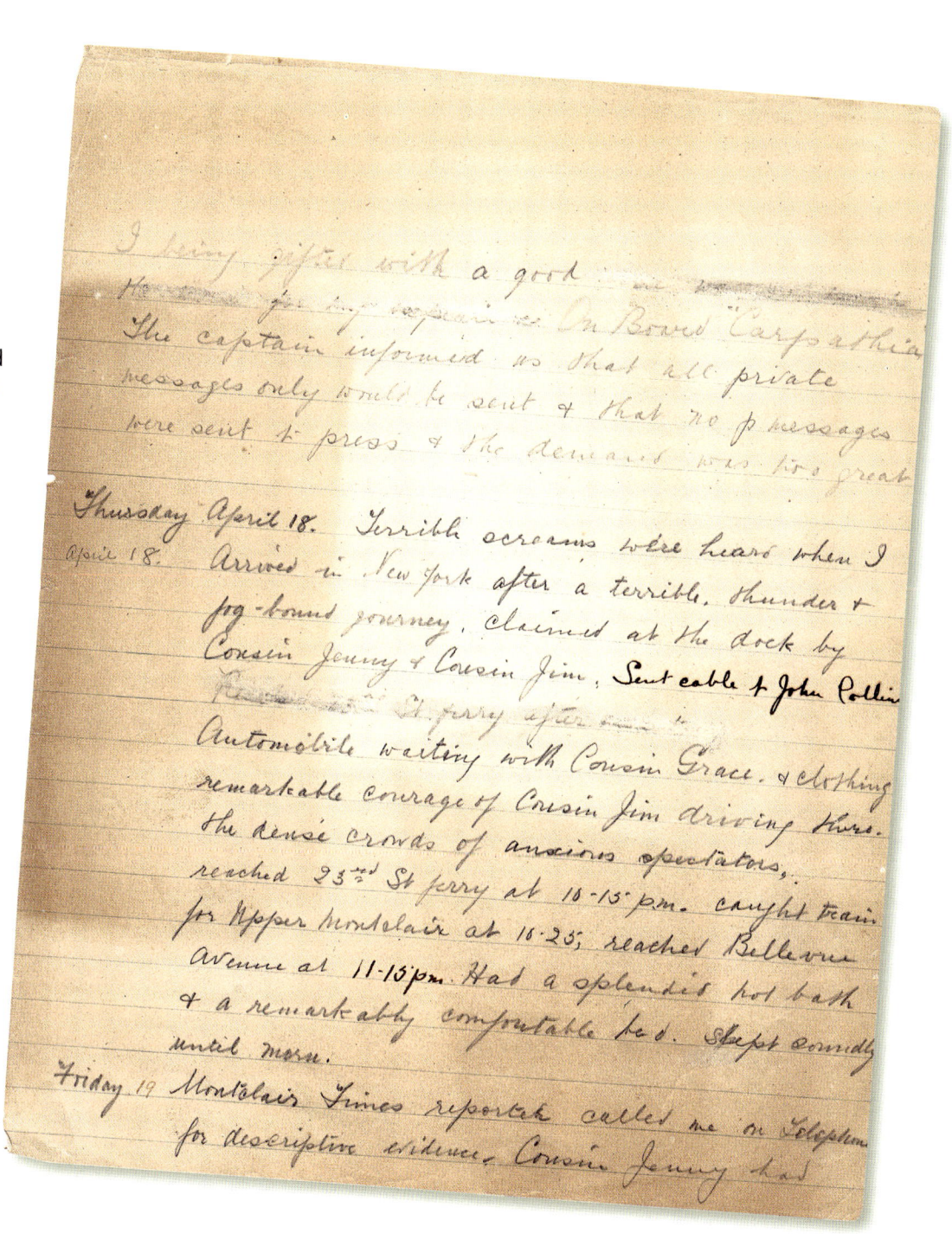

Then ere I cross the bounding sea
The White Star line's the line for me
As round the Titanic you proudly roam
You'll find every comfort just like home.
Whilst coal strikes play their dirty tricks
The white star line can send their ships
Not one alone but a fine old fleet
Of seagoing giants like the Olympic

Nov 8th continued. Left Boston 8 p.m. on Express to Trenton said Good Bye to Elsie. Elsie promised to send telegram. Just after leaving Back Bay a sudden noise like an explosion caused me quite a little anxiety. I began to wonder if the xpress would deliver me safe & sound. No Titanic troubles. Nov 9th. Reached Trenton after a somewhat tiresome journey, but greatly enjoyed the lunch Elsie had fixed for me. To my very great surprise no one to meet me. I hailed a Cabby. he knew not the time finally I telephoned then cabbed to the office. Fisher & Norris. As I arrived the secretary ushered me into the office awaiting the arrival of Mrs Andrew.

Mrs Andrew arrived with Mr Brookes. My, what a different woman to what I had pictured. Anyhow I was very warmly greeted. & after a little chatting was in the Auto en route for home. Reached home, an Ideal Farm house. There I met a Miss Fisher. had lunch then I went to rest. My how I slept. I don't think an earthquake would wake me. Finally I was called as Mrs Andrew would like very much to see me. We had a Tête a Tête before dinner cocktails being served. All were very much interested in my story. Had dinner being five at Table. Mr B being my escort.

▲ **Poem**

Despite the *Titanic* disaster, Troutt apparently still favoured the White Star Line, with which she had crossed the ocean previously. Though not a particularly gifted poet, here she penned a ditty about the *Titanic* and *Olympic*, even mentioning the coal strike that had caused her to be aboard the *Titanic* in the first place. The light-heartedness of this poem belies the emotional trauma she was suffering when it was written. (Don Lynch collection)

▲ **Diary**

One of Troutt's table companions, Edgardo Andrew, had sailed on the *Titanic* to attend his brother's wedding. Alfredo Andrew did not know his brother was on the sunken liner until Edwina called to tell him of Edgardo's death. Later that year she was invited to visit Alfredo and Harriet Andrew, and afterwards wrote an account, several pages of which are shown here. In it she mentions an issue with the train, and is relieved that there are 'No Titanic troubles'. She also expresses surprise upon meeting Mrs Andrew, for although Alfredo was roughly Troutt's age, his bride was much, much older. (Don Lynch collection)

▲ Cruise Documents

Troutt loved the sea, despite her experience in 1912, and returned to England a number of times over the years. In October 1954 she took the opportunity to sail on the fastest ocean liner in history, SS *United States*. Among the items she saved from the crossing were the rate booklet and the Abstract of Log. Her strongest memory of the voyage was that the ship vibrated its way across the Atlantic. (Don Lynch collection)

◀ Cruise Ticket

In 1969 the relatively young firm of Princess Cruises decided to attempt their first extended cruise – a month-long voyage from Los Angeles to Australia and back aboard the *Princess Italia*. Among the passengers was Edwina MacKenzie (née Troutt). Considered a maiden voyage of sorts, she discovered that the superstitious Italian crewmen would literally turn and run when they saw a *Titanic* survivor approaching on deck. Although these unexpected antics might have amused her, what she did not care for was how calm the Pacific Ocean was for the crossing. She never felt she was at sea. This copy of her passenger ticket is significant as Princess Cruises does not have an example of a ticket from that long ago in their archives. (Don Lynch collection)

▼ White Star Line Pin

After Edwina Troutt MacKenzie's death in 1984 at the age of 100, this White Star pin was found among her possessions. It is unusual as it does not have a banner with a ship's name across it as most souvenir pins had. It is estimated to date from before the First World War, which prompts the question of where MacKenzie got it. She never claimed to have saved such a thing from the *Titanic*, and if it had been from her voyage on the *Arabic* in 1907 it would have gone down with the *Titanic* along with all her other possessions. She did not sail on a White Star ship again until 1923. Did someone give it to her, or did she obtain what would have been an outdated souvenir when on the *Majestic* in the 1920s? We'll surely never know. (Don Lynch collection)

AUGUSTUS WEIKMAN

▶ **Augustus Weikman Marconigram**

Philadelphia native Augustus 'Gus' Weikman worked as a barber for the White Star Line starting around 1892. By 1911 he was one of their top barbers working the line's newest and greatest ship, *Olympic*, and he transferred to the *Titanic* to work in first class as chief barber during her maiden voyage. Weikman made a harrowing escape from the *Titanic*, being one of the few to go down with the ship and survive. On board the rescue ship *Carpathia* he sent this wireless message home to his family in Palmyra, New Jersey, that he was saved. (Mike Beatty collection)

▶ **Uniform Button**

This brass White Star Line button, manufactured by Rayner & Sons of Liverpool, was worn by Weikman during the sinking. Weikman, reportedly the only American crewman aboard, was one of the few individuals to survive being in the frigid waters of the North Atlantic before being hauled aboard the partially submerged collapsible A. A few years after the disaster, Weikman's daughter gifted this button to one of her teachers at her high school in Palmyra. (Trevor Powell collection)

EDWY WEST

▲ **Edwy West Painting**

A watercolour by Edwy Arthur West, who was travelling on the *Titanic* in second class with his pregnant wife and two children, intending to emigrate from Cornwall to the United States. He died in the disaster. (Kalman Tanito collection)

GEORGE WIDENER

▶ **George Widener Business Letter**

George Widener worked for the Philadelphia Traction Company, his father's company, which operated streetcars throughout the city. He was involved in other businesses as well, and he wrote this letter in 1889 regarding a vote for the charter of the People's Bank of Philadelphia. (Mike Beatty collection)

▼ **Widener Christmas Card**

The Wideners were among the wealthiest passengers on the *Titanic* and lived in Lynnewood Hall, a 100-acre, 110-room Philadelphia estate known as one of the most glamorous in the United States. The family had a well-known art collection, and each Christmas they would hire the famous engraver Timothy Cole to make a wood carving of one of their paintings for use on a signed, limited edition, oversized Christmas card. The card pictured is of a van Dyck painting. (John Lamoreau collection)

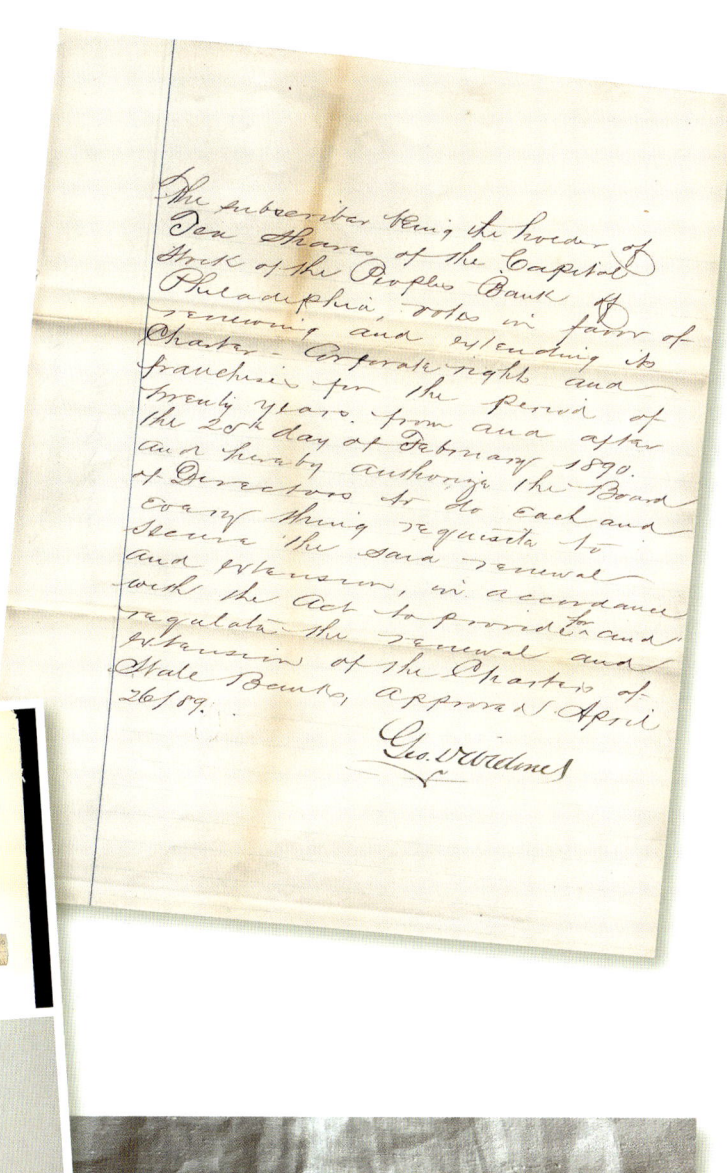

▶ **Widener Linen Napkins**

This large linen napkin, measuring over 2ft square, is monogrammed with a Widener 'W'. From a set of eight. (John Lamoreau collection)

◄ Stock Certificate

George Widener was one of the wealthiest passengers on the *Titanic* and died in the sinking. This stock certificate for 100 shares of the Philadelphia Traction Company was signed by Mr Widener and is dated 15 April 1902, exactly ten years before the *Titanic* went down. (John Lamoreau collection)

HARRY WIDENER

▶ Bookplate

Bookplate of Harry Elkins Widener, a first-class passenger on the *Titanic* and a well-known bibliophile. He perished in the disaster, and his mother donated the Harry Elkins Widener Memorial Library to Harvard University in his memory. (Kalman Tanito collection)

HENRY WILDE

▶ **Henry Wilde 1894 Letter**
Henry Wilde wrote to his future wife, Mary Catherine 'Polly' Jones, while working as third mate on the *Hornby Castle*. The couple would be married four years later. (Mike Beatty collection)

◀ **Henry Wilde 1911 Letter**
On 28 March 1911 Henry Wilde was chief officer on board the *Megantic*. He wrote this letter to his sister-in-law on *Megantic* stationery that bore advertising for both *Olympic* and *Titanic*, on the latter of which he would also serve as chief officer. Henry writes of stopping in Halifax and of his plans to see the family and his children when he arrived back in Liverpool. (Mike Beatty collection)

On board R·M·S· "OLYMPIC."

10th March 1912

My dear Annie

I have just received your letter returned from Belfast which I was glad to have but I am sorry to hear that you are not well again I hope you will soon be better I am disappointed not being able to come to Liverpool this time but hope to do so on our return from New York. I have had a very busy time here since getting back from Belfast on board today Sunday & it is now 5 pm I won't know what to do with myself when

Henry Wilde 1912 Letter

From August 1911 to March 1912 Henry Wilde served as chief officer under Captain Smith on *Titanic*'s sister *Olympic*. Wilde regularly mailed letters home to his wife, children, his sister-in-law Annie and her husband Owen Williams. On 10 March 1912 he wrote to Annie about having just returned from Belfast, where the *Olympic* had a propeller blade repaired (an incident that contributed to the delay of *Titanic*'s maiden voyage). After the next voyage he wrote that he was to leave for the *Cymric*, where he would be promoted to captain. This anticipated event never occurred due to a coal strike that affected shipping during the next month, and in his next letter he informed his family that he was being transferred to the *Titanic* for a voyage. Wilde would not survive the sinking, leaving his four orphaned children to be raised by Annie and Owen. (Mike Beatty collection)

ARTHUR WILLIAMS

◄▼ **Arthur Williams Postcard**
First-class storekeeper Arthur Williams sent a portrait postcard for Christmas 1909. He'd previously worked on the *Celtic* before transferring to the *Titanic* for her maiden voyage. He did not survive the sinking, leaving his wife Ellen a widow. (Mike Beatty collection)

RICHARD WILLIAMS

▶ **Richard Williams Photo**
This previously unpublished photo shows Richard 'Dick' Williams playing in a tennis tournament at Forest Hills, New York, in August 1914. (Mike Beatty collection)

▶ **Richard Williams 1914 RSVP**
This RSVP was declined and returned by Williams in 1914. Williams had Colonial America heritage, being a direct descendant of Benjamin Franklin. (Mike Beatty collection)

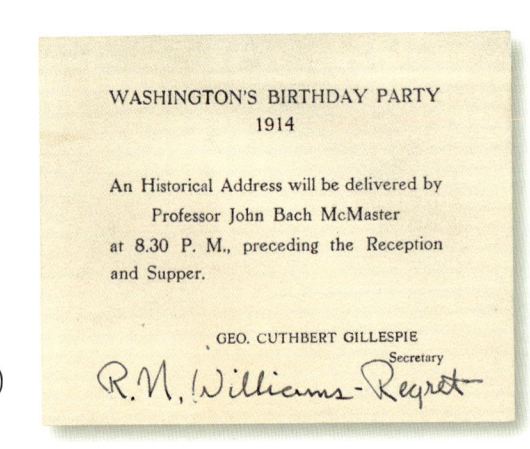

▲ **Richard Williams 1916 Photos**
These unpublished photos were taken of Williams while playing at the Newport Casino in August 1916. Williams would win the US Championship for the second time in 1916. (Mike Beatty collection)

▲ R.N. Williams Sports Card
One of two sports cards that Williams was featured on in the 1920s. (Mike Beatty collection)

▲ R. Norris Williams Press Photo
A September 1928 press photo of *Titanic* survivor R. Norris Williams (left), who was an up-and-coming tennis star in 1912. In 1911 Williams won the Swiss Championship, and after entering Harvard University he became the intercollegiate tennis champion in singles in 1913 and 1915. He also won two men's singles titles at the US Championships in 1914 and 1916. (John Lamoreau collection)

HUGH WOOLNER

▲ **Passenger List**

A *Lusitania* passenger list for 29 May 1912, a voyage on which *Titanic* survivor Hugh Woolner was a passenger. (Don Lynch collection)

HENRY WORMALD

▶ **Relief Fund Cheque Envelope**

This rare Titanic Relief Fund envelope shows how recipients would have received their cheques. This one is made out to Henry Wormald's wife Emily. Henry was working as a first-class saloon steward on board *Titanic* and did not survive, leaving his wife and several children. When his body was recovered, it was mistakenly buried in the Jewish cemetery in Halifax; Emily decided to go retrieve his body, so she and her children travelled to New York on board the *St Louis*. When they arrived, the family was refused entry through Ellis Island and was forced to return home. Upon their arrival back in England, they found their home had been rented out and their belongings gone! Fortunately, neighbours were looking out for them and had stored their property during their absence. Cheques like this one provided great assistance to the family during a desperate time. (Mike Beatty collection)

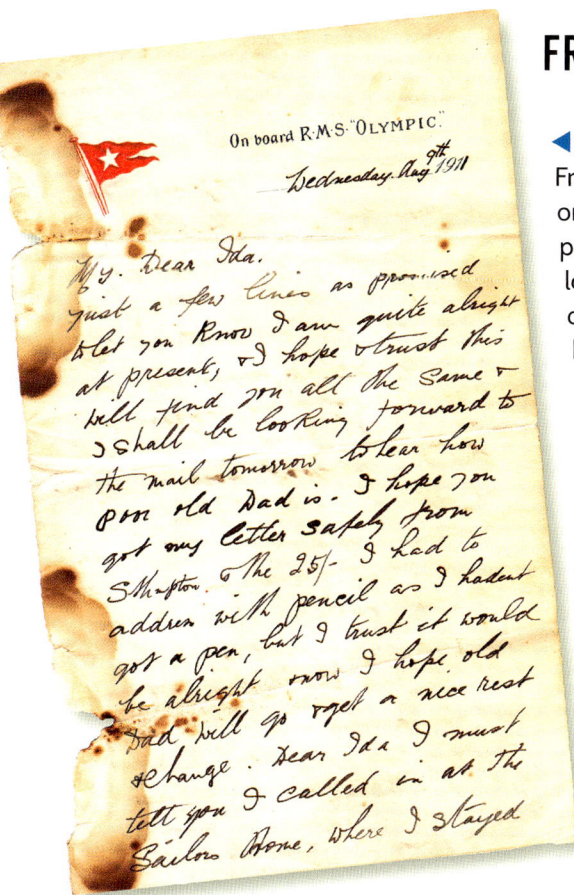

FRED WRIGHT

◀ **Frederick Wright Letter**

Fred Wright was hired by the White Star Line in 1911 to be the squash court attendant on their new ship *Olympic*. Fred had never worked on ships before and was rather paranoid of being out at sea in general and especially on such a large ship. In this letter written to his sister Ida on 9 August 1911 he shared his concerns as well as an opinion from a certain captain ... 'there was an old Captain there, been to sea and he says he wouldn't go on the Olympic for anything, he says she is top heavy and thinks she will go over, he says and I thought I expect to be on her for every trip, and I heard someone else say the same thing last trip, but it is no good worrying about it, only I thought about it this morning.' The following April, Fred was transferred to *Olympic*'s sister ship *Titanic* to run her squash court, and it was there that his worries came to fruition. Fred did not survive the sinking. (Mike Beatty collection)

CARPATHIA PERSONNEL

JAMES BISSET

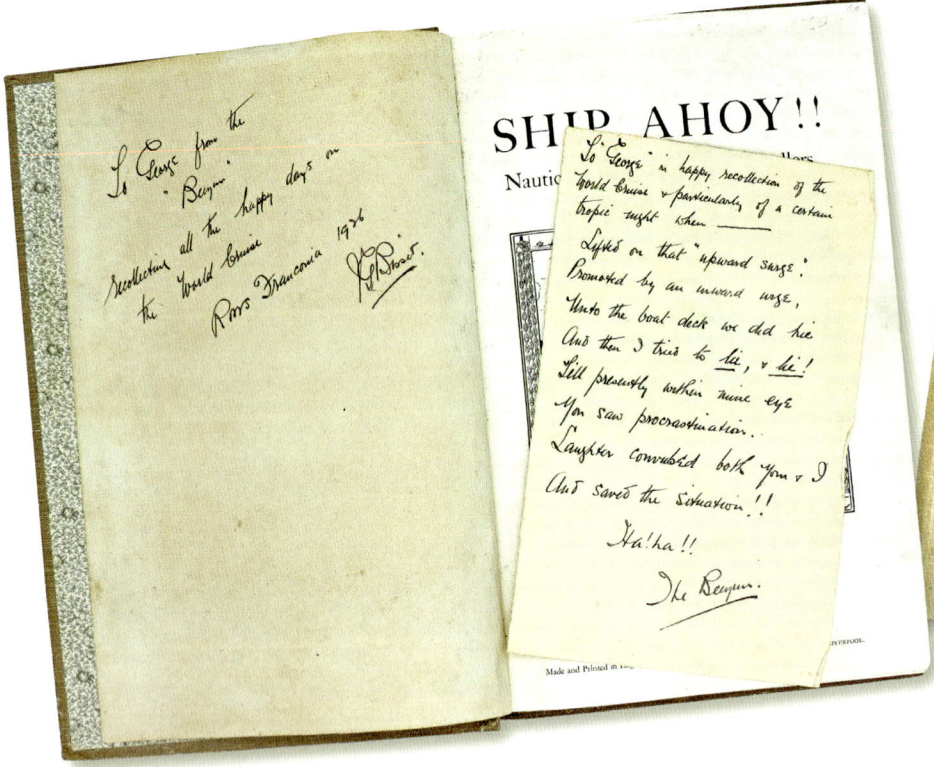

▲ *Ship Ahoy!!*
Carpathia's second officer James Bisset was a captain for Cunard in 1926.
Here he has written a humorous letter in a copy of his book *Ship Ahoy!!*
for a passenger who was on his round-the-world cruise on the *Franconia*.
(Mike Beatty collection)

▶ Bisset Autobiography
In 1959 Bisset published an autobiography containing his description of the rescue
ship's dash towards the sinking *Titanic* in 1912. He also wrote that a young *Olympic*
officer had previously told him about *Olympic*'s many safety features and had assured
Bisset that the *Titanic*'s elder sister was unsinkable. (George Behe collection)

DR FRANK BLACKMARR

▶ Marconi Receipt

Cash receipt for sending a telegram from the *Carpathia*. Dr Frank Blackmarr worked as a physician in Chicago and was a passenger on board the *Carpathia* during the *Titanic*'s rescue. On the receipt, he says he bribed the operator to send the message. (Kalman Tanito collection)

HAROLD COTTAM

◀ Harold Cottam Postcard

One of the heroes of the *Titanic* story was Harold Cottam. He received the distress signal from *Titanic* and worked for days after with no sleep manning the heavy wireless traffic *Carpathia* had to deal with. The following year, on 13 October 1913, while working on the *Gaika*, he signed a souvenir postcard to William Shaw. (Mike Beatty collection)

JAMES AND MABEL FENWICK

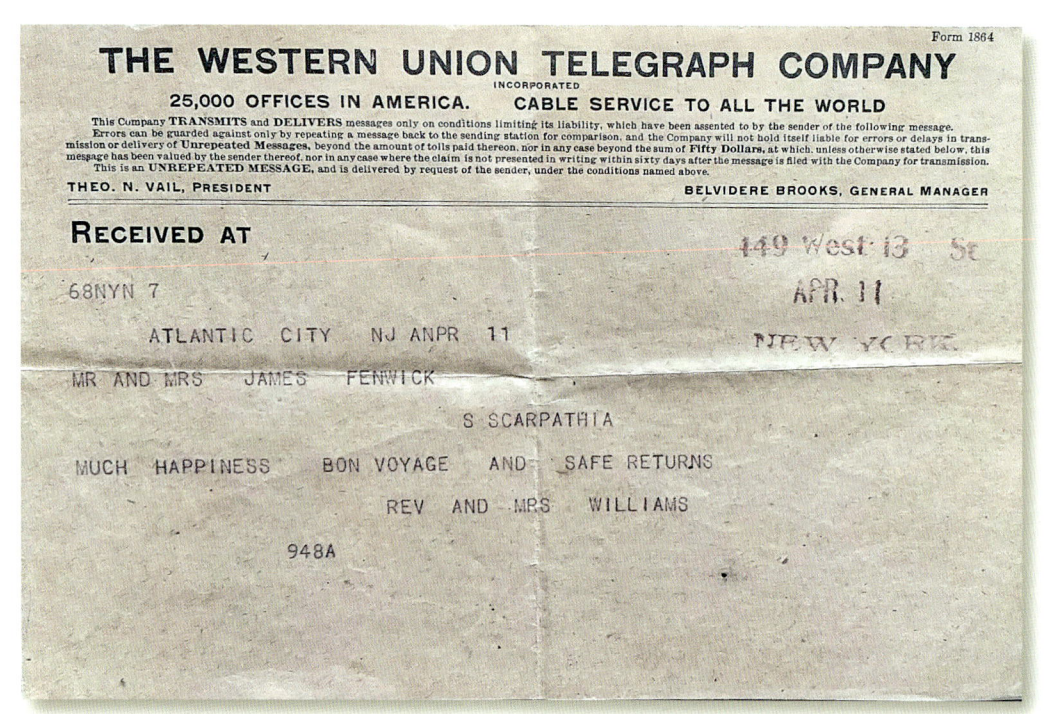

Fenwick Telegrams
Honeymooners James and Mabel Fenwick received a telegram delivered to the *Carpathia* on 11 April 1912. They were headed to Italy, where they would then go on an extended tour of Europe before returning home from Queenstown, Ireland, a month later. Three days after their departure from New York their honeymoon was interrupted when the *Carpathia* received a distress call from the *Titanic* and changed course towards the stricken vessel's reported location. After rescuing the *Titanic*'s survivors, the *Carpathia* headed back to New York and arrived there on the evening of 18 April 1912. (Trevor Powell collection)

Fenwick Negative
On the morning of 15 April 1912 James and Mabel Fenwick witnessed the rescue of *Titanic*'s survivors. The Fenwicks were among the very few *Carpathia* passengers to document those scenes with their camera, and this negative shows survivors Lawrence Beesley, Hilda Slayter and Fanny Kelley on the afternoon of the rescue. (Mike Beatty collection)

On the morning of 19 April 1912, the Fenwicks received this telegram checking on their welfare. The *Carpathia* left New York later that same day with the Fenwicks on board to continue their interrupted honeymoon. (Mike Beatty collection)

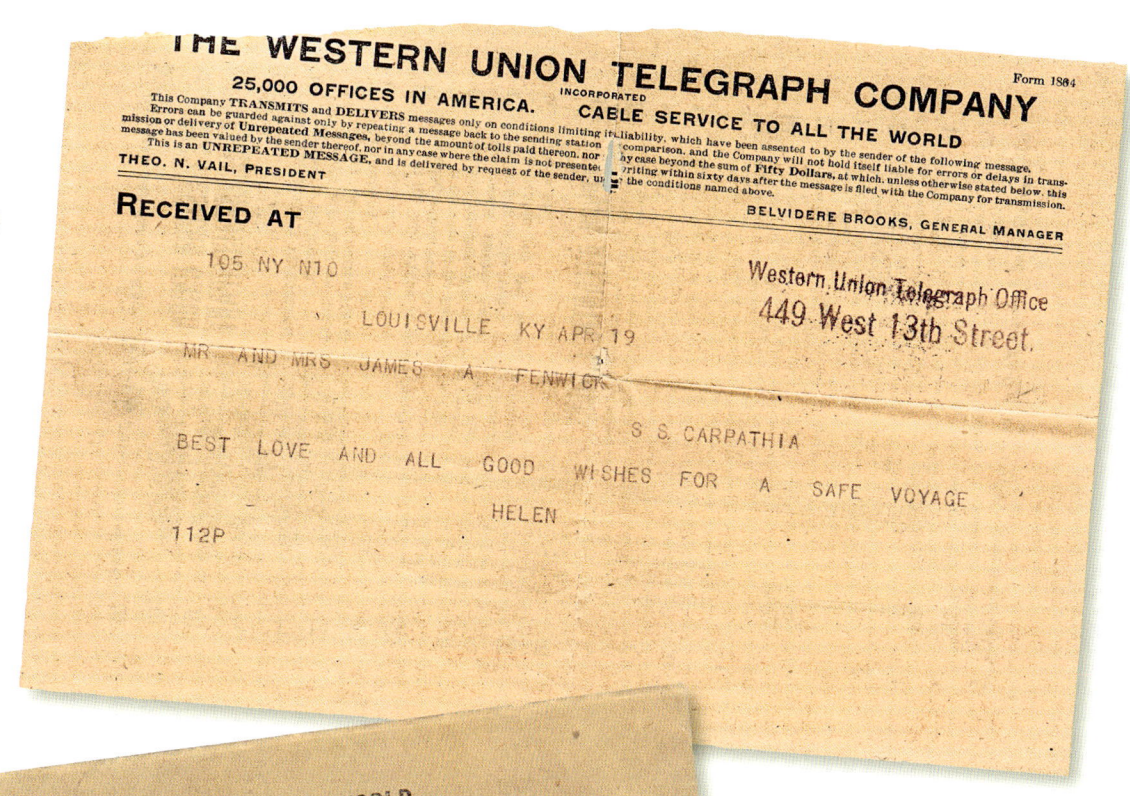

ÁRPÁD LENGYEL

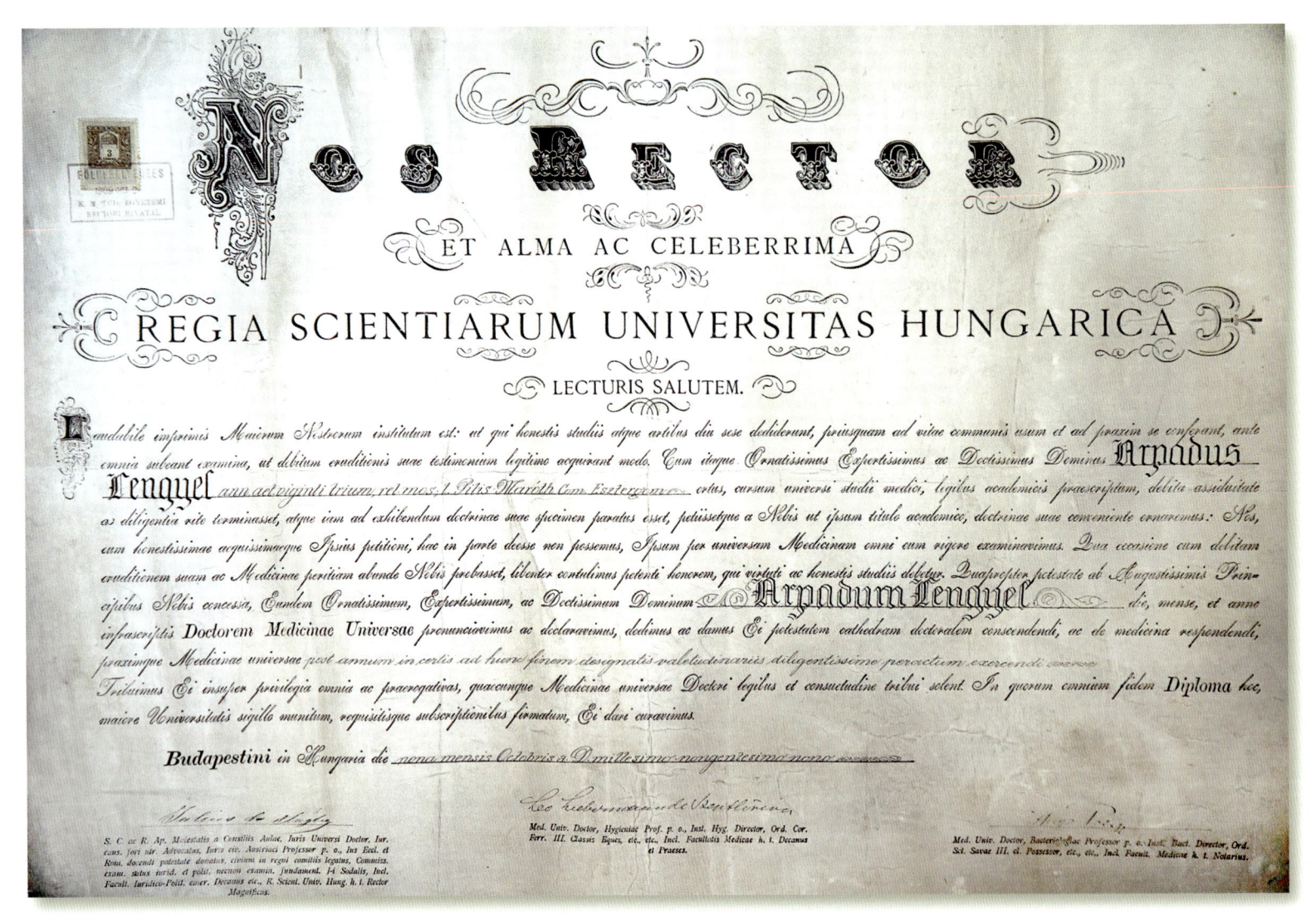

▲ **Árpád Lengyel Diploma**

Árpád Lengyel was one of the *Carpathia*'s doctors who served on the ship for just the rescue voyage. He was 26 years old at that time, and he never went to sea again. This is his original doctor's diploma from 1909. (Kalman Tanito collection)

▶ **Public Address**
The account of Dr Árpád Lengyel aboard the *Carpathia*, which was read as an address at a special event of the Budapest Doctors' Casino's special event on 17 May 1912. (Kalman Tanito collection)

A BUDAPESTI ÖNKÉNTES MENTŐ EGYESÜLET KIADVÁNYAI.
Igazgató-főorvos: Dr. Kovách Aladár, kir. tanácsos.

TITANIC és CARPATHIA.

IRTA

DR. LENGYEL ÁRPÁD, A CARPATHIA VOLT ORVOSA.

Felolvastatott a »Budapesti orvosi kaszinó« 1912. május 17-én tartott rendkivüli ülésén.

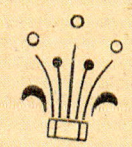

PESTI KÖNYVNYOMDA RÉSZVÉNYTÁRSASÁG.

PHILIP MAURO

▶ **Mauro Booklet**

Philip Mauro and his daughter Margaret were travelling as first-class passengers on *Carpathia* when the vessel made its historic rescue. Philip was deeply affiliated with religious work, and shortly after the disaster he wrote this rare booklet about the lessons of the disaster from a religious viewpoint. (Mike Beatty collection)

LOUIS OGDEN

◀ **Rostron Portrait**

A 1926 engraving of Captain Arthur Rostron, formerly the property of Mr and Mrs Louis M. Ogden. The Ogdens were passengers aboard the *Carpathia* during the rescue voyage and remained close friends with Rostron in the years following. (Trevor Powell collection)

CAPTAIN ARTHUR ROSTRON

▶ **Rostron Photograph**

This period photograph shows Captain Arthur Rostron, master of the rescue ship *Carpathia*. Rostron's wireless operator received *Titanic*'s distress call at 12:37 a.m. (*Titanic* time), and three and a half hours later the *Carpathia* arrived at the scene of the disaster and began picking up survivors from lifeboat 2. (George Behe collection)

◀ **Article**

A 1912 article titled 'The Rescue of the "Titanic" Survivors', by Captain Rostron. (John Lamoreau collection)

H.M.S. "MAURETANIA."

Pier 54. N.R.,
New York,
31.12.18.

My dear Mr. Ramsdell,

Just received your letter written in Cunard office.

I am sorry I missed you to day, as I shall not be able to go 'Home' to Newburgh – I should love to have seen you. Your other letter of Dec. 2 w.cd I got on arrival yesterday. I want to wish you all a 'Happy New Year' –

◀ **Captain Rostron Letter**
A 1918 New Year's Eve letter from Captain Rostron, written on stationery from HMS *Mauretania*. Part of the letter reads: 'The horrors of the past we can leave behind us … We can hope for brighter, happier and more wholesome times to come. We can hope for the best.' (John Lamoreau collection)

to Tuxedo in August.
You'll have a jolly
luncheon party I know
& I can assure you I
shall be thinking of you.
— I'm off to Redfield
this morning to stay with
some friends for a week.
— End.
It is pretty warm here
to day — & was yesterday
too.
Hope you both keep
well. — I'm sorry to say

ON BOARD THE
CUNARD
R.M.S. MAURETANIA

New York.
June 26th. 26.

Dear Brother,
Many thanks for
your nice welcoming letter.
— You only mention Bob
Bartlett & myself — surely
you forgot yourself.
So we must be the
Trio.
Hope Bob has a good
time up in Greenland.
— I'm hoping to get out

Mrs Rostron was none
too grand when at home
last time. She had
been unwell & the maid
put a hot-water-bottle
to her feet, either it
was too hot or it leaked
at any rate — she had a
badly scalded leg & foot.
— Poor girl it looked
awful & was painful
too. — She was getting
better when I left.
The children are O.K.
& Rob — seems O.K. in Chile.

I wish the Coal Strike
could be settled at home
it is becoming a nuisance.
— Bravo — America!
— Yes — the photo was taken
at City Hall — just before
I received the Freedom of
the City of New York.
You didn't know that!
Cheero & Keep well &
I'm looking forward to
seeing you both again.
— How are the ribs? —
better I hope.
Yours
most sincerely,
A.H.Rostron.

◄▼ Captain Rostron Letter
The Ogdens were lifelong friends of Captain Rostron and always sailed on his ships. On 26 June 1926 Rostron sends a letter on *Mauretania* stationery to Louis Ogden with news about his having recently been awarded the 'Freedom of the City of NY' award. (Mike Beatty collection)

▶▼ Captain Rostron Letter
Captain Rostron sent another letter
to Louis Ogden on 20 July 1926.
(Mike Beatty collection)

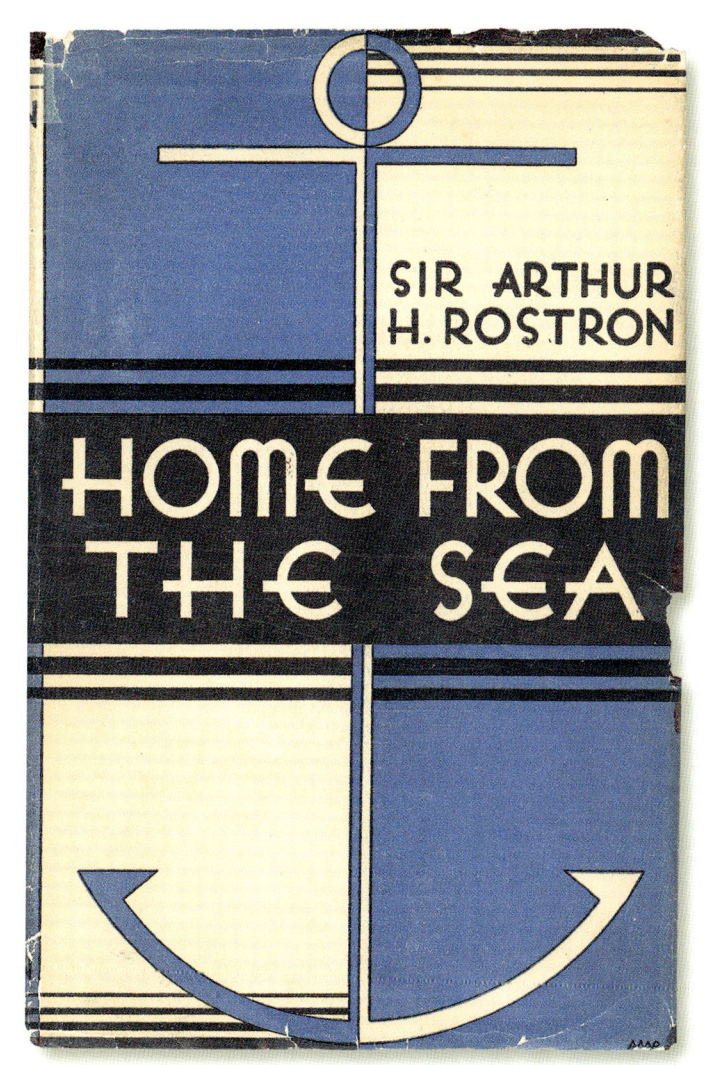

▲ **Rostron Autobiography**

In 1931, after a storied career, Captain Rostron published his memoir under the title *Home from the Sea*. The volume on the left is a UK first edition that includes the rare original dust jacket and contains Rostron's signature. (Mike Beatty collection)

Dear Commodore Randall.

— I have fulfilled my promise to autograph over page. Please allow me to extend to you my highest regards, admiration, and sympathy in your command.

Only those who have commanded these huge vessels can possibly understand the anxiety, worry, trubles and responsibilities of the Captain with my best wishes for your good health, happiness & success.

Yours sincerely,

A. H. Rostron.

Commanding
Mauretania - 1915 - 26.
Berengaria. 1926 - 30.

SOUTHAMPTON
FEB. 15 1933

◄ **Book Inscription**
Captain Rostron's inscription in the copy of his autobiography that he presented to A.B. Randall, Commodore of the United States Lines and captain of the *Leviathan*. (Kalman Tanito collection)

LEWIS SKIDMORE

▶ Painting

Lewis Palmer Skidmore was a passenger on the *Carpathia*'s rescue voyage and is known for his sketches of the *Titanic*'s sinking based on John Thayer's eyewitness account. When he arrived in Europe, he painted this view in Venice in July 1912. (Kalman Tanito collection)

AUTHOR BIOGRAPHIES

MIKE BEATTY was born, raised and still lives in the Philadelphia region with his wife Jessica and daughter Mira. Having had an early interest in history, he started reading about the *Titanic* around 1983 and his interest only grew from there. In 1987, he was lucky enough to meet six survivors; around the same time, he started collecting items related to the *Titanic*, *Olympic* and *Britannic*, a hobby that he still actively pursues. In 2017, he wrote the book *Sincerely Harry: The Letters of Henry Tingle Wilde*, a compilation of letters written by the *Titanic*'s Chief Officer Wilde during his career; twenty-eight of these letters are in Mike's collection. Mike currently runs the Facebook page 'White Star Memorabilia', where collectors display their original items and provide helpful advice to steer buyers away from fake items that are so prevalent today. He is currently a Titanic International trustee and contributor to their journal *Voyage*. His other interests include restoration: he has restored antique cars and radios and has been restoring a 1906 house for fifteen years, which has earned him the local Historic District Preservation Award in 2010. He works in the power industry as a controls and instrumentation technician and is also a part-time antiques dealer.

GEORGE BEHE became interested in the *Titanic* as a small boy in the 1950s when he found a 1912 book about the disaster on his grandmother's bookshelf. One of the book's illustrations depicted a dying swimmer raising his arm in futile supplication towards passengers in a lifeboat that was being rowed right past him, which made George wonder how he might have felt if he and his mother had been in that lifeboat and the dying swimmer were his father. After completing his hitch in the army in 1972, George began researching the disaster in earnest and eventually attended a Titanic Historical Society convention, where he met several *Titanic* survivors in person. He also met Don Lynch, with whom he began exchanging research information, and with whom he

eventually made research trips to England and The National Archives. George became friends with several of the *Titanic* survivors, including Winnifred Quick Van Tongerloo, who happened to live only a few miles from his home. He is a prolific author and contributor, and has written numerous articles for the Titanic Historical Society, as well as several books for The History Press, including *Fate Deals a Hand*, *Voices from the Carpathia* and *On Board RMS Titanic*. George is now retired and spends as much time as possible researching the *Titanic* disaster and sharing his newest discoveries.

JOHN LAMOREAU lives with his wife in rural Oregon, surrounded by children and grandchildren. His interest in history and ships comes naturally: his genealogy includes Myles Standish (9th great-grandfather), who sailed on the *Mayflower*, and Andre l'Amoureux (8th great-grandfather), a ship's captain who escaped persecution in France and arrived in the American colonies in 1701. From an early age, Lamoreau was fascinated by the stories of the *Titanic*. As a collector of historical documents, his interest in the *Titanic* was further inspired after obtaining a handwritten letter from passenger Francis D. Millet, which was the start of his collection. An educator, Lamoreau brought his interest in the *Titanic* to his classroom: one class project became a cover story for the Titanic Historical Society's journal *The Titanic Commutator* ('Edith Rosenbaum: World War One Letter from France', Issue 218). Lamoreau has also teamed up with a local chef to host a popular annual recreation of the last first-class dinner served on the *Titanic*. Called 'a taste sensation', the dinner offers guests every item served that night and has attracted international guests including relatives of the *Titanic*'s passengers. He enjoys sharing his collection with others, as well as collaborating with other researchers and family members of passengers.

DON LYNCH was born in Coeur d'Alene, Idaho, and raised in Washington State, where he began researching the *Titanic* while still in high school in Spokane. In the five decades since, he has travelled to museums and archives throughout the United States, Canada, England and Ireland to conduct his research. He has met and interviewed twenty passengers from the *Titanic*, as well as numerous relatives of survivors and victims. For many years he has been the official historian for the Titanic Historical Society. In 1992, Don wrote the text for the book *Titanic: An Illustrated History*, which went on to spend twelve weeks on the *New York Times* bestseller list. Director James Cameron hired Don as the historian for the 1997 movie *Titanic* and also as a consultant on his 2003 *Ghosts of the Abyss* project, for which they dove to the *Titanic* in a Russian submersible to film the wreck for Cameron's 3D, large-format documentary. Don wrote the text for the companion book and was a contributor for Cameron's book *Exploring the Deep: The Titanic Expeditions*.

TREVOR POWELL lives in Philadelphia, Pennsylvania, where he attended college at Temple University. His interest in maritime history began at the age of 7 after reading a book on the *Titanic* disaster in elementary school. He began collecting ocean liner memorabilia twenty years ago and has a primary focus on the Olympic-class liners as well as the *Lusitania*. His other interests include genealogy and historic architectural preservation. Trevor is a member of the Titanic International Society.

KALMAN TANITO lives in Budapest, Hungary, with his wife and two sons. As a child, he moved with his parents to Finland, where he became interested in the *Titanic* and researched the many Scandinavian passengers on the ship. This resulted in correspondence with several experts in the field, as well as meetings with survivors at different conventions. He has also published several articles in the Titanic Historical Society's magazine, *The Titanic Commutator*. As fate would have it, when James Cameron's *Titanic* came out in 1997, Tanito happened to sit next to a woman whose relative didn't survive the disaster. This led to a research trip to northern Finland with his friend Juha Peltonen, where they met family members of other passengers. With Phillip Gowan, a fellow researcher, good friend and best man at his wedding, he followed the *Titanic* trail in the Balkans. He has specialised in rare publications about the *Titanic* catastrophe, especially those not in English, but he is also interested in other ocean liners of the past. In his spare time, he is a keen photographer and spends time on modern cruise ships, where he is able to combine these two passions.

BY THE SAME AUTHORS

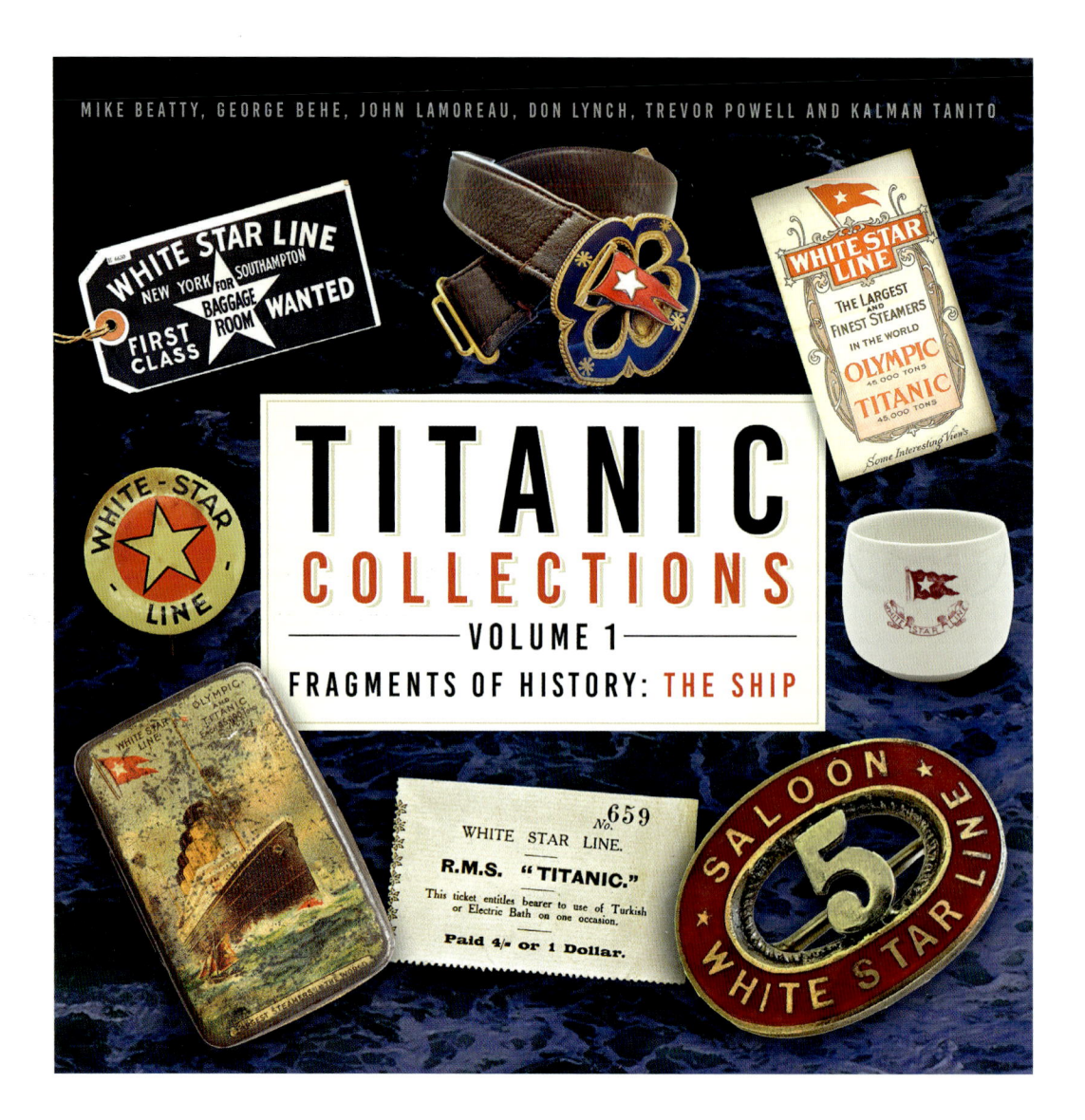

978-1-80399-333-1

The History Press
The destination for history
www.thehistorypress.co.uk